T0381090

INUVIK

A HISTORY, 1958 –2008

The Planning, Construction and Growth
of an Arctic Community

by Dick Hill

Order this book online at www.trafford.com
or email orders@trafford.com

Most Trafford titles are also available at major online book retailers.

Dick Hill moved to Inuvik with his family in 1963 and spent 33 years there. He served as the director of the Inuvik Research Laboratory and was the Town's first Mayor. He was active in many community organizations including the Chamber of Commerce, the Territorial Experimental Ski Training program, the University of Canada North and the Western Arctic Tourism Association. On retiring, he donated his substantial collection of northern books to the Inuvik Centennial Library. *Inuvik: A History*, acompanion volume to *Inuvik In Pictures*, is published to mark the 50th birthday of this planned arctic community.

Contact Dick Hill at 43 Niagara St., Collingwood ON L9Y 3X1, or email to dickhill@rogers.com for any corrections or suggestions.

Editing, design and layout by Bart Kreps.

Front Cover photographs: top, Inuvik from the air, 1995, photo by Staffan Widstrand/Corbis; bottom left, the Firth twins, photo by Dick Hill; bottom centre, loading gravel at Twin Lake gravel pit, 1955, photo by Curt Merrill, NWT Archives/N-1992-192: 0180; bottom right, RCMP officer Gerry Kisoun, photo by Raymond Gehman/Corbis.

Print information available on the last page.

ISBN: 978-1-4251-5973-3 (sc)

Trafford rev. 10/21/2019

www.trafford.com

North America & international
toll-free: 1 888 232 4444 (USA & Canada)
fax: 812 355 4082

Foreword

Inuvik is a fascinating community that kept me fully involved in community activities from the day I arrived in 1963 until retirement and departure in 1995. The Hill family moved to Inuvik from the Toronto suburb of Don Mills, as early environmentalists wanting to get away from big city life and to better nurture our young children. Also, I assumed that I could be more productive in a small community rather than continuing with the big city problem of spending at least half of my time behind a steering wheel. My 1950s urban experiences in the planned new community of Don Mills, and rural weekends with farm folk in Nottawa, prepared me for the challenging situations encountered in Inuvik on the Arctic frontier, such as the rural to urban movement, youth unconcerned with their elders and new employment directions.

The Inuvik activities were exhilarating as I was able to learn life wisdom from Northerners and to feel I was making a positive contribution to the community. As director of the Federal government's Inuvik Research Laboratory, I became a scientific dilettante through involvement with researchers, in all disciplines from anthropology to zoology, who came to Inuvik from around the world. As a participating citizen, I was active in the formation of Inuvik's responsible government and was elected as the town's first mayor in 1970. When the northern petroleum exploration activities arrived, I participated in many Mackenzie Delta and Beaufort Sea economic and business projects including the Inuvik Chamber of Commerce, the Mackenzie Business Opportunities Board and the Beaufort Sea Community Advisory Committee.

As a researcher by nature, I believed that I had a responsibility to document the Inuvik story for all the Northerners and Southerners who contributed to Inuvik's development, and for students and visitors who might have an interest in how Inuvik evolved.

My thoughts in presenting the Inuvik story can be compared to the drifting snow of an Inuvik blizzard, where millions of snow flakes move around erratically, with some forming drifts and others moving beyond the town boundaries. As there are infinite Inuvik information bits drifting around in my mind, I have tried to assemble this knowledge in a logical sequence and to present it objectively without biases. However, as the activities and people mentioned are limited to my personal experiences, I can fully understand that many residents will see the Inuvik story with a different perspective.

When active in Inuvik politics and speaking to visiting groups and journalists, I often related the "two hand" problem of presenting the Inuvik story. On one hand I would extol Inuvik's positive aspects of being a modern arctic community with all groups working together for a better life, while on the other hand I would ask for assistance and advice on Inuvik's real life social and economic problems. I still have this "two hand" enigma while writing about Inuvik.

INUVIK: A HISTORY

I believe that I played a significant role in Inuvik's development, and I'm proud of the accomplishments that I assisted such as the utilities extension throughout the community, town planning, the TEST cross country ski program, Eskimo dancing, the Inuvik Centennial Library, Northern Information Services, land claims, tourism development and spinoff benefits from northern petroleum exploration. I am still actively involved in Inuvik's current activities through regular contact with many friends, regular visits and reading the *Inuvik Drum.*

As one is a fool to generalize about the Canadian North with its vast geography and many cultures, I have to tried to restrict global comments about Inuvik and to be both specific and realistic. The information comes from many sources which are noted where appropriate. Much of the "bulk" data is presented in the Appendices so the community story will not be too heavy for light readers.

This study is intended to be of general Inuvik interest and to serve as a reference on the people, projects and happenings. Only activities related to Inuvik are included, and no attempt is made to cover the broader aspects of development in the surrounding communities or in the North. As I am not an aboriginal and have no special expertise on native affairs, the coverage of land claims and social philosophy is shorter than some might think is warranted. I did have practical experience in community government, but purposely stayed away from the issues of aboriginal self-government.

This is a personal odyssey involving historical aspects that I was involved in and leaves out much significant information that I was not familiar with. Personal opinion is not included except for the final chapter, Retrospect. More detail is provided for the early period in respect to those who have contributed to Inuvik's success and have passed on. Although as many names as possible are included, I feel that for every name mentioned, another 20 worthy residents have been missed. I take responsibility for any errors, and I hope that many people will find the book interesting and a basis for further study and comment.

Dick Hill
Collingwood Ontario
April 2008

Table of Contents

Introduction

Inuvik is a new Arctic community conceived around 1950 through a getting together of Aklavik and Federal officials who wanted to improve living conditions in the Mackenzie Delta area. The decision to create a new town was made by the Federal Cabinet on December 3, 1953. The name "Inuvik" was chosen by the Northwest Territories Council and officially proclaimed on July 18, 1958 at its 50th Session in Ottawa.

The social forces that created Inuvik and urbanization of the Mackenzie Delta region during the 1950s and '60s were happening naturally at the same time across rural Canada. Small communities generally had little control over their destiny and could only react to distant political and economic forces. As a new planned community, Inuvik's main advantages were its remote northern location and the Federal government paying all the costs. In the early years when someone complained too much, they were quieted by suggesting that they go back to where they came from, whether it be from other Northern communities or from the South.

The Hon. John Diefenbaker, Prime Minister of Canada, attended the town's official dedication ceremony on July 21, 1961 and unveiled the Inuvik monument in Mackenzie Square with a plaque reading:

> *This was the first community north of the Arctic Circle built to provide the normal facilities of a Canadian town. It was designed not only as a base for development and administration but as a centre to bring education, medical care and new opportunity to the people of the Western Arctic.*

The Prime Minister's dedication set policy for Inuvik's evolution. Included were the following directives:

1. First modern Canadian community north of the Arctic Circle.
2. Notable social progress in education, health, housing and employment.
3. Introduction of democratic self-government institutions.
4. Recognition of indigenous cultures and rights.
5. Application of community planning to improve life quality.
6. Technical success of building a community on permafrost.
7. Practical application of frontier development theories.
8. Research studies documented community activities.
9. Extensive economic benefits for residents.
10. Indians, Eskimos and Southerners working together.

This Inuvik study reviews these development directives. Also, the community's unique developments, successes and failures are examined. The town is known mainly for its Igloo Church, utilidors, buildings on piles, native crafts, noon moon and 24-hour sun. However, the community offers much more in the areas of culture, technology and economics that deserve elaboration. This information on Inuvik's first half century is presented with a brief overview of the setting, followed with a chronological narrative in six arbitrary time sections, plus a concluding retrospective:

1. Mackenzie Delta Setting
2. Beginnings 1950-1955
3. Construction 1956-1963
4. Adjustment 1964-1970
5. Resource Support 1971-1982
6. Local Control 1983-1992
7. Consolidation 1993-2008
8. Looking Back: 50 Years

Each section begins with a timeline chart with dates and distinctive happenings. Significant community aspects are discussed in detail, and many lesser events are also noted in the main text or as insets. There are several overlap situations where community activities extended into several sections. A final retrospective section comments on Inuvik's first fifty years and reviews the original community goals and evaluates their effectiveness on the community's successes and failures.

It has been difficult to be fully objective and to present all sides of discussion without becoming verbose and opinion-less. The intent is to provide a balanced review and coherent narrative.

Many details on Inuvik people, activities, organizations and data are included in the Appendix. An extensive Inuvik Reference and Bibliography of books and reports is included, to provide sources for references cited and a basis for original research for future Inuvik documentaries.

The original Mackenzie Delta residents are presented as Eskimo, Inuit, Inuvialuit, Indian, Dene, Loucheux and Gwich'in where appropriate, without retroactive cultural sensitivity. "Eskimo" is the traditional convention that in the 1970s, with land claims and native sovereignty challenges, has been changed to "Inuit". The Siberian and Alaskan Inuit still refer to themselves as Eskimos. The Eskimo Lakes are still shown on maps. During the formative years the newcomers from away were counted simply as "Others". From the beginning, Inuvik activities involved its three main populations of Inuvialuit, Gwich'in and Others.

The logo of the Town of Inuvik incorporates an igloo, a teepee, and a frame house, representing its three main populations – Inuvialuit, Gwich'in and Others.

Inuvik Time Line to 1949

20,000 BC	Earliest Gwich'in occupation of Mackenzie Delta area
2,000 BC	Earliest Inuvialuit occupation of Mackenzie Delta area
1789	Alexander Mackenzie paddled by site of Inuvik on his return from the "Polar Sea"
1825	John Franklin traveled through the Mackenzie Delta to the Arctic Coast
1858	Archdeacon James Hunter visited the Mackenzie Delta to establish Anglican missions
1860	Bishop Grollier initiated the first Catholic mission in the Western Arctic
1889	Count Edouard de Sainville begins four-year stay in the lower Mackenzie area
1892	Frank Russel made plant and animal collections in the Mackenzie Delta area
1905	Alfred Harrison spent two years surveying and mapping the Mackenzie Delta area
1906	Vilhjalmur Stefansson traveled extensively in the Mackenzie Delta and Beaufort Coast area
1912	First HBC building at Pokiak Channel across from present day Aklavik
1917	First buildings at Aklavik
1919	Anglican mission house built at Aklavik
1920	Mackenzie Valley petroleum well at Norman Wells
1921	Indian Treaty No. 11 signed, including Mackenzie Delta and Inuvik townsite area
1922	RCMP opened a detachment at Aklavik
1925	Royal Canadian Corps of Signals established base at Aklavik
1925	Governor General Lord Byng visits Aklavik on HBC's SS Distributor
1925	Roman Catholic Mission established in Aklavik
1929	Punch Dickens made first flight to Aklavik flying for Western Canadian Airways
1930	Search began for Mad Trapper of Rat River
1932	CKCU radio station opened in Aklavik by Signals staff
1937	Governor General Lord Tweedsmuir (John Buchan) visits Aklavik, arriving on HBC's SS Distributor
1939	All Saints Anglican cathedral consecrated
1943	Jim Sittichinli ordained by Anglican church in Aklavik
1944	Imperial Oil set up first Delta exploration camp at Arctic Red River
1947	CHAK radio begins broadcasting in Aklavik as a first northern CBC affiliate
1947	Governor General Viscount Alexander visits Aklavik
1949	Royal Canadian Navy communications base established at Aklavik

CHAPTER ONE

Mackenzie Delta Setting

Inuvik is an Arctic community on the eastern side of the Mackenzie Delta, 150 km north of the Arctic Circle and 80 km south of the Arctic Ocean. The town's location, along the East Channel of the Mackenzie River, combines the traditional preference of Dene to live south of the treeline and the Inuit who choose the Arctic tundra.

Inuvik's 1961 dedication monument has three gracefully curving arms representing the town's tri-racial character, where Gwich'in, Inuvialuit and Southerners live harmoniously together. The Gwich'in are the most northerly of the five Dene tribes living in the Mackenzie River Valley and are part of 11 Athapascan bands living in the Northwest Territories, Yukon and Alaska. Most of the Inuvialuit living in the region migrated in recent times from Alaska and settled along the Beaufort Sea coast. Their ties remain closer to the Alaskan Eskimo than other Inuit to the East. The terms "Inuvialuit" and "Inuit" are relatively new and are politically correct expressions for the Eskimo residents.

"Inuvik", an Inuvialuit word originally translated as "The Place Of Man", is now considered to translate as the more gender-neutral "Place of People" or "Living Place". The new name was officially assigned to Inuvik by resolution of NWT Council on July 18, 1958.

Historical Background

By the time Alexander Mackenzie made his "Voyage To The Polar Sea", the Western Arctic had been inhabited for 3000 years. On his return from the Beaufort coast, Mackenzie paddled up the East Channel of the Mackenzie River past the site of present-day Inuvik. His diary indicates that on July 16, 1789 he over-nighted at what is now the East Three Park, in the area above Inuvik's town dock (Mackenzie 1801). Mackenzie was searching for a route to the large river which Captain James Cook's 1776-78 North Pacific expedition assumed flowed from the West into Alaska's Cook Inlet (Mackenzie 1801).

When Franklin and Richardson explored the Mackenzie Delta in the summer of 1826 many "Eskimos" were encountered. Jenness figured about 2,000 were inhabiting the area in 1826, while Stefansson estimated the total population of the Delta and Beaufort Coast in 1848 to be approximately 4,000. Due to the devastation of the native population after European contact from smallpox and other diseases, by the early 1900s only about 200 native Inuit remained in the area (Morrison 1997). Jenness estimates that in 1929, only about 12 Eskimos were really native to the district between the Alaska-Yukon border and Cape Bathurst, the remainder of the existing population of 800 having migrated from Alaska (Jenness 1958).

The Dene have lived in northern Boreal forest area for 3,000 or more years, having arrived from Asia over the Bering Land Bridge. The northernmost group, the Gwich'in people of the Mackenzie Delta region, were called "Loucheux", meaning "slanted eye people", by the early European explorers. The Mackenzie Valley Dene were collectively referred to as "Indian" along with all other aboriginal Canadians.

Prior to 1900 and the establishment of trading posts, residents traveled seasonally through their territories and gathered at many sites. Fort McPherson, at the southern end of the Mackenzie Delta, was one of the original Hudson Bay Company trading posts founded in 1848. The Tetl'it Gwich'in began using Fort McPherson as a gathering and trading place and subsequently their seasonal movements began to focus more on the Delta and its valuable fur-trapping potential. Many early travelers passed near the site of Inuvik while taking the traditional portage between Campbell and Sitidgi Lakes connecting the Mackenzie Delta to the Husky Lakes and the Arctic Coast.

Aklavik is a relatively young community that started when Pokiak, an Eskimo trader, set up a camp in 1910, along the Peel Channel midway between Fort McPherson and Herschel Island. The Hudson's Bay Company and the Northern Company set up adjacent posts in 1912, and a small settlement developed. Gradually the community spread across the channel to the area known as Aklavik, which in Eskimo means "Place of the Brown Bear". Over the years, a small town grew up with government offices, medical services, schools, military, churches and stores. Many Inupiat Eskimos from Alaska migrated into the region in the 1920's.

By 1930 the population of Aklavik and the surrounding area had reached 400, and in 1950 was about 1500. The population of the delta and adjacent areas in the 1950 to 1960 period was over 2000 of whom about 50% were Eskimo, 30% white and 20% Indian (Mackay 1963).

Aklavik had become the Canadian government's administrative center of the Western Canadian Arctic. However, Aklavik's unique location in the heart of the Mackenzie Delta made it susceptible to flooding and limited the expansion options.

Geography

Inuvik is located at 68° 18′ N × 133° 29′ W on the East Channel of the Mackenzie River Delta. This is comparable to the latitude of Fairbanks in Alaska (65° N), Reykjavik in Iceland (64° N), Narvik in Norway (68° N), Murmansk in Russia (69° N) and Norilsk in Siberia

AIR DISTANCES FROM INUVIK			
Edmonton	1970 km	Aklavik	37 km
Vancouver	2197 km	Tuktoyaktuk	130 km
Winnipeg	2844 km	Norman Wells	444 km
Los Angeles	3940 km	Sachs Harbour	325 km
Chicago	3981 km	Kugluktuk	475 km
Toronto	4116 km	Whitehorse	848 km
New York	4630 km	Yellowknife	1096 km
		Source: www.convertunits.com	

(69 °N). On the world air map, Inuvik is centrally located between New York and Tokyo, Los Angeles and Moscow, Honolulu and London.

The meridian due South from Inuvik passes one time zone west of Vancouver Island, so based solely on that criterion Inuvik would be in the Pacific-plus-one time zone. But Inuvik operates on Mountain Time as do other Northwest Territories communities including Yellowknife. Hence Inuvik is two hours ahead of "sun time", and the high point of the sun's traverse is mid-afternoon. Since residents do not see the sun for 30 days in the winter, and in the summer the sun does not set for 56 days, this two-hour time difference is hardly noticed.

Inuvik is close to all major Canadian geologic formations. The community sits on the western sedimentary basin (Mackenzie Delta), the Rocky Mountain Cordillera (Richardson Mountains) is across the Delta to the west of Aklavik, and the Canadian Shield is to the east (Airport Lake outcrops).

The Mackenzie River is Canada's longest river, and drains around 20% of Canada. At Inuvik the average water level is 15 metres above sea level. Hence although Inuvik is often described as being "Up North" based on the usual Canadian map, Inuvik residents are really "Down North" relative to the Mackenzie River's headwaters in Alberta and British Columbia.

The Mackenzie Delta, measuring 210 km long and around 62 km wide, is a vast convoluted network of interconnected lakes and channels covering 13,000 sq. km. It is the largest delta in Canada and twelfth largest delta in the world. It contains approximately 25,000 lakes. When viewed from the air it is difficult to ascertain whether the Mackenzie Delta is "water on land" or "land on water".

The delta was formed by the slow and still ongoing deposition of sediment into a shallow bay, following the retreat of the continental glaciers between 12,000 to 13,000 years ago. Differing from other deltas in the world, the Mackenzie Delta is confined on two sides by high land forms: the Richardson Mountains to the west and the Caribou Hills to the east. These boundaries prevent the delta from increasing in width.

Climate

Inuvik's combined arctic and subarctic environment provides short, warm summers and long, cold winters. The average temperature in July is around 14°C. High temperatures of 32°C have been recorded. The lowest temperature on record is −57°C. The average total annual precipitation is 25 cm with an average annual snowfall of 175 cm. Since the air is dry with little wind at low temperatures, Inuvik winters are quite pleasant with generally clear skies.

The warmest month is July and the wettest month is August. There can be a snowfall any month of the year. Technically, Inuvik is classed as having a "subarctic" climate as the treeline lies just to the North, but with a total annual precipitation of only 25 cm the Inuvik area is considered an arctic desert.

Inuvik winters extend from September to April with an average January low temperature of −40°C (at 40 degrees the Centigrade and Fahrenheit scales meet). Residents spend little time shoveling snow as it is dry and does not drift much. Vehicles seldom get stuck in the snow. The Inuvik snow cover lasts for up to eight months a year and remains pristine white until summer. Inuvik and the southern Mackenzie Delta are relatively calm for long periods, with only one or two winter wind storms a year which could be considered as a blizzard.

Inuvik experienced an extreme cold spell in February 1965 with the minimum temperature –52°C (-62°F) and warming to no more than -22°C (-8° F) for an entire month. The monthly average minimum was –42.4°C (–44.4°F), average maximum was -31°C (-23.8°F), and the mean monthly average was –36.7°C (–34.1°F) . For Inuvik residents who experienced this cold snap, the current winters are relatively mild.

A sundial for Inuvik would have all 24 hours marked, because the sun at Inuvik never sets from May 25 to July 19 – a period of 55 days. Nor does the sun rise from December 7 to January 5 – a period of 30 days. The difference between the number of days without sunset and the number without sunrise is due to the thickness of the sun and the earth's wobble. Even at the winter solstice on December 21st, the sun comes close enough to the horizon to provide twilight for several hours, which is bright enough for most daytime activities including taking pictures.

The Inuvik twilight is enhanced due to the sun's rays bending through the atmosphere, by moonlight, "light of the night sky" and snow reflection. Inuvik's pristine snow cover reflects the available light to make winters quite pleasant, 24 hours a day. The moonlight can be quite bright. Total darkness only occurs during rare times in winter when there is a heavy cloud cover. At the beginning and end of the "dark period" there can be fantastic solar effects on the southern horizon from the blending of sunrise and sunset.

The short summers can be warm and wonderful, a time when most of the community is involved in outdoor activities. The continuous daylight reduces the feeling of fatigue and the need for sleep. Many residents working regular hours have trouble retiring in time to get up for work. With the sun shining around the clock, Inuvik doesn't cool down at night as in southern communities. There's no comfort and relief after the occasional hot and humid day. The average first frost-free day in Inuvik is June 23rd.

Inuvik has a moderate climate, according to Environment Canada's "Climate Severity Index", which rates communities according to human comfort and well being. The index

CANADIAN CLIMATE SEVERITY				
Vancouver	18	**Inuvik 53**	Quebec City	53
Calgary	35		Dawson City	54
Toronto	38		Sudbury	54
Montreal	43		Whitehorse	56
Ottawa	44		Yellowknife	57
Regina	49		Churchill	82
Winnipeg	51		Alert	84
Data from Canadian Encyclopedia website, Oct 2001				

ranges from 1 to 100 and takes into account environmental stress, mobility, safety and hazards. With a severity rating of 53, Inuvik is in the middle for Canadian communities. Inuvik's dry continental climate, clear skies and freedom from severe storms make it a more pleasant place to live than communities much further south such as Sudbury, Whitehorse, Yellowknife and Churchill. Inuvik's climate severity is comparable to Winnipeg and Quebec City.

The annual mean temperature at Inuvik averages around −10°C but varies considerably, from a low of −12°C in 1974 to a high of −6°C in 1993.

Permafrost

Although there is a very low total precipitation, the Inuvik area can be quite muddy when it rains due to the permafrost which results in poor drainage.

Beneath Inuvik the ground is frozen solid all year to a depth of 350 metres due to the average annual below-freezing temperature. There are large pure ice "lenses" measuring a metre thick with areas of several acres. This permafrost ground is as hard as cement but, if thawed, turns into an inhospitable quagmire.

The permafrost necessitates engineering adaptations, but with a mean annual temperature of nearly −10°C , the ground can easily be kept frozen and can support a modern community (Leggett 1959). Also, some permafrost areas are solid rock and dry gravel, without significant ice content, so they would cause no foundation problems even if temperatures rose above 0°C.

The surface soils that melt every summer and freeze again in the winter are known as the "active layer". Under insulating vegetation, the active layer will thaw only 15 cm, while under a disturbed area, such as a playground, the thaw depth could be 2 metres.

Around Inuvik there is no permafrost below lakes and river channels with a water depth greater than 2 metres, which is the usual maximum for ice thickness each winter. This unfrozen water and the soils below create permafrost-free areas much like the holes in a Swiss cheese. Due to vegetation or water level changes small lakes are often formed where permafrost ice formations have melted.

At Inuvik the presence of permafrost is very positive as it has stabilized the high ice content Deltaic silt that much of the community is built on. With an average ground temperature of −8°C, a considerable amount of thermal imbalance is require to cause any melting problems other than those at the surface active layer. In comparison, high ice content permafrost is

---

'NORTH OF THE NORTHERN LIGHTS'

The northern lights are always active over Inuvik but they cannot be seen during daylight periods, and generally they are fairly pale coloured at night. There have been spectacular displays over Inuvik but they are rare. Many a local person claims to have heard the northern lights. It is said that Inuvik is "north of the northern lights", as the area of peak auroral activity is to the south along a band joining Fairbanks, Whitehorse, Yellowknife and Churchill.

a considerable problem in the more southern Mackenzie Valley communities where the permafrost layer is shallow and the average ground temperatures are -0.5°C at Fort Providence, -1.0°C at Wrigley and -2.0°C at Norman Wells (Brown 1970). The usual construction practice in this area is to clear away insulating brush and allow the permafrost to melt away before building starts (Brown 1970).

Vegetation

The Inuvik townsite straddles the line between Boreal forest and Arctic tundra. The sparse spruce forest to the east of Inuvik is the start of the Barrens. These trees are mainly around 70 years old, dating from a severe forest fire in the 1930s. The Arctic tree line is just 2 km north of Inuvik, but in the Mackenzie Delta proper it extends around 50 km further north due to the warming influence of the north-flowing Mackenzie River. White spruce is the dominant tree in the community with black spruce in the lower wetter areas. Groves of white birch in the Happy Valley area and at Chuk Park indicate drier gravel areas. Northern tamarack (larch) around Airport Lake are the world's most northerly of this species. Low Arctic vegetation is typified by dwarf shrubs, sedges and herbs, with sedges and willows dominating the wet sites.

Scrub vegetation, characterized by willow and ground birch, occupies a transitional zone between the treeline and the tundra. Cranberries and blueberries are abundant throughout Inuvik along with bog blueberry, crowberry, cloudberry, knotweed, sweet pea, and mountain sorrel. Sedges, usually called cotton-grasses, grow luxuriantly in wet areas. There is an abundance of wild flowers, with arctic crocus being the first to show in late May. Blue Arctic lupins come next followed by an array of an estimated 100 wildflower varieties in the area.

Wildlife

Fifty-four species of mammals, 169 species of birds, one amphibian, and a total of 55 fish species are known to occur in the Inuvik area. Many of these species are migratory and play an important role in the traditional lives of peoples living in and around the Mackenzie Delta. The area's natural productivity is considerably greater than many areas to the South with less favorable ecological conditions. Muskrats, beavers, fox, black bear and moose are particularly abundant, and mink, lynx, red fox, wolves, grizzly bears and wolverine are also often found within the Delta.

Of the 169 recorded bird species, 17 are in the region year round, 101 come for the summer and nesting, 12 are uncommon transients and 39 are incidental observations. A flourishing raptor population – bald eagles, golden eagles and peregrine falcons – lives in the Delta during the warmer months. Ravens are plentiful in Inuvik, especially in the winter when their capers and sounds are fascinating. Six gull species frequent the area, and many species of waterfowl appear near Inuvik every spring. Included in these species are the tundra swans, snow geese, white-fronted geese, surf and white-winged scoters, and mallards.

Another bird often recognized in the Delta is the belted kingfisher. Rock ptarmigan, spruce grouse, and the gray jay – often called the "whiskey jack" or "camp robber" – can be found year round.

A great variety of fish such as whitefish, inconnu, jackfish, lake trout, grayling, cisco and dolly varden char are commonly found in nearby lakes and streams. In summer, thousands of beluga whales migrate from Alaska to the outer Delta to give birth to their calves. The region's only amphibian is the wood frog.

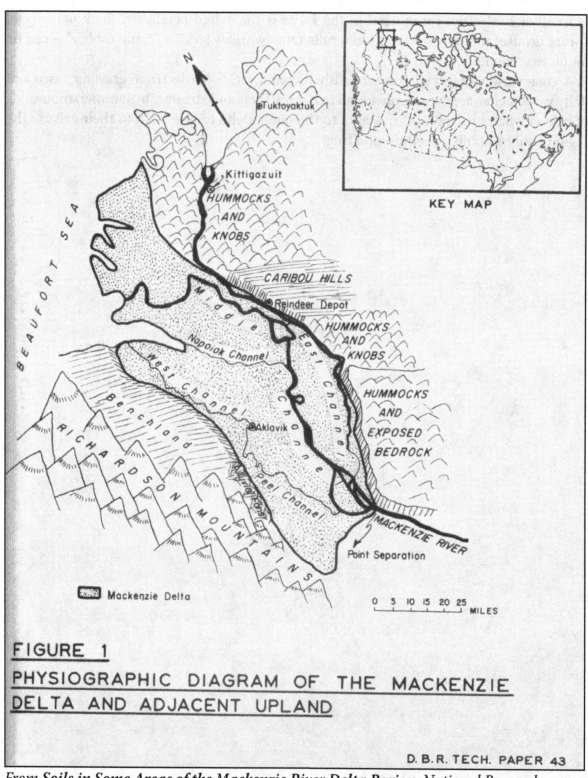

KEY MAP

FIGURE 1

PHYSIOGRAPHIC DIAGRAM OF THE MACKENZIE
DELTA AND ADJACENT UPLAND

D. B. R. TECH. PAPER 43

*From Soils in Some Areas of the Mackenzie River Delta Region, National Research
Council, October 1956*

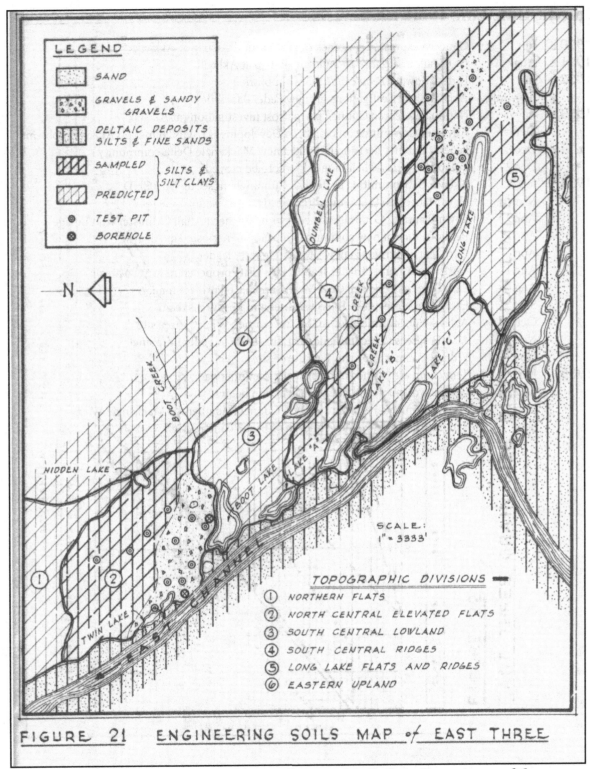

FIGURE 21   ENGINEERING SOILS MAP of EAST THREE

*Results of site testing at East Three site, as illustrated in **Soils in Some Areas of the Mackenzie River Delta Region**, National Research Council, October 1956*

Inuvik Time Line 1950-1955

1950	Jun	Concern expressed over lack of year around airstrip at Aklavik
1951	Aug	DOT fails in attempt to build an airstrip at Aklavik
1952	Jul	Farley Mowat's *People of the Dear* published
	Jul – Aug	Aklavik site investigations for new Federal facilities
1953	Jun	National Research Council permafrost investigations at Aklavik
	Oct	Advisory Committee on Northern Development (ACND) met on Aklavik problems
	Dec 3	Federal Cabinet decision to build a new Mackenzie Delta community
	Dec 23	*Edmonton Journal* headline "Aklavik to be moved"
1954	Jan 22	Aklavik Subcommittee under F. J. Cunningham set up by ACND
	Mar	New Mackenzie Delta townsite investigations begin
	Apr 9	Town Planning Committee meets with Northern Affairs Minister Jean Lesage
	Apr 15	Public Notice of new community development posted at Aklavik
	Apr	Curt Merrill arrives as new site search party leader
	Aug 11	Northern Affairs Minister Jean Lesage visits proposed new townsites
	Aug	East Three site chosen, Curt Merrill appointed project manager
	Sep	East 3 site surveyed by Energy, Mines and Resources team
	Oct 12	Aklavik Subcommittee of ACND recommends East Three site
	Nov 8	ACND agrees to recommend East Three site to Federal Cabinet
	Nov 18	Federal Cabinet approves East Three site
1955	Jun	Tent camp established and construction underway
	Aug	Garage workshop and dock construction begins
	Aug	Frank Carmichael elected as NWT Council Member for Mackenzie West
	Sep	Tent school organized for children of East 3 construction workers

CHAPTER TWO

Beginnings, 1950–1955

In the decades after Aklavik's founding in 1910, the town grew from primarily a fur-trading post to the administrative centre of the Canadian Western Arctic. But as the village developed, it became obvious that the site was not suitable for a major community.

By 1931 Aklavik had an area population of 411 listed as 180 Indians, 140 Eskimos and 91 others. With the expansion of the Anglican and Roman Catholic missions, hospitals and residential schools and intensive Mackenzie Delta trapping, Aklavik's population increased steadily and in 1952 numbered around 700.

With this concentration of activities, the Federal government opened up administration offices to provide more efficient services for the Western Arctic region. Government assistance to individuals had been rare in Aklavik (Brown 1999, p 22). But after a severe drop in Aklavik's trapping income, the Northern Affairs Department organized a program for cutting Delta portages and dog team trails. More work could have been provided if plans to build a large airstrip had been carried out, but they were abandoned in 1948, by which time there was already consideration of moving Aklavik to another site (Honigman 1970). The permafrost conditions at Aklavik were also a major challenge to construction of a new airstrip.

Community broadcasting had been initiated on May 1, 1947 with the designation CHAK. In 1949 the Royal Canadian Navy opened a "communications research" base in Aklavik. Also in 1949, the Royal Canadian Navy established a small wireless station at Aklavik. Its mission was to conduct research into the basic problems associated with Arctic communications techniques and to provide independent High Frequency Direction Finding (HFDF) support for Search and Rescue (SAR).

In 1950, with the enlarged military facilities requiring improved services and resupply, the Federal government's increasing interest in northern activities, and a burgeoning population with a need for improved facilities for communications, administration, education and medical care, there was a strong impetus for the creation of a new Aklavik townsite.

It was apparent to northern planners that the Western Arctic was growing in national significance. But the site problems at Aklavik precluded the spending of large sums of money to modernize and enlarge the existing facilities.

Expansion Limitations

Aklavik had nowhere to expand as lakes, streams and marshes hemmed in the site against the Aklavik Channel, which every spring flooded the community and was continually eroding its banks. High ice content soils were found at the site where a new Federal school was proposed. Aklavik's government administrator reported that "It's impossible even to build a suitable outhouse on the permafrost. Once a hole has been hacked out of the frozen ground, it begins to thaw and the hole widens. Eventually an outhouse would disappear into its own cesspit" (Hunt 1983). Sewage was collected in honey buckets which were picked up by a honey wagon. Disposal was a problem. There was no year round supply of fresh water for the growing community.

Similar sentiments had been expressed by Governor General Lord Tweedsmuir, who visited Aklavik on August 1, 1937. He thought the settlement was "a complete mistake" in the middle of the Delta with "no proper sanitation and the foreshore was foul." His impressions of the Delta found their way into his Canadian novel, *Sick Heart River* (Galbraith 2005).

As there were no gravel deposits near Aklavik, proper roads could not be built or reinforced. When Pierre Berton visited Aklavik in August 1954 he reported that the community was known as the "Mudtropolis of the North" (Berton 1964). It was said that Aklavik was enveloped by swirling waters and shifting channels. The opinion that Aklavik was actually sinking in the mud gained wide support in the South, though locals, accustomed to the permafrost and spring floods, ridiculed this disaster scenario.

A study team from the National Research Council's Division of Building Research was sent north in 1953 to study Aklavik's permafrost and to assess the possibilities for community expansion (Pihlainen 1954).

During the summer of 1953 the permafrost research staff of the National Research Council's Division of Building Research carried out extensive investigations of Aklavik soil conditions relating to the proposed construction of a new ten-room school and apartment teacherage. Sixteen test cores were drilled to an average eight-metre depth. The investigation revealed that the Aklavik soils have an extremely high ice content that would make the construction of large buildings costly (Pihlainen 1954).

At the new Aklavik Navy Base there was a growing need for improved communications and supply, as they were cut off for at least six weeks during freezeup and during breakup each year. In the summer of 1951, more efforts were made to construct an airport landing strip. This failed miserably: after the bush was cleared from the site with a bulldozer, large ice lenses melted, leaving gaping holes (Webster 1987). The undulating muddle remains visible to the north of Aklavik's present-day Esso tank farm. Pierre Berton writing on his 1954 visit to Aklavik said "Below us lay dramatic evidence of the need for moving Aklavik: carved into the yellow muskeg were the faint lines of an airstrip that hadn't worked. One of the bulldozers that tried to scrape it out had been swallowed by the silt when the permafrost melted" (Berton 1956).

By the early 1950s, there was already an investment of about $3 million in Aklavik facilities, with around 40% coming from the federal government, 27% from church missions and the rest private (*RCMP Quarterly* 1954). With the increasing demands for northern administration, education and medical services, the Federal government was under pressure to provide many new facilities. Beginning in 1950, the possibility was raised to seek a better townsite for Aklavik. This possibility was also strongly influenced by external factors, involving protection of northern sovereignty, concerns about indigenous peoples, and northern resource development.

External Influences

Northern Sovereignty

In 1953 Prime Minister Louis St. Laurent made the classic statement in the House of Commons that "we have administered these vast territories of the north in an almost continuing state of absence of mind". He added that there was concern for the "security of the North American continent" (Commons, 8 Dec 1953). Plans were made to augment the Navy facilities at Aklavik with a year-round airstrip and with improved radio reception away from the Richardson Mountains. A decision to move the military operations away from Aklavik was the first factor in finding a "New Aklavik". The Mackenzie Delta miracle is that other government departments and the churches agreed to go along with the military in developing a new northern community.

In 1954, before the era of the Kennedy-Kruschev cold war détente, with the threat of Soviet aircraft coming from the North and submarines passing around the Arctic Islands, Canada and the United States agreed on the construction of the Distant Early Warning (DEW) Line, a series of 41 radar stations along the Arctic coast. Joint Arctic Weather Stations (JAWS) were established at Mould Bay, Isachsen, Eureka and Alert. A Strategic Air Command (SAC) base was built at Frobisher Bay. The construction of Beaufort region DEWline stations at Shingle Point, Tuktoyaktuk, and Cape Perry had a great effect on the Mackenzie Delta residents. These very large "American" projects opened up the North but were operated mainly by foreigners. Part of Canada's response to maintain northern sovereignty and to provide some balance to the US-controlled DEWline activities was to bolster arctic communities, such as Aklavik.

Concern for Indigenous Peoples

The arrival of the Canadian "welfare state" in 1940s had a great effect on the Mackenzie Delta region, especially in the areas of family allowances, medical services, tuberculosis eradication, and education. The Indian Affairs Department became active with new programs to assist the concerns of indigenous people throughout the North. Aklavik's population grew considerably, as these programs attracted many Delta residents off the land to benefit from health, education and social services.

Aklavik "was the only settlement at that time in which Indian, Metis and Inuit and whites lived together and where all the agencies active in the north – government, religious and private – provided their services or traded their goods to a confusing mix of humanities in transition" (Robertson 2000).

Farley Mowat's popular 1952 book *People of the Deer* denounced Canada's treatment of the Eskimos and gained considerable sympathy for the serious plight of northern residents ignored by the Federal government. Social activists were proposing that more be done. The new Department of Northern Affairs was created in 1953 partially in response to Mowat's popular writings. This well-intentioned Federal support for northern indigenous people played a significant role in the founding of a "New Aklavik".

Resource Development

In 1789 Alexander Mackenzie had reported petroleum seepage along the Mackenzie River near Fort Norman. In 1848 Sir John Richardson, while searching for the missing Franklin, observed that "Point Atkinson is a flat, low piece of ground ... marshy pond, the water of which being ... greasy from the quantity of ... oil with which the ground was saturated..." (Richardson, 1851). Oil was discovered by Imperial Oil at Norman Wells in 1920. Shortly afterwards Indian Treaty No. 11 was signed on June 27, 1921. This Treaty covered an area extending along the Mackenzie Valley from the Alberta border through to the Arctic Coast, and included the Inuvik townsite.

The Mackenzie Delta resource development thrust was for oil and gas. Following the development of the Norman Wells oilfield, petroleum exploration activities proceeded down the Mackenzie Valley and reached the Mackenzie Delta in 1944, when Imperial Oil set up a field camp at Arctic Red River (Byer 1977).

The mining and petroleum industries were becoming active throughout the Canadian North in the 1950s. New mines were developed at Pine Point, Yellowknife and Rankin Inlet. Plans for the Great Slave Railway north from Grimshaw to Hay River, and the Dempster Highway north from Dawson City, were considered. In 1953 political debate on Mackenzie Valley oil developments in the House of Commons speculated that "if oil and gas development goes ahead at a reasonable rate, the population of this area could be up to 5,000 and beyond 5,000" (Commons 1959). This popular Canadian enthusiasm for northern resource development was another strong element for creating a "New Aklavik".

A Decision is Made

New Town Committee

The decision to move the government facilities from Aklavik to a new location was not taken lightly. The federal government's Advisory Committee on Northern Development (ACND) was formed in January 1948 and involved all federal Deputy Ministers with northern activities. Its purpose was to coordinate the federal government's overall responsibilities in Northern Canada. Hugh Keenleyside was the first ACND Chairman. The committee met in October 1953 under the chairmanship of Major General H. A. Young, then Deputy

---

MAJOR GENERAL HUGH YOUNG

Major General Hugh Young (1899-1982) is sometimes referred to as the founder of Inuvik since he was responsible for the federal government's decision to move the settlement of Aklavik to a new site. He was Commissioner of the Northwest Territories from 1950 to 1953, Deputy Minister of NA&NR, and chairman of the ACND. Mr. Young had a long association with Aklavik and the Mackenzie Delta beginning in 1924. As a young lieutenant with the Royal Canadian Signal Corps he traveled in the Arctic establishing radio stations. On one trip to build a Signals station at Herschel Island, his ship sank in the Mackenzie Delta, and so he built the station at Aklavik instead.

Minister of Resources and Development, to discuss the need for establishing a new Mackenzie Delta community (Jenness 1964). At this meeting a study was commissioned to review a new and more stable site for Aklavik, with coordination by an ACND Aklavik Subcommittee under F.J.G. "Frank" Cunningham, Director of the Northern Affairs & National Resources (NA&NR) Northern Administration Branch. Also on this project steering committee were J.P. Carriere of Public Works and R. F. Legget of the National Research Council. Later this sub-committee included J.K. Fraser (Mines & Technical Surveys), K.C. Berry (Public Works), J.A. Pihlainen, G.H. Johnson & R. Brown (NRC).

Gordon Robertson was appointed ACND Chair on November 23, 1953. A submission was made to the Federal Cabinet which, at its December 3, 1953, meeting agreed that a new townsite was required to enlarge the school, hospital, airport and administration facilities at Aklavik. The ACND was given the responsibility of selecting the new location and coordinating the move. When Gordon Robertson was appointed Northern Affairs Deputy Minister, Ernest Cote from External Affairs took over as ACND chairman.

On December 8, 1953, the Hon. Jean Lesage, Minister of Resources and Development, announced in Parliament the decision to investigate the possibility of relocating the government facilities at Aklavik to a better location. At the time there were three elected NWT Representatives present in the Commons Visitors Gallery. The *Edmonton Journal* headline of December 23, 1953 read "Aklavik to be moved".

Also in December 1953, the *Canadian Weekly Bulletin* stated:

> The plan for relocation of Aklavik, the largest community in the Canadian Arctic, is announced to have been approved in principal by the Canadian Government. The town is to be rebuilt in a location safe from erosion of the Mackenzie River and from sinking through the melting permafrost, with conditions permitting proper sanitation and water supply. The new site will be chosen by experts during 1954; after roadways, water and sewage system, etc., are installed, transfer of buildings will begin in the winter of 1955-56. The move is estimated to require four years' time (11 December 1953 "Plan To Move Aklavik" AB33993).

There were several 1954 news reports on the Aklavik relocation in the *Edmonton Journal*, including

"Possibility Of Oil In Yukon Outlined By Hon Jean Lesage":

> ... One of the matters that the Minister will look into in the Northwest Territories is the proposed transfer of the Town of Aklavik to a new location ... (July 28, 1954).

"Jean Lesage Tours North":

> ... Hon Jean Lesage, Minister of Indian Affairs & Northern Development, travelling with Deputy Minister R. G. Robertson, Maurice Lamontagne and G. W. Stead tour began June 22nd. Aklavik Relocation: referring to a government plan to relocate Aklavik, Mr. Lesage

said he investigated the site previously proposed on the West Channel of the Mackenzie Delta and found it would be no great improvement over the present townsite. There would still be a problem with mud and the construction of an airport would be out of the question. He said another site is now being considered on the East Channel at the same latitude as Aklavik but 50 miles distant. He said the distance would present a problem in moving the town but felt the advantages would outweigh the disadvantages... (August 11, 1954).

The Aklavik study team was assembled in December 1953 with the directive to prepare an assessment of new town sites in the Mackenzie Delta, in time for the arrival of Northern Affairs Minister Jean Lesage in August 1954 (Robertson 2000). This team was composed of experienced "northern" experts with responsibility to design and implement Canada's first planned community. They started work in Ottawa assembling data and studying Mackenzie Delta aerial photos. In March 1954 the team traveled to the Mackenzie Delta by air and began the search by dog team, canoe and helicopter.

Justification for the Decision
Early in the search, the site that was eventually picked was labeled "East 3," after its location on the East Channel of the Mackenzie. National Defence officials supported the move to East 3, as there was space for expansion, a good airport for resupply, and better radio reception in all directions as compared to Aklavik, where the nearby Richardson Mountains blocked signals from the West. Education and religion officials agreed to the move as an opportunity for improved schooling. An education agreement for the new townsite schools was negotiated in 1953 between the northern bishops of the Catholic and Anglican churches and Prime Minister Louis St. Laurent and Minister of Northern Affairs Jean Lesage. For the first time in the North, the new school was to be non-denominational, although church-run student hostels were continued.

Gordon Robertson, the Northern Affairs Deputy Minister at the time of the Aklavik move, commented on the 1953 decision at a meeting of the Standing Committee on Mines, Forests and Waters in 1959. He said that the situation

> was all right as long as Aklavik was simply a trading post, but it became clear about 1953 that, if the North was going to develop at all, there had to be an administrative centre at the lower end of the Mackenzie.... They could not recommend making further expenditures at the old site of Aklavik ... basically, it is not a move of Aklavik. I think Aklavik is going to stay where it is ... what we were recommending was the establishment of a new administrative centre.... The ACND recommended to Cabinet that East 3 should be selected.... The Cabinet approved that decision. The population was in the neighborhood of 700 when we considered the move.... We have planned it on a possible maximum of 5000.... Not residential schools. The system that has been devised is to construct hostels, and then the children would attend the day school.... If oil and gas development goes ahead at a reasonable rate, this area could be up to 5,000 and beyond 5,000 (Robertson 1959).

Later Mr Robertson commented in a 1983 CBC interview that

> We needed a larger base, a more secure base, than Aklavik on an alluvial island could provide.... Frequently it has been said that the idea was that Inuvik would be created and Aklavik would vanish. I don't think we really thought that.... We wanted very much to have a town that was not ethnically divided and in which there were not areas that were Inuit, areas that were Native of any kind or other areas that were White.... It hasn't entirely worked out that way ... the houses on the utilidors by necessity had to be more expensive to live in and to maintain than the places that were not.... At the time, there were few Natives who were earning an income that would permit them to live in the places that were on the utilidors ... a degree of segregation that was not part of policy. It was sort of an economic accident (CBC Inuvik 25 May 1983) (McDermit 1983).

Nevertheless, there was considerable antagonism to the proposed Aklavik move, both from Ottawa opposition politicians and from local Aklavik residents. For one thing, some people preferred a site on the Delta's west side as "best for social, educational and health purposes and also for the gradual introduction of the local people into the new employment opportunities that we hoped would come" (Robertson 2000). The cost of the move was also an issue. In the Senate Hansard of 1 August 1956 the Hon. T. A. Crerar said, "I remain quite unconvinced of the need to spend several million dollars to move 600 or 700 people from their present location in Aklavik to some point 40 or 50 miles distant" (Brown 1999).

Almost 30 years later, Yukon MP Eric Nielsen recalled

> The raison d'etre for the policy was the unavailability of sufficient solid land to build an airstrip at Aklavik, the closest such land being at what is now known as Inuvik. In my view, that airstrip should have been built at the closest available land and if a community and a gathering of people naturally grew up around the airstrip, fine. That's the way things should develop. But to spend the taxpayer's dollar to influence the location of any community I thought personally was wrong. ...
>
> There was a natural feeling of resentment on the part of the people in Aklavik. In the first place, commercial values would drop. ... Also, I think, there was some feeling that the people who had trap lines in the immediate area might not have as good facilities. And, I suppose, another consideration was that Aklavik had been there for a long time, and the residents had an emotional attachment to Aklavik. ...
>
> The mistakes were made and still are being made ... mistakes were made because southern Canadians were making the decisions. Decisions were made in Ottawa by people who really did not know the Territories. They didn't know the people, they didn't know the geography, they didn't know the climate, they didn't know the economy, they knew nothing about the North (CBC Inuvik, 25 May 1983, McDermit 1983).

However, strong proof of the need for a new townsite occurred even as Inuvik was being constructed. As the ice broke up in the Mackenzie River in the spring of 1961, there was exceptionally severe flooding, and an estimated 98% of the delta land was under water. In Aklavik, at the flood peak, only a level strip about 100 yards long remained as dry land (Mackay 1963).

New Townsite Criteria

On January 22, 1954, an ACND Aklavik Subcommittee under Frank Cunningham set up guiding principles for the New Aklavik site as:

1. the new site would be planned as a modern community with appropriate zoning
2. the National Building Code would be enforced
3. solid foundations would be constructed at the new site
4. worthwhile government buildings in Aklavik would be moved to the new site
5. interested Aklavik residents would receive equivalent lots and be assisted to relocate.

Also, the main selection criteria for the new site were established as:

1. suitability for economic and social aspects
2. suitable ground for permanent roads, water and sewer systems
3. access to a navigable river channel
4. access to a suitable airfield site
5. satisfactory water supply.

ENERGY SERVICES

The secondary criteria for establishing a new Mackenzie Delta townsite involved availability of wood, access to a coal deposit and reasonable access to hydroelectric power. All of the 12 sites targeted for study from air photos had access to wood supplies both around the sites and in the Mackenzie Delta.

Hansen's Coal Mine, 90 km Northwest of Aklavik off Moose Channel near Mackenzie Bay, had supplied the Aklavik missions with around 2400 tons a year of coal. This operation used a 50 ton barge and made 48 trips over 16 weeks between July and October. Three trips were made each week taking one day each way with one day off. The coal deposit was checked out in 1955 by Geoff Galloway, an expert on the geology of coal deposits from England. He reported that the extent and quality of the coal was not suitable for large scale extraction (Galloway 1955).

Hydroelectric power potential for the Mackenzie Delta region was studied as part of the new townsite. A project was considered to divert Porcupine and Peel River waters across the continental divide to generating plants on the Rat River. This project would develop in five stages costing $1 billion, and would provide about 1.1 million kw of prime power at 6 mills per kwh at site. Another plan without river diversion would involve projects on the Porcupine and Peel Rivers. The Porcupine River project would cost $180 million and would process 175,000 kw of prime power at 7.5 mills per kwh at site. The Peel River project would cost $290 million and produce 310,000 kw of prime power at 6.5 mills per kwh at site. None of these projects were considered seriously.

Secondary criteria for the new site were:

1. within the treeline for the availability of wood
2. access to a coal deposit
3. reasonable access to hydroelectric power.

These principles and criteria were presented to the site search team that would start working immediately and proceed to the Mackenzie Delta in early Spring.

Search Team

Curt Merrill was appointed leader of the New Aklavik search team. He was a geologist who participated in several Arctic Island expeditions beginning in 1949. In March 1954 he was seconded from the Defence Research Board to the Department of Indian and Northern Affairs. Other team members were appointed from participating Federal departments. Local community advisors were appointed from the Aklavik Navy base and Aklavik community organizations.

The search party depended on local people. Dan McLeod served as cook. Leffingwell Shingatok, an Aklavik elder, was a special advisor to the townsite search party (Grainge 1999). Fred

SEARCH TEAM FOR NEW AKLAVIK 1953	
C.L. "Curt" Merrill (Leader)	Dept. of Northern Affairs and National Resources
K.C. "Ken" Berry	Dept. of Public Works
R.J.E. "Roger" Brown	National Research Council (DBR)
G.H. "Hank" Johnston	National Research Council (DBR)
J.A. "Johnny" Pihlainen	National Research Council (DBR)
J.K. "Ken" Fraser	Dept. Mines & Technical Surveys
E. "Eli" J. Garrett	Dept. of Transport
J. W. "Jack" Grainge	Dept. of National Health & Welfare
Aklavik Ex-Officio Members	
Lieut. A. P. Johnson	Royal Canadian Navy
W.O.D. Allison	Canadian Army (Signals)
Aklavik Local Advisory Committee	
Canon R. K. Gibson(chair)	Anglican Mission
Father A. Biname (sec)	Roman Catholic Mission
Karl Gardlund	Trappers Representative
Charles Smith	Eskimo Representative
Rev. Jim Sittichinli	Loucheux Representative
Insp. W. G. Fraser	Royal Canadian Mounted Police
S.M. "Stan" Peffer	Local Traders Representative
Herb Figures	Local Traders Representative
Frank Carmichael	Territorial Government
L.B. "Lee" Post	Dept. of Indian Affairs & National Resources

Norris transported crew and equipment by tractor-drawn sleigh. Mike Zubko of Aklavik Flying Services provided air support and Dan Landell flew helicopter transport (Grainge 1999).

In 1952 Lt A. P. Johnson was the first officer to take up this arctic posting. He assisted in the search for and selection of the New Aklavik site.

Site Investigations

In early 1954 a Mackenzie Delta map, made at a scale of 1 inch = 1 mile, was made from 1947 aerial photography and was assembled in Ottawa. This map and air photos were reviewed to find likely sites for a new community. Twelve sites were targeted as worthy of detailed study in the field – six on the west side of the Delta and six on the east side. These were narrowed down to nine possible sites before the main search party set out from Ottawa in April. When the survey party assembled in Aklavik during March 1954, four sites with the most potential were selected for field investigations until the end of August. These were named:

West 1 – Husky site. 19 km SW of Aklavik on Husky Channel near where it joins the Peel Channel, below Red Mountain on an alluvial fan running east from the Richardson Mountains.

West 2 – Black Mountain site. Along the Husky Channel, 10 km south of the Husky site on an alluvial fan below Black Mountain.

East 3 – East Channel site. 40 kilometres east of Aklavik, with relatively high glacial terrace extending 5 km along the East Channel and around 1.5 km wide. A gravel knoll at the river's edge provided a natural location for docking facilities and an initial construction camp.

East 4 – Reindeer Hills site. On East Channel 25 km north of East 3, to west of Noel Lake, site ran six kilometres along East Channel and extended inland for about 1.5 kilometres, terrain flat to north, series of rounded knolls to south, general rise to northeast, many hummocks, scattered birch up to nine metres high, plus scattered spruce, small lake in area.

Other sites that were reconnoitred but not fully investigated included Fraserville on the West Channel, 25 miles north of Aklavik where the Richardson Mountain benchlands intercept the Mackenzie Delta. As the Aklavik RCMP Inspector, Bill Fraser, had recommended this location, it was nicknamed Fraserville (Grainge 1999). On the East side of the Delta three other East Channel sites were considered in the area of Big Rock and Gull River where the Norris camp was located.

The team used a three-seat Associated Airways Hiller helicopter piloted by Dan Langile, which flew at 110 kph and had sufficient fuel for three hours flying with one passenger. Four base camps were established and the helicopter was used for 201 sorties and a total of 164 flying hours.

Roger Brown went to Aklavik ahead of the main study team, and then on to East 3, to observe the East Channel during 1954 spring breakup (Brown 1954).

The study team completed their work in late August and, in consultation with local residents, recommended the East 3 site as it had the highest criterion rating. This 110-hectare site was well above flood levels, within the treeline, on a navigable waterway, had large gravel sources identified, had access to wood and had ample space for airstrip construction. Minister of Indian and Northern Affairs Jean Lesage visited Aklavik and toured the proposed new townsite on the East Channel in August 1953. He was accompanied by Gordon Robertson, Deputy Minister, and L.A.C.O. Hunt, Administrator of the Western Northwest Territories. The survey team set up maps and reports in the Aklavik school for the meetings. Then they flew from Aklavik to East 3, with Max Ward of Wardair piloting an Otter, accompanied by Frank Carmichael, NWT Council Member, Merv Hardie, first MP for NWT, and Lee Post, Area Administrator for Aklavik.

Robertson later wrote about this visit, "Aklavik was both fascinating and depressing. The fascination was in the cultural mix. It was the only settlement of that time in which Indian, Metis, Inuit and whites lived together.... The depressing part was the confirmation of the utter unsuitability of Aklavik as the location for administration and services for the Western Arctic. [A move] would be best for social, educational and health purposes and for the gradual introduction of the local people into the new employment opportunities that we hoped would come. Lesage required convincing that no west site would do. We flew to the four proposed townsites" (Robertson 2000).

During this visit Curt Merrill was advised that the townsite move was approved and that building supplies were already underway.

Several years later Merrill commented on his August 1954 directions for developing East 3: "Gordon Robertson told me to remain in the Delta as long as useful work could proceed and to get on with developing a townsite. Some lumber and a few salvaged prefab buildings from Yellowknife were on barges headed for the Delta. There were willows to be cut at East 3. There were questions to be pursued about an airport site and gravel to be developed as source of road fill. Mr. Robertson suggested I hire any suitable help and purchase any available supplies. Despite certain limitations on the availability on short notice, of such things as tents and tools, a work party was quickly assembled using our survey camp tents, etc. and hiring local trappers able to supply their own tents" (Merrill 1985).

East 3 Examination

The East 3 site was originally known as Kigiak, the Inuit word for beaver, from the beavers living in Twin Lakes. (An Inuvik service company later operated as Kigiak Services.) The gravel knoll by the river was assumed to be where Alexander Mackenzie camped overnight on July 16, 1789. There were several trading posts and camps along East Channel. At Little Gull Creek to the south of Inuvik a post was operated by Adolphus Norris (1937-1963). Further south at Big Rock, Hudson's Bay Company had operated a post as a satellite to their Aklavik operations (Aquilina 1981). Several camps operated around Campbell Lake, including one belonging to Adolph Koziecek. Molly and Tom Goose had a camp on the East Channel just downstream from the site.

Registered Trapping Area No. 68, from the East Channel to Dolomite Lake, had been issued in the early 1950s to Jimmy Adams, a Cree Métis trapper, when the entire Delta area was divided up into trapping areas. Mr. Adams camp was along what became Airport Creek, and he ran a trapline through the present Inuvik townsite. For many years he and his son asked the federal goverment for compensation but he received none.

At the East 3 site a detailed terrain analysis and soil sample collection was made in late August and part of September 1954. Louis Jacobsen, an Aklavik elder and an employee of the Stefansson Arctic Expedition of 1913-1918, performed many tasks around the camp including tent repair. Peter Thrasher was the master of the D-6 Cat tractor and did most of the early roadwork. Logs for Inuvik were obtained from Gillis River near Fort Good Hope by Fred Norris with his boat "Barbara Jean." Buck Storr also delivered logs. There were 25 test pits dug for soil and permafrost investigations.

NRC's drill rig was brought into Boot Lake in summer of 1954 and hauled up a steep trail to the bench terrace. Near the eventual site of the Zubko house on Spruce Hill Drive, there was gravel down to a six-metre depth.

Consultations with Residents

Aklavik residents were already familiar with change from the outside, after the Beaufort Coast whaling days around 1890, the Klondike gold rush of 1900, the influx of Southern trappers during the 1920s and Alaskans during the 1940s, and DEWline construction along the Arctic Coast in the 1950s, especially the stations at Shingle Point and Tuktoyaktuk.

On December 7, 1953 the news came to the Delta that Aklavik was to be moved. The scientifically planned replacement for Aklavik would rehouse the people, and provide a better, more modern base for government services and operations as well as allow room for future expansion (Aquilina 1981). "The benefit of local experience was obtained through a Local Advisory Committee. This committee included representatives from each racial group and from the traders and missions. The first meeting was held before the team established a camp; other meetings were called at intervals as required. In this way, not only the local experience was made available to the survey team, but the residents of Aklavik were kept directly advised on the survey's progress" (Merrill 1960).

The apprehensions of residents on the location of a new townsite and transfer of services to this site were considered by the Aklavik Relocation Advisory Committee. The 1954 site search team was based at Aklavik and its members held regular meetings with the Advisory Committee and the Town Planning Committee.

DIGGING HOLES AND FILLING THEM IN

During the initial E3 site investigations local crews were commissioned to dig several test pits to examine the subsurface soils and permafrost ice content. Victor Allen recounts this difficult digging in rock-hard frozen soils and how he thought the "white man" was really crazy to have all these holes dug and then just fill them in.

At Aklavik a Citizen's Committee to review the East 3 activities was formed with Karl Gardlund, spokesman, Herb Figueres, chair, Bert Wallace, secretary. Four letters from Commissioner Robertson on liquor distribution were considered along with Native rations.

On April 9, 1954 Northern Affairs Minister Jean Lesage and Deputy Minister Frank Cunningham held a meeting in Aklavik with the Town Planning Committee, to answer questions and objections for the move of Aklavik to the East Three site. Present at this meeting were Jim Edwards, Charlie Gordon, Andrew Stewart, Alec Stefansson, Karl Gardlund, Dave Allison RCCS, Dave Jones IOL Agent, MLA Frank Carmichael, Capt. McDonald RCN, Stan Peffer, Insp. Wm. Fraser RCMP, Wally Burton, Archdeacon Webster, Fathers Biname and Brown (Brown 1996, 15 May 57). Lesage and Cunningham responded to questions on a prepared sheet read by Karl Gardlund. At this meeting Karl Gardlund was elected Chairman to replace Herb Figueres. Father Brown was elected secretary to replace Father Biname.

At this meeting the timing and terms for the relocation were agreed on as follows (Brown 1996):

1. Timing: 1956 – pick your lot
               1958 – build your new home
               1959 – move your old home over from Aklavik
               1960 – deadline for moving all government buildings

2. Homeowners in Aklavik who wish to move will be paid what their house would cost to build in E-3, less depreciation, plus 15% for disturbance. A government inspector will be in to do this job this summer.

3. Lots at the new townsite will cost nothing and present lot owners in Aklavik will get first choice.

4. The Eskimo cabins will be used to house labourers and then depreciated and sold afterwards.

5. There will be a property tax.

6. Individuals may build their own homes provided they can pass the building standards set up. Every individual supplies his own piles.

7. There will be a town laundry but as yet no one has offered to run it. There will be no charge for soap for showers at the main laundry as this item will come under the heading "education".

8. Recreation centre and radio station will be left for the people to build.

9. Each householder pays for installing surface pipes from his cabin to the main utilidor.

Aklavik residents generally were not pleased with the proposed East Channel site, as they thought the trapping was not as good there, it was far from familiar hunting areas in the Richardson Mountains, and, since it was within the Reindeer Grazing Preserve, they could not hunt caribou (Berton 1956). The Reindeer Grazing Preserve had been authorized in 1929, in an effort to start a Canadian reindeer industry comparable to practices in

Scandinavia and Alaska at the time. Also, there was speculation of a road being constructed to Aklavik from the Yukon, and local residents assumed this road couldn't be extended across the delta to the East Channel site (Brown 1999).

Aklavik was facing several social and economic problems in addition to the townsite relocation. These are succinctly reported in Pierre Berton's 1956 book *The Mysterious North*. When Berton visited Aklavik in summer of 1954 he found that the town

> was grappling with a depression as black as the one that hit the outside world in the thirties.... In 1950, three hundred thousand muskrat pelts poured through Aklavik. Each sold for an average of two dollars. But by 1954 the caprices of fashion had forced the price down to fifty cents. At the same time the muskrat's mysterious life cycle had reached its ebb and only half as many were trapped. Aklavik's income had dropped by seven-eighths in just four years.

> This was only half the story of Aklavik's dilemma: the rest was more ironic. All the building planned for the town was government construction work – either out-and-out government buildings or government-subsidized buildings such as the schools and hospitals. It was absolutely necessary to build them, because the native population is increasing so swiftly. The old people are living longer, more babies are surviving, tuberculosis has been controlled by free chest X-rays and improved medical services, mothers are getting better prenatal care, family allowances are encouraging bigger and healthier families, and old age pensions have made grandparents a blessing instead of a burden.

> There are more natives than ever before. There is less income for them.... The situation is complicated because over the years, in boom times of the past the Indians and Eskimos approached a Coca-Cola standard of living.... But now the schooners sat on the Aklavik beach, the paint peeling from their hulls, and the natives went hungry. All of them found it painful and bitter to revert to the primitive standards of living (Berton 1956).

The Minister of Northern Affairs had arrived in Aklavik a few hours before Pierre Berton. "Aklavik was making news. The government had announced its intention of moving the entire settlement out of the muddy peninsula into which, the newspapers said, it was slowly sinking.... The Minister said, simply, that it would be easier and cheaper to trundle the entire town fifty miles away to the river's eastern channel, where the ground is high and hard. Then he mentioned casually what is undoubtedly the main reason for the move: a modern airstrip capable of landing jet planes would soon be built here on the Arctic's rim. The new town would be a long way from most of the trapping lands, but for a few years at least there would be plenty of work for everybody at the airport and in the new town" (Brown 1996).

On February 7, 1955, the Town Planning Committee was given a draft plan for the new townsite. This plan included the instructions that "Natural conditions should not be interfered with in any way and, in areas where permafrost exists, excavations should be prohibited." Sixty lots were reserved for Aklavik residents expecting to move to Inuvik. There were no charges for these lots.

There was a free draw for these lots at the Aklavik Administration Building on 20 and 22 December 1956. Only 22 people showed up for the draw on the first day but, when it closed, 49 lots had been chosen, 8 for the serviced area and 41 for the unserviced.

The Local Advisory Committee had three members – Karl Gardlund, Jim Edwards and Stan Peffer – on hand to handle disputes, but no disputes arose. (Brown, Jan 1957, 1996). When this Aklavik Citizens Committee met on 27 December 1956, Karl Gardlund was spokesman, Herb Figueres, Chairman, and Bert Wallace, secretary. Andrew Stewart was interpreting for the Indians and Charley Gordon in place of Chief John Keevik interpreting for the Eskimos.

A New Town Advisory Committee was formed in Aklavik in January 1957 with Karl Gardlund, Jim Edwards and Stan Peffer as members (*Aklavik Journal* January 1957).

But many Aklavik residents remained opposed to the move. During this period of change a resistance spirit developed that was led by the Aklavik school principal A.J. Moose Kerr. A " Never Say Die" resistance song became popular:

> *Sing a song of toy town,*
> *Glossy, bright and new,*
> *But the people, not the buildings,*
> *Make a spirit true.*
>
> *Oh, you can have your airport,*
> *Roads and cars and all,*
> *But loudly and forever,*
> *You will always hear us call,*
>
> *Aklavik, Aklavik, ever we will cry,*
> *Aklavik, Aklavik, never say die.*

Dan McLeod (left) and Curt Merrill cross the delta aboard a 16′ Peterborough Cedar Strip boat powered by 25hp kicker. McLeod was cook for the site search party as well as during construction at East 3. Merrill was leader of the site search party and project co-ordinator for construction in 1955 and 1956. (Photo by Curt Merrill, NWT Archives/N-1992-192: 0099)

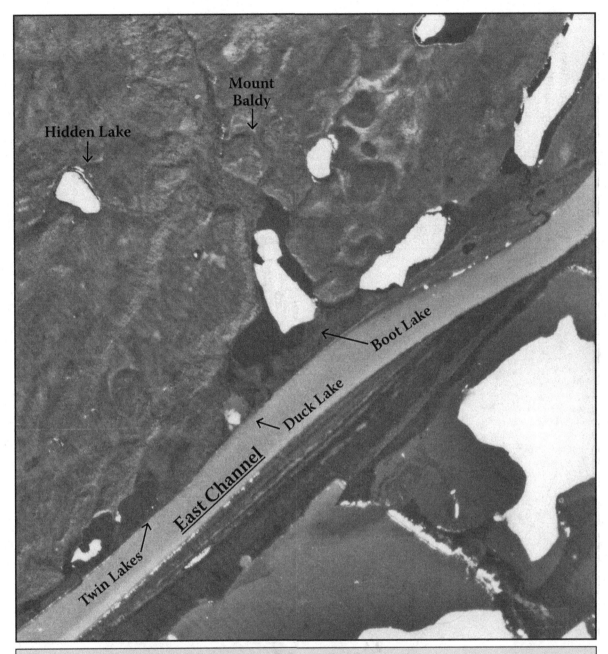

AERIAL PHOTO OF EAST 3 SITE
Taken in June 1952, when many of the lakes were still partially ice-covered, this photo was the basis for the initial maps of the site. (Photo # A13406-283, Department of Energy, Mines & Resources)

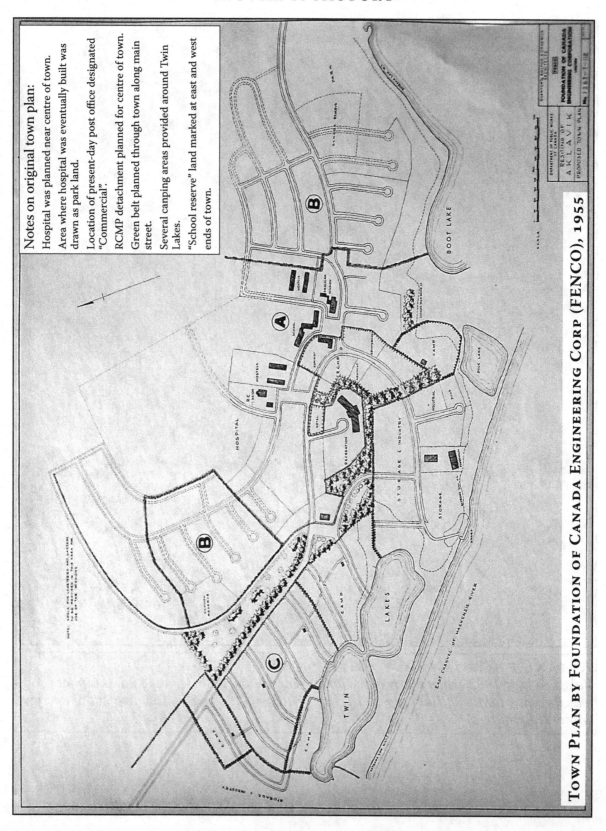

Notes on original town plan:

Hospital was planned near centre of town.

Area where hospital was eventually built was drawn as park land.

Location of present-day post office designated "Commercial".

RCMP detachment planned for centre of town.

Green belt planned through town along main street.

Several camping areas provided around Twin Lakes.

"School reserve" land marked at east and west ends of town.

TOWN PLAN BY FOUNDATION OF CANADA ENGINEERING CORP (FENCO), 1955

PERSPECTIVE OF ROAD CROSS OVER
TYPE 'C' UTILIDOR

The town was planned to minimize intersections between roads and utilidors. Where a crossing was necessary, roadways were to be routed over or under the utilidor, so as to avoid grade changes in the utilidor. From "Re-siting of Aklavik" blueprints done by Foundation of Canada Engineering Corporation (FENCO), 1955

Inuvik Time Line 1956 – 1963

1956
	Mar 30-Apr 2	Gov Gen Vincent Massey and party visit Aklavik and East 3
	Jun	New town plan approved by Aklavik Relocation Committee
	Jun	Slim Semmler opens tent store on East Channel shore
	Jul	First baby born at East 3, Shirley to Bertha and Victor Allen
	Jul	Fred Carmichael is first Western Arctic local to obtain pilot's licence
	Aug 23	NWT Council Session at East 3, first meeting north of Arctic Circle
	Aug 26	First wedding at East 3, Father Brown married John Pascal & Rosie Pokiak
	Aug	HBC opens new store on Water Street next to the government garage
	Sep 9	First "512" classroom setup by Connie Miller and Ella Shanahorn
	Sep	New Catholic mission opens
	Nov 3	First CPA ski plane lands on East Branch

1957
	Apr 23	First East 3 Spring Carnival
	May	Nursing Station and RCMP operations begin
	May	Royal Canadian Legion moves to East 3 from Aklavik
	Jul	Agriculture Canada experimental vegetable crops behind Stringer Hall
	Jul	Anglican Mission opens on Distributor Street under Capt. Ken Snider

1958
	Apr	Bank of Commerce opens first "512" bank on Mackenzie Road
	May	East 3 post office opens as "New Aklavik"
	Jun	Igloo Church construction starts
	Jul 18	NWT Council proclaims name "Inuvik" to replace Aklavik East 3
	Jul	NCPC installs 150 KW generator for construction camp
	Sep 15	Peffer's Rec Hall complex opens with cafe, pool hall & theatre
	Nov 24	Inuvik Airport licence issued by Ministry of Transport

1959
	Feb	Inuvik Community Association organized for recreation activities
	May	RCMP district headquarters relocated from Aklavik
	Jun 25	Jim Koe appointed to Nelson Commission on Indian Treaties 8 & 11
	Sep	Federal Day School completed with 30 classrooms and two student residences
	Oct 9	Inuvik proclaimed a NWT Development Area by NWT Council
	Dec	Inuvik Laundry and wash house completed

1960
	Jul 31	First Mackenzie Delta oil well spuded, Richfield Point Separation No. 1
	Aug 5	Igloo Church consecrated with Ceremony of Blessing by Bishop Paul Piche
	Oct	Mackenzie Hotel opens
	Nov 25	CBC's CHAK radio station opens in Inuvik
	Nov	Royal Canadian Navy transfers from Aklavik to new Inuvik facilities
	Nov	Inuvik Curling Club opens in Butler Building with two sheets
	Dec	Government liquor store moved from Aklavik to Inuvik Federal Building

1961
	Jan 15	Inuvik General Hospital and Nurses Residence opened
	Jan 23	First birth at Inuvik Hospital, Katherine May, to Rowena and William Edwards
	Jun 5	Extremely high flood with about 98% of Mackenzie Delta under water
	Jun 30	Inuvik Lions Club founded
	Jul 21	Prime Minister John Diefenbaker officially dedicates Inuvik
	Sep	Federal Day School name changed to Sir Alexander Mackenzie School (SAMS)

1962
	Oct	New Legion building of Delta logs
	Nov	Inuvik Christian Assembly opens in a "512" building
	Nov	Government Liquor Warehouse and store opens

1963
	Jul 8	NWT Council's 25th Session in Inuvik in SAMS gym
	Sep 10	Polaris Theatre opened on Mackenzie Road
	Sep 10	Navy communications facility commissioned as HMCS Inuvik
	Dec 31	Inuvik Research Lab opens with a community drum dance in cosmic ray room

CHAPTER THREE

The Construction of Inuvik, 1956 – 1963

Building a new town from scratch on the permafrost in the Arctic was a major undertaking. Workers had to be hired and trained, the landscape had to be transformed into roadways and building lots, a transportation infrastructure had to be developed to handle the shipping of all the materials, and the buildings had to be designed, contracted, and constructed. There was necessarily a lot of overlap between these tasks, as a large workforce could not be assembled until buildings were in place to house and feed them, and even this initial construction required shipping of materials and development of landings along the river bank. And of course, a town is more than a collection of buildings and roads, and even as the physical infrastructure of East 3 was under construction, elements such as schools, churches, commercial enterprises and social clubs were also developing.

Northern workforce

People from the North and from the South worked together at East 3 from the outset. The local workers were recruited mainly from Aklavik, Fort McPherson, Fort Good Hope, Tuktoyaktuk, Old Crow and Fort Franklin. Most of the southern workforce was recruited in Edmonton. In 1957 the Federal Department of Public Works in Inuvik had 130 employees working under Charlie Walrath. (In 1957 it was agreed that the Department of Public Works would be responsible for all Inuvik construction projects, and that the Department of Indian Affairs would deal with all matters concerning administration.)

The early days of construction coincided with another important project in the history of the northern economy: the Distant Early Warning Line (DEWline). This was a set of radar installations built across the US and Canadian arctic to provide advance detection of Soviet

LOCAL EAST 3 TEAM/CONTRACTORS 1954		
Jimmy Adams	George Harry	Jimsey McLeod
Colin Allen	Dan Hubbs	Rosa McLeod
Victor Allen	Nels Hvatum	Fred Norris
Red Anders	Louis Jacobsen	Pat Patrick
Sam Arey	Ed Kikoak	Jake Peffer
John Carmichael	Adolph Koziecek	Johnny Semple
Malcolm Firth	Pat Martin	Leffingwell Shingatok
Charlie Gordon	Dan McLeod	Buck Storr
Cliff Hagen	Ellen McLeod	Peter Thrasher
Jim Harrison	Eddie McLeod	

43

bombers or missiles. When nearby DEWline work was completed in November 1956, many Eskimo workers came to Inuvik looking for work on the townsite and nearby airport construction. Moose Kerr, the Aklavik school principal, had the job of hiring for East 3 and DEWline work during the summer of 1956.

From the start East 3 provided employment for native girls and women. This helped many families after they lost their productive role in the trapping economy (Honigman, 1970, p 59). The Inuvik construction program was initially planned for five years but was later extended to 10 years mainly to provide more local employment (Kettle 1956).

The first tasks were primarily in transportation and site preparation, and training programs were set up at the beginning to foster local participation. During the 1954-55 winter several Mackenzie Delta residents were given work experience in operating earth-moving equipment in a school at Leduc, Alberta managed by Bert Boxer. In the following years, the training programs branched out into many other areas.

The East 3 project provided the opportunity for a continuous course in building skills including carpentry, heavy equipment operation and electrical services. There was opportunity for Delta residents to learn a new trade and to live in a modern community with full conveniences such as education, medicine, transportation, communication and employment. Contractors were obliged to provide employment and training for every interested local resident. Local residents were hired directly or given training for employment before any Inuvik construction positions were made available to outsiders (*Aklavik Journal* January 1957).

During the winter of 1956-57 and the winter following, large groups of local workers were given vocational training programs by Northern Affairs as carpenters, painters, mechanics and drivers, while their wives and daughters learned cooking and service skills. On-the-job training was encouraged. Most local people trained in their various trades readily took up permanent residence in Inuvik and participated in the future of the town they helped build.

The Education Department's Continuing Education Section provided extensive programs to assist local residents in upgrading and trades training. Adult literacy was strongly encouraged as many of the initial East 3 workers had not had the opportunity of schooling. Also, money management, home economics and family enrichment services were provided. The training programs sometimes had to face language barriers, and sign language was common.

As the years went on, and a more permanent infrastructure was in place, additional programs were made available. The Inuvik Rehabilitation Centre was set up in 1959 to provide a "halfway house" between living on the land and participating in the modern wage economy offered by East 3. The facility, located on Lot 17 (Samuel Hearne Secondary School site), offered accommodation, training and counselling. There were several small buildings made from Delta log construction, providing an office, training, trades activities and participant housing. The Centre was operated by the Rehabilitation Section of the Northern Administration Branch for people who suffered from physical or psychological disabilities or were socially disabled as a result of cultural or economic change. The Centre was designed to provide experience in community living and employment routines to help restore participants to a useful, normal and gainful life. Many individuals and families were helped to bridge difficult periods.

Charley Soupy had the opportunity to go south for watch repair training. He returned and operated his watchmaker's shop in a Rehab Centre building. The Centre operated the snack concession at the Inuvik General Hospital. A barber shop was operated by a participant from Old Crow in the Yukon. A Woodcraft Workshop made sleds, toboggans, sleighs, rat boards and coffins. A Sewing Shop sought to develop home industries, arts and crafts, and provide a sales outlet. The Fish and Game Shop purchased Delta whitefish, trout and rabbits and resold them. Chickens were raised. A full time teacher from SAMS was employed to work with rehabilitants. Driving lessons were provided.

Tom Butters was Rehab Centre superintendent in 1962 with Dave Sutherland as projects manager. Tom Butters was replaced by Olive Chesworth in November 1964.

In March 1963 a decision was made to phase out the Rehab Centre and to locate the new high school in its place (Langford 1966). Some of the former Rehab log houses are now at Dave Button's lot on Carn Road.

From the earliest stages of work, local people worked not only as labourers, but also as contractors, providing not only their labour but also project management and machinery.

In December of 1956, the *Aklavik Journal* reported that Leo and Albert Norwegian, Eddie McPherson, Archie Hardisty and George Villeneuve had recently returned to Fort Simpson from work at East 3, and Michael Coyne, Barney Natsie, Pierre Bluecoat, Rudolph Cardinal and Martin Niditchie had returned to Arctic Red River (Brown 1996, December 1956).

Colin Allen worked on log booms and general carpentry. Elijah Allen was involved with the airport construction. Sam Arey operated a steam point. Jim Biggs was a D8 Cat operator. Cliff Hagen was a Cat skinner. George Harry worked the pile driver. Cliff Moore was a steam point operator. John Carmichael operated a soil sampling drill. The *Aklavik Journal* of March 1957 reported 22 men from Good Hope out cutting logs for East 3 (Brown 1996).

Planners had tried to anticipate and prepare for possible social problems. "No one will be encouraged to drift into Inuvik and hang around on the chance of picking up a job. Slum areas and unemployment are two scourges that those responsible for the town will strive to avoid at all costs …. This is not a place that people from the 'outside' came in and built, single handed and unhelped. It is a town that people from the North and South worked on together from the outset" (Baird 1960). Nevertheless, not everything worked smoothly. In the view of one observer, "The government was unwittingly disturbing the tranquility of those communities and alienating some of the best workers from them …. It might have proven better for the natives involved if as many jobs as possible were filled by complete strangers to the North. This view would not have been politically agreeable at the time, for it was argued that work on these projects should first benefit the people of the North" (Brown 1999).

There were some problems with local workers not showing up for work regularly and some weekend parties which could go on all week (Brown 1999). At the 1962 NWT Council session in Ottawa, Mackenzie Delta Councilor Knute Lang said "too many Indians and

Eskimos spend their time at Inuvik playing poker, drinking, waiting for pay cheques and living on welfare payments." (*Nuna* Winter 1962). "

At one point one of the workers from the South was promoting a strike for higher wages. When the white man asked the Indian truck driver to join, he replied "Are you crazy? We never had it so good" (Webster 1987).

There were few amenities for workers in the early years. The initial workers pitched their tents along the East Branch shoreline. Then they moved up to the next level to the site of the present day Happy Valley campground.

During the summer of 1955 there were more than 100 in the East 3 work force, 30 of them local hire. At the start of construction in Spring 1956 there was still no worker accommodation. A qualification for local hire was having a tent. There were still around 200 locals living in tents in late summer 1956.

Feeding the work crews was an early priority. To make a cookhouse, two 512s (a standardized wood-frame building measuring 16′ × 32′, or 512 square feet) were put together with one half for cooking and the other half for eating. Later a third 512 was added for food storage and trash handling.

Within a short time, many local hires moved into more 512s as they became available.

Local supplies and suppliers

From the beginning of work, year-round transportation between Aklavik and East 3 was essential. "The Eskimo Loan Fund together with Indian Affairs have advanced $5000 for the construction of a winter road from Old Aklavik to the new town site of E3. Reconnaissance of the route was made by Adolph Koziesak in March (1955). The distance is about 40 miles [65 km], 70% of which is over water. Fred Norris received a contract to grade the cutbacks where the road will cross rivers" (Brown 1996).

A historic trip was made on November 4, 1956, when a jeep driven by Dr. Ian Black and RCMP Inspector Huget made 115 km from Aklavik to E3 and back. This was the first time a wheeled vehicle traveled between Aklavik and East 3, on ice as smooth as the Trans Canada Highway, according to the *Aklavik Journal* (December 1956).

Air travel was also important. Fred Carmichael obtained his pilot's licence in 1956 and flew a Stinson aircraft to Aklavik. Danny Norris returned to Aklavik after two years at an Edmonton trade school (Brown 1996, 15 February 1956). In November 1956 CPA Otter service began twice weekly flights between Norman Wells and E3 (Brown 1996).

During East 3's preparation stage there was considerable boat activity across the Delta, as the East 3 site was over 100 km from Aklavik by unmarked Delta channels, with 21 critical "Y" turns (Brown 1999).

Some lumber and a few salvaged prefab buildings from Yellowknife were sent by barge to East 3 (Pennington 1994). Harry Harrison used his schooner, the Golden Hind, to haul empty 45-gallon drums from the abandoned military base at Kitigazuit, 65 km to the north. These drums were used to build road culverts and for many other construction projects.

Felling saws were used to cut down trees for power poles in April 1956, as powered chain saws were not yet available. Dick Bullock arrived at East 3 towing a raft of 100 logs for pilings that he had cut at Tree River.

Fred Norris obtained logs from Gillis River, near Fort Good Hope, with his tug boat "Barbara Jean". Merrill described Norris with these words: "The energetic and resourceful Fred Norris, owner of a 5-ton truck, D2 cat, Barbara Jean tug boat and a CANOL barge, a veritable local Dep't of Public Works". A Delta scow was leased from Jim MacDonald, and Hans Hansen's boat "Kings Highway" was busy hauling freight. Buck Storr, an Aklavik trapper turned timber entrepreneur, hauled logs to East 3 from around the Mackenzie Delta. During the summer of 1957 Fred "Jake" Jacobsen traveled by boat every Saturday for a load from the Aklavik liquor store.

Red Anders and Jake Peffer were the first East 3 contractors hired to find, fell, square and deliver timbers, suitable for wood sills on which to pile the lumber enroute from Swanson's Mill in Wood Buffalo Park. Late in the summer of 1954, several million board feet of lumber were barged down the Mackenzie River to East 3. Also in 1954, several prefab buildings that had been used during the construction of Norman Wells and the Canol Pipeline were knocked down and shipped north to East 3. A bulldozer, back hoe and several trucks were also sent. The decision to ship these items in 1954 cut a year off the construction time for the new town (Grange 1999).

By the end of the shipping season in 1954, deliveries to the site included $300,000 in supplies and equipment, in preparation for construction in 1955.

The original site plan

In September 1954, Dick Snowling and Dick Bower of Energy, Mines and Resources surveyed the East 3 area and produced a large map with one-foot contour lines.

On May 17, 1955, Foundation of Canada Engineering Corporation (FENCO) of Toronto signed an agreement with the Federal Public Works to implement planning for the new townsite for 275 acres (110 hectares) and an initial population of 2,500, with possible expansion to 5,000 people. There was to be a central heating plant, services distributed in above-ground utilidors, methods to preserve the permafrost and a community layout. Preparation of the plans were assisted by architects Durnford, Bolton & Chadwick of Ottawa, design engineers Rule, Wynn & Rule of Edmonton and geotechnical engineers R. M. Hardy & Associates of Edmonton. On August 16, 1955 FENCO Vice President Per Hall submitted the East 3 report on the "New Town Site for Aklavik, NWT" to the Department of Public Works in Ottawa (FENCO 1955). This report was prepared by FENCO staff – N.D. Lea, assistant to Vice President, A.H. Thompson, mechanical studies, E.J. Bartley, electrical studies and B.I. Maduke, soils work. The report was reviewed by R.E. Bolton, R.M. Hardy and Per Hall. This detailed new town pan included novel recommendations for community heating and municipal services.

Montreal Engineering Limited was commissioned to design the power plant and the architect firms of Rensaa and Minsos and Rule, Wynn, and Rule were hired to design the main buildings.

A new aerial survey of the East 3 site was made in August 1955 to establish the basic topography and drainage. Two gravel deposits were located at Twin Lakes and Boot Creek. Samples of the limestone outcrop at Dolomite were evaluated for crushing. The gravel sources in the Caribou Hills to the north of Inuvik were not considered close enough to be utilized.

Site soil conditions were classified into shallow organic, deep organic, sandy till and fine-grained soils. High ice content, segregated ice and ice lenses were found in all soils throughout the townsite confirming that special foundations would be required to avoid thawing the permafrost. Test piles confirmed that wooden posts would provide the most satisfactory and economical foundations. Steam point penetration was suggested as the most effective way to set the piles.

The town plan was designed to fit the existing topography and was in the form of a 'T' along the higher and more desirable ground. The bottom stem of the 'T' was at the wharf on the East Channel, with the arms extending above Boot Lake and Twin Lakes. The town centre was placed at the junction of the stem and the arms. The streets were laid out along the natural topography to accommodate gravity-flow of sewage in utilidors. Building locations were selected to maintain vista and serve as wind breaks. As the service utilidors were more expensive than roads, additional roads were included to keep the utilidor length to a minimum. Crossing of roads by utilidors was avoided where possible. Major fire breaks of at least 150 feet (46 metres) between building zones were set as a safety measure. The zones were laid out radially from the town centre to accommodate future expansion.

The town wharf was designed with a deck elevation of 8 feet (2.4 metres) above summer levels allowing for the spring floods to carry most of the river ice over it without damage to the structure. A central 25 acre (10 hectare) storage and industrial area was located close to the wharf. A second industrial area was located at the west end of Twin Lakes for a possible saw mill, boat haulup and storage yard which would involve dredging a channel from East Channel to Twin Lakes.

A town square was shown near the town centre, with a Federal building and a school between the two mission properties. A hospital, with provision for a nurses residence and other single hospital staff, would be on the high ground northwest of Mackenzie Square where Samuel Hearne Secondary School is now located. Residential areas included space for regular housing and for camps. Accommodation allowance was made for 424 families with 1878 persons. A considerable part of the town was zoned as a green area to accommodate parks and recreational areas. It was considered important to restrict construction operations so that the natural cover was not disturbed. Consideration was given to transplanting birch trees to the townsite.

There was provision for dog pounds to accommodate the dog teams used by the RCMP and local residents. At the time dog teams were as important as cars were to a southern society. There was a need for a community "parking lot". As Aklavik's summer population swelled from an influx of people from Delta camps, provision was made in the new townsite plan for "transient" accommodation. The airport location was still under study when the FENCO report was issued. Two locations were considered, one northwest of the town site and the other alongside Long Lake (Shell Lake).

Roads were designed with a minimum 4% grade, except for the ramp from the wharf which had a 9% grade. Cuts were completely avoided except for the wharf approach. Dead end streets in the residential areas avoided crossing the utilidors which were usually at the rear of the lot lines. The road gravel was to be placed on top of the undisturbed moss cover. Except for a small area requiring stripping and drainage, the moss cover was to be preserved throughout the entire site. Where it was disturbed, it was to be covered with gravel. A surface drainage system was developed to handle the spring runoff and summer rains on the impervious permafrost soils.

With the concept of concentrating buildings close to the town centre, central heating was considered attractive economically and was a practical way to keep the utilidors from freezing. In addition to economy, the advantages of central heating were listed as:

1. Convenient means for heating utilidors.
2. Reduces fire hazard.
3. Reduces cost of buildings serviced.
4. Reduces the staff required for heating.
5. Makes possible a steam driven electrical generating plant.
6. Makes possible conversion to atomic fuel.

Consideration was given for using Norman Wells fuel oil and Bunker "C" fuel. Coal from the Hansen Mine at the northwest corner of the Delta was evaluated but considered too expensive. The location of the power plant close to the river was justified on the savings of both capital and operating costs.

Water supply was proposed from a combination of Hidden Lake and East Channel. The domestic water would be treated, filtered and chlorinated with provision to bypass the treatment for steam system and fire protection. Sewage disposal was considered using Duck Lake

Atomic Power in the North

At the time the central power plant concept was introduced, it was thought that a small, efficient and economic atomic reactor would soon be available. The Atomic Energy Company Ltd. (AECL) was developing a modified "CANDU" reactor which might be utilized. A small reactor was operating at McMaster University and a nuclear-powered weather station was installed at Axel Heiberg Island. In 1960 the US Army installed a PM-2 portable nuclear power plant at Camp Century located in the Greenland ice cap 140 miles east of Thule to provide electricity, steam heat and fresh water. A similar nuclear plant was installed for the Cold Regions Test Centre at Fort Greely near Fairbanks.

and Twin Lakes but these were considered too close to the community. Simple dilution into the East Channel was recommended with a sewage outfall 300 yards downstream from the water intake. Consideration of a complete treatment plant was to be considered later should one be required. For garbage disposal controlled dumping and burning with subsequent burying was recommended at a location along the East Channel west of the community.

The 1955 construction schedule called for building the wharf, 11 camp buildings and a workshop garage. Some gravel was to be stockpiled from a pit at the west end of Twin Lakes and piles were to be gathered for the 1956 construction program. It was proposed that a contractor be selected as soon as possible to carry out the 1956 construction program, so the site could be visited before freezeup and materials procured during the winter for early spring delivery. Surface grubbing of 50 hectares for the town site and 25 hectares for an airstrip and for laying the base for roads and the airstrip was planned. Piles would be installed for the 1957 construction projects.

It was anticipated that the main construction program would be carried out during 1957 and 1958 with a labour force that could exceed 500. With the completion of the roads and airstrip in 1957, the 1958 program would be exclusively buildings. Individual government functions would be transplanted from Aklavik at various times through the two years. It was proposed to have the town functioning by the beginning of 1959 with a cleanup of construction operations completed that year. Based on the preliminary recommendations, a total cost for providing services was estimated at $5.5 million.

Site Preparations at East 3

Curt Merrill was sent to the East 3 site in April 1955 as Project Manager. He was an engineer and geologist working on northern problems with the Defence Research Board and was leader of the 1954 New Aklavik Search Party.

Inuvik's environmental ethic was initiated by Merrill, when he instructed all construction crews to minimize vegetation disruption when building roads and building pads. A bulldozer operator could be fired for knocking down trees unnecessarily. Of particular note was the preservation of elegant spruce trees along Mackenzie Road between the central area and the hospital. These trees were protected from the contractors, but all died by the early 1960s after drainage programs changed the soil conditions.

In June 1955 vegetation was stripped off a gravel deposit at the southwest end of Twin Lakes, with the willows used as a base for the roads being constructed at the time. Fred Norris stripped the moss from another gravel deposit, at the north end of Twin Lakes, where there was 1 – 1.3 metres of thawed gravel. Most of the Inuvik roads were built with gravel from this pit.

During the summer of 1955, road building equipment was delivered by Northern Transportation Company Ltd. (NTCL), including a D6 Caterpillar dozer, a two-yard back hoe that could be converted to a dragline, seven GMC five-ton dump trucks, a steam jenny and a Bombardier snowmobile. Jerry Tracz was the equipment foreman. Peter Thrasher was the bulldozer operator. Peter had a good eye for grade and built most of the East 3 roads in 1955-57.

Detailed site investigations were carried out for the Department of Public Works by Foundation of Canada Engineering Corporation (FENCO). When test pits were dug several large ice lenses were found. Early construction projects included an access road to the main borrow pits, and buildings for warehousing and contractor quarters.

In March 1956 two miles of gravel roads were constructed and the garage/workshop and eleven worker accommodation units had been built. These units measured 16′ × 32′ and were known as "512s" after their square footage. Seventy-five 512s were planned to be built

EAST 3 SITE CREWS

Kitchen crews:

DPW Kitchen: Margaret White Chief Cook, Mary Harley, Louis Greenland, Rosa McLeod, Emily Nazon, Florence Hagen, Susan Harley, Elizabeth Firth, Ida Irish.

Poole Kitchen: Ellen Martin, Myrtle Harrison

Gardlund's Cafe: Eliza Greenland, Astrid Gardlund, Persis Stewart, Patsy Louie, Kay Mitchell, Mary Kendi

Semmler's Store: Esther Rufus, Rosalie Greenland, Dorothy Joe, Agnes Moses

Aklavik Constructors: Blanche Jeski chief cook (AJ Summer 1957)(Brown 1996)

Operating Crews:

Dick Bower: Survey assistant to Charley Gordon

Roger Brown: National Research Council, Division of Building Research

John Dusseault: carpenter foreman, from St. John, Quebec

John Gilbey: Dep't of Agriculture, Fort Simpson

Charley Gordon: Dominion Land Surveyor for legal survey of East 3

Hank Johnston: National Research Council, Division of Building Research

Per Hall: Construction consultant

Bob Langdon: Northern Affairs representative in 1958

Dan Landells: Pilot, Bell G-47 helicopter for site search team

Bill Lawlor: Carpenter, helped on building Igloo church

Norm Lee: Consultant with Foundation Engineering Company

Bud Maduke: Engineer with Foundation Engineering Company

Curt Merrill: Northern Affairs Project manager in 1956

Ray Oancia: Resident Engineer

Charlie Olson: DPW on East 3 dock construction

Lee Post: Northern Affairs Administrator

John Pihlainen: National Research Council, Division of Building Research

Joe Pinsonnault: Carpenter, helped on construction of Igloo Church

Tom Taylor: Northern Affairs Project Manager in 1957 replacing Curt Merrill

Jerry Tracz: Equipment Foreman

Charlie Walrath: DPW Construction Manager in February 1957

for use by the construction program, and they were to be sold later to local residents at low prices after project completion.

Engineers from the DPW Edmonton office designed and supervised the construction of the wharf, which was finished in late September 1956 by Charlie Olson and his pile driving crew. A steam jet and pile driver were used. One large warehouse was constructed on a mud sill foundation using 4″ flattened and treated spruce sills. This construction variation without piles was considered an experiment.

In 1957, "[Charlie] Walrath's construction crew tried stripping away the organic overburden .... This created a 3m wide boggy trench of mud and water ... switching to laying willows on the un-stripped ground crossways of the road and dumping gravel on top was no less a headache .... Finally they dumped almost a metre thickness of gravel on the natural ground. If sags developed, they filled them in with more gravel. With this the roads have stood up well but were dusty" (Grainge 1999 p 95).

Many roads were already constructed before the FENCO recommendations came in. Culverts were made by welding oil barrels together. Roads were built with shallow ditches to allow natural runoff.

SOME OF THE 1957 NORTHERN CONSTRUCTION TEAM MEMBERS

Isaac Alanik	Malcolm Firth	Richard Kendi	Martin Niditchi
Colin Allen	R. Firth	George Kunnezie	Fred Norris
Hubert Allen	John Francis	Clayton Jewell	Leo Norwegian
Elijah Allen	P. Francis	Audrey Joe	Garret Nutik
Victor Allen	Jack Frost	Peter Joe	Jake Peffer
William Allen	Jack Goose	Joe Johnson	P. Peterson
Harry Amos	Irene Greenland	Donald Kaglik	Bobby Porritt
Red Anders	Chester Hagen	Jack Kalinak	Nels Pulk
Antoine Andre	Cliff Hagen	Alfred Kendi	Frank Rivet
Porter Arey	Florence Hagen	Peter Kiktorak	Bib Jim Rogers
Sam Arey	Roy Hamilton	John Koe	Little Jim Rogers
Johnny Avaganna	Rod Hardy	Adolf Koziesak	Louis Roy
Alfred Bernard	Mary Harley	Archie Lennie	Mike Salamio
Jim Biggs	C. Harry	Johnny Lennie	Buck Semmler
Effram Bonnetplume	George Harry	Eric Lester	Isaac Simon
Billy Cardinal	Harry Harrison	Lazarus Lester	Alex Stefansson
Rudolph Cardinal	Hans Hansen	James Lord	Melvin Stensby
E. Cheezee	H. Hodgins	Steven Loreen	Noel Stewart
Billy Day	N. Hurd	Jim McDonald	Charlie Thrasher
Herbert Dick	D. Husky	Wilfred McDonald	Peter Thrasher
Al Derosier	Nels Hvatum	Dan McLeod	Tommy Thrasher
Tom Dillon	J. Illasiak	Eddie McLeod	Rufus Tingmiak
William Edwards	Pat Illasiak	John McPhail	John Vehus
Frank Elanik	Alec Irish	Eddie McPherson	George Villeneuve
Richard Ethier	Ida Irish	Mary McPherson	A. Vittrekwa
John Firth	Henry Isaksen	Cliff Moore	
Lazarus Firth	Louis Jacobsen	Barney Natsie	

Airport construction

Airport construction was also an early priority, but the location of the proposed new airstrip retreated away from the community. "Word has trickled in from East 3 that a new airstrip location is being sought some 9 miles out of town. Reason given is that the location 4 miles out was condemned by the Department of Transport because the approaches were dangerously low" (*Aklavik Journal*, May 1956).

Originally the airport had been proposed on the ridges just north of the townsite. Then a location was suggested on the flat area north of Long Lake. The final location was chosen on solid rock by Dolomite Lake. Some locals commented then that the entire community should have been built around Dolomite Lake, which might have been a superior location to the East Three site since it had solid foundations, gravel supply, fresh water and was linked to the Mackenzie Delta.

The new airport site was located 12 km from the townsite in a well wooded area that rested on a base of limestone. Locals referred to the airport construction camp as "East 4".

While there were two construction crews working in the twenty-four daylight, the airport crew had top priority in men and materials. The inability of the large transports, like the DC3, to use skis or floats on the river made cargo transfers to smaller crafts, in Norman Wells, necessary. It was therefore imperative that the airport begin operations as soon as possible.

In May 1956 the 12 km road to the airport was completed except for a bridge over Boot Creek just below Hospital Hill. As the large culvert purchased for the site would not arrive by barge until later, a timber culvert to handle the spring run-off was constructed using local materials.

In August 1956 Aklavik Constructors were awarded the contract to build the East 3 Airport involving a cost-minus arrangement with a ceiling of $5 million and a 70-30 split on all savings under that amount (Brown 1996). Aklavik Constructors was a consortium under President Bill Venables.

In August 1956 Venables began making onsite preparations. Construction equipment for the airport was mobilized in the summer of 1956 and shipped by barge to arrive in September. By late October 1956 the ground had frozen enough to permit moving crews, accommodation and equipment to the airport site. The airport quarry was opened, with a cone crushing plant for runway construction located at the west end of the strip.

Henning Jensen, formally underground shift boss at the Gunnar Mine, Lake Athabaska, was in charge of the Aklavik Constructors airport crew. In 1956 they started off dynamiting rock for fill on the airport end of the road to East 3.

Starting in March 1957 the crushed rock base for a 1520 metre runway was placed, with the initial layer up to one metre thick, plus a 0.3 metre top layer; this was completed by the end of August. It was decided to extend the runway to 1800 metres by adding east and west ends. Some slumping was found over a wet area at the west end, and this was corrected. In some areas the runway crushed rock pad is 2 m thick. All the runway work was completed by the fall of 1958.

The Ministry of Transport issued the airport operating licence on November 24, 1958, and Barney MacNeil became airport manager. The Inuvik airport's call sign was designated as "CYEV" which is usually shortened to "EV" and often used as a short form for "Inuvik".

A Visual Omni Range (VOR) transmitter was built just west of the airport. It is a Very High Frequency (VHF) omnidirectional range beacon for aircraft flying into Inuvik. Visitors coming to Inuvik from the airport are often told that this is Inuvik's official landing site for UFOs.

Initial streets

In 1958 there were a total of 21 streets in the various stages of construction. Twelve streets, namely Distributor Street, Water Street, Mackenzie Road (the main street of town), Mackenzie Square, Council Crescent, Franklin Road, Millen Street, Firth Street, Reliance Street, Union Street, Bompass Street and Breyant Street, had buildings and were named. Three streets, Kingmingya Road, Camsell Place and Spruce Hill Drive had buildings but weren't named until later. Six more streets were planned but construction had not been completed.

Utilities

The construction camp's water supply came from Hidden Lake above the town by siphon through a 1-1/4 inch plastic hose. This lake is now Inuvik's water reservoir. A winter water supply was constructed from the East Branch to the construction camp at Council Crescent. From a small pump house on the river, the water was pumped periodically up to a storage tank through a self-draining pipeline. There was a septic tank in a heated area under the wash house, which emptied in pulses from a self-discharging Anthes Syphon arrangement, without any additional heat supplied. Waste water exited the camp in a naturally draining insulated pipe to Duck Lake. This was Inuvik's first utilidor system, unofficial and improvised, which worked well and served everybody on the site on a completely equal basis.

D.R. Stanley and Associates Ltd. of Edmonton designed the water supply system (Grange p 98). The Inuvik water supply still comes from Hidden Lake in the summer and during the winter months comes from the East Channel.

HIDDEN LAKE

There are two accounts on the naming of Inuvik's Hidden Lake water supply, from Roger Brown and Jack Grainge.

While camped along the East Branch to check spring water levels in 1954, Roger Brown was instructed to investigate a small lake shown on air photos to the north of Inuvik. He wandered around looking for it but couldn't find it. He called it Hidden Lake (Brown 1957).

In 1955, Jack Grainge wanted to check out a possible water supply for the new community from air photos. With assistant Richard Ethier, Grainge had great difficulty in finding the lake, especially as they were carrying an inflatable boat and paddles. After spending most of a day on the chore they referred to the Lake as Hidden (Grainge 1999).

With a larger population and increasing water use, additional summer water supplies were needed. An 8″ surface steel pipeline was laid three miles from Hidden Lake to the much larger Lake B which acts as a natural reservoir. The water supply in the summer is not taken from the Mackenzie River because the water is too silty, but in winter the Mackenzie River water is crystal clear under the ice.

Bide Clark, a Northern Canada Power Commission (NCPC) supervisor, was in charge of the water supply system in the early 1960s. He ignored the directive to put fluorine in the Inuvik water supply as he was a Mormon and didn't believe in fluoridation. Jack Grainge, the NH&W environmental officer for the NWT commented that "Clark had one hang up. When fluoridation of the water supply was ordered, he did not agree with the policy. Therefore he ignored instructions to operate the fluoridator. It did not surprise me. At that time many critics, including a few doctors and dentists, were claiming fluoride to be a dangerous poison" (Grange 1999 p 102).

Sewage from Inuvik buildings and homes flowed by gravity in the utilidors to the central disposal lagoon along East Channel, downstream from Inuvik, which was known as Anuk Lake. Lagoons were the most common community sewage treatment system in the prairie provinces. In the summer the sun stimulated algae growth to oxidize the lagoon and keep it virtually odour-free. As the lagoon was shallower than expected, there was a sludge build up. Improvements were made in the late 1960s to build two sludge pits, with overflow into the main lagoon, and to increase the lagoon depth by building retaining walls on the west side of the lagoon (Grainge 1999). A stop-log dam at the north end was designed to hold a year's sewage. In the spring, the stop-logs were removed to allow the sewage to be washed away by the spring flood. Several studies have shown satisfactory performance for the lagoon.

For health reasons, many considered Anuk Lake too close to the community, and it was proposed to pump Inuvik's sewage by a pipe buried beneath the East Channel to a large lake in the Delta. Other people objected because they used that lake for trapping and recreation. Tests showed that the lagoon was performing well.

There was another small sewage lagoon at Navy Operations west of Inuvik; waste was pumped to it in a heated line.

Where water and sewer systems are usually buried, this could not be done for Inuvik as any underground pipes would be frozen due to the permafrost. Inuvik's water and sewage pipes are in above-ground "utilidors" with insulated walls which snake throughout the community. This construction technique was used in several northern Canada locations, usually at mine sites on solid rock where it was uneconomic to put them underground. Inuvik was the first full community to have above-ground utilidors.

To keep the water and sewage pipes from freezing, central heating pipes were included for all the government buildings. There are no chimneys in these buildings. In the original town layout, roads crossed the utilidors in ten places (Brown May 1956). Where a road and a utilidor crossed paths, a bridge was built over the utilidor. These arched bridges over the utilidors gave an appearance of canals, which allowed Inuvik to be jokingly referred to as the "Venice of the North".

The original utilidor network contained water and sewage lines plus a circulating high-temperature hot water system to heat buildings. These structures were metal-clad and heavily insulated. Lost heat from the heating pipe kept the water and sewer line above freezing at the coldest outside temperatures. Later an econo-utilidor was introduced which only carried water and sewer lines, as building heat came from oil-fired furnaces. Hot water was added to the water line as necessary to keep this system from freezing in the winter. The smaller connections from the main utilidor to each building are called utilidettes.

In the beginning several private home owners did not want to connect to the utilidor even though free connections were offered and a minimal $10 per month was charged for both water and sewage services. Coming from Aklavik or Delta camps they had not experienced running water and were provided with free water delivery and sewage pickup. For many years the government sector was charged more than the private sector for electricity, water and sewer services and in effect subsidized private users.

The utilidor system has functioned well, providing the "normal facilities of a Canadian town" of running water and sewage, but had a high capital cost and operating expenses. The standard utilidor initially cost $600/metre to construct, or $600,000/km. The high cost arises from the design concept for high-temperature, high-pressure heating lines which have to be solidly anchored, the large 12''' water lines, and the initial prohibition of the utilidor passing under buildings. Although well insulated, there is a high radiation heat loss from the sides, which is about 3.9 square metres for each lineal metre of utilidor.

For several small buildings, the utility services cost more than the building being served. As a standard Inuvik lot is about 25 metres ft wide, it requires at least $7,500 per lot assuming the $15,000 cost will serve two houses – one on each side of the utilidor.

There are 17 km of utilidor services. Should the utilidor break down and become frozen, the community would have to be evacuated.

There were some design problems in buildings with utilidor heating that, in the middle of winter and especially in summer, made many buildings unbearably hot. This situation provided for many jokes about the "hot Arctic".

In response to complaints on the lack of waste and sewage services for the "unserviced area" of Inuvik, the administration constructed three "Service Centres" around 1961 with water and sewage services under one roof. Each unit had a toilet, a tap for drinking water and a disposal chute for emptying "honey" pails and bags. These three facilities were located side by side at the top of an 8′ flight of stairs. The two-story buildings contained both water and sewage tanks. There was a water tap at the lower level. To empty a toilet bucket one had to climb outside stairs to a second story chute. The service centres were not used extensively.

This service centre concept was wrong in principle and unsatisfactory in practice. In winter, the stairs became too hazardous from spillage to be of practical use. Also there was a serious health hazard from the potential mixing of drinking water and human wastes. On October 7, 1964 Gene Rheame, MP for the NWT, wrote a letter to Northern Affairs Minister Arthur Laing requesting immediate action to improve or eliminate the service centres.

When trucked water deliveries and "honey" bags pickup were introduced in late 1964, the service centres were demolished (Grainge 1999).

The original utilidor provided 241 buildings – major government buildings and some private facilities – with high temperature steam heat, from four large boilers in the Northern Canada Power Commission (NCPC) power house. (Smaller buildings in the new town were heated with fuel oil or wood.) The bypass heat from the steam generators was used to heat high pressure hot water, which was circulated through the utilidors. (This system was used until 1999, when natural gas distribution was introduced.) A similar concept was utilized at the large mining community of Norilsk in Northern Siberia, at the same latitude as Inuvik, with large buildings on permafrost connected to the central heating plant by utilidors.

The Aklavik Power Company, owned by Stan Peffer and Carl Gardlund, considered setting up a private electrical plant in East 3 in 1956 but was not encouraged. In Aklavik, under the management of Carl Gardlund, they operated a 250 KW plant with a $75,000 investment. Also in 1956 there was a "proposal from an Aklavik resident to install a private telephone system at Inuvik" (Rowley 1959).

In October 1958 the Northern Canada Power Commission (NCPC) installed a 150 KW diesel generator to supply Inuvik's construction requirements. Additional capacity was provided as required by two 375 KW units. A power line was run 400 yards to the main camp.

Montreal Engineering designed the permanent power plant with electricity generated by steam turbine generators burning Bunker C or "heavy ends" oil barged from the Norman Wells refinery. Poole Construction Ltd, later PCL, from Edmonton, constructed the power plant as well as the water and sewage systems. The new power plant had total installed capacity of 1500 KW, with 600 KW from a back pressure steam turbine and 900 KW from diesel units. By 1990, the total installed generating capacity for the Inuvik power plant was 12,200 KW.

Construction of buildings

Because of the high ice content of frozen soils underlying most of the Inuvik townsite to a depth of 350 m, special engineering considerations had to be applied for buildings. The permafrost created a unique challenge for architects and engineers to build modern facilities safely and economically. The basic principle was to preserve the permafrost by allowing air circulation or using a gravel base. Nearly all major facilities were built on pile foundations with at least one metre of air space. (Relatively small structures such as the 512 accommodation units were placed on gravel pads up to a metre thick.)

> **"Building In The North"**
> This National Film Board film shows the techniques of northern site selection and building construction. It outlined the important measures that must be taken to build successfully in the Arctic. Included are sections on permafrost and early Inuvik construction. The film shows the 1959 scene of the burning nurses residence. The film crew spent most of the 1959 summer in Inuvik. (1961, 25 minutes, Director Gordon Spirling.)

A steam jet and pile driver were used to place the 5 metre piles to a depth of 4.3 m, but there were some problems when large boulders were encountered. The piles obtained were mainly black spruce from the Mackenzie Delta and Peel River Valley.

In May and June the ground temp at 3.7 m was at its annual low, so the piles froze in quickly. Some piles set in September froze at the top and some heaved up later.

During the winter of 1959, 4,474 piles were driven, with much of the work taking place at -35° C and during the period of darkness. (*Education North of 60*).

The pile-driving program was accelerated in the winter and spring of 1957 to accommodate the increased demand and not slow up the construction program. During 1957 many private and commercial interests made urgent requests for permission to build in the townsite, but they were held back until the essential town services could be provided.

An Inuvik Research Lab survey in October 1967 counted 25,849 piles under Inuvik buildings. By 1970 an estimated 80,000 foundation piles had been installed. This number probably increased to around 100,000 by 1995.

Strict rules were made to protect the natural moss and vegetation and to prevent random movements of equipment around the community. Wherever vehicles moved or materials were stockpiled, gravel pads were first laid to avoid disturbing the natural cover.

National Building Standard codes were applied to avoid a shack town situation for Inuvik. All Inuvik buildings were of wood frame construction except for the steel clad power house, Northern Transportation's warehouse, a Bay warehouse, Bruno Wiedmann's garage, and the Inuvik Community Association's two-sheet curling rink.

Inuvik buildings had no basements, but many homes have "suspended" basements with the main living areas on the second floor.

Contractors and suppliers

Many companies, large and small, from the south and from the local area, played important roles in the construction period.

E.M. Rensaa, engineer with the firm Rensaa and Minsos in Edmonton, was responsible for the design of school and hostel buildings in Inuvik, and the firm also supervised

---

INUVIK CONSTRUCTION TECHNIQUES

A digest on Inuvik construction was summarized in the *Arctic Bibliography*. "Describes the construction of three wooden buildings, the largest at Inuvik, each divided into three sections by fire-resistant cross walls and equipped with sprinkler systems. They have sloping roofs (18°) covered with aluminum interlocking shingles, stop fences along the eves to prevent snow sliding. The interior sheetings are mostly fir and poplar plywood; the exterior wall-finishing consists of color-stained cedar shingles. The buildings rest on piles, steam jetted into the permanently frozen ground and have approx. 2.5 ft. free air space below the lowest floor. The ground floors are about 7.5 ft. above the ground and a 4.5 ft "crawl" space is provided under the main ground floor to house ducts, piping, etc. Pipes for water and sewage are laid in utilidors together with hot-water pipes from the community's central heating plant" (Rensaa, E. M., Canadian Consulting Engineer, 1959, AB61164).

construction of these buildings.

Bird Construction Company built the hospital, navy base, and DOT Station. Houle Electric had the electrical contracts. The Bird Construction camp was located across from the hospital where the Finto Hotel is now situated.

In May 1957 a contract was awarded to Poole Construction for the construction of the 20-classroom school and two hostels, each providing accommodation for 250 students. The contract was for $5.5 million, which beat out a McNamara Construction bid of $8.5 million and an Aklavik Constructors bid of $6 million. The second major building contract, for Federal building and accommodation units, was awarded on June 30, 1958. The goal was to allow the contractor to move in as much material as possible before the close of shipping, so that most of the buildings could be closed in before cold weather, and materials would be on hand for an early start the following spring.

Homes and offices

The 16′ × 32′ "512" cabins used for the construction workers were later moved to residential sites and sold to those who had accepted compensation for moving from Aklavik. (Grange 1999). The cabins were rented for $50/month, which was to go to the final purchase

---

SOME OF THE NORTHERN CONTRACTORS AT EAST 3

Adolph Red Anders: First contractor at East 3 with Jake Peffer

Bob Baetz: Freighting

Ray Cox: Contractor

Carl Gardlund: Cafe/Coffee Shop

Harry Harrison: Schooner freighting

Hans Hansen: Schooner "Kings Highway"

Nels Hvatum: Schooner freighting, equipment supply

Louis Jacobsen: Schooner freighting

Dave Jones: Esso Agent

Adolph Koziesak: Crew foreman in 1954 and 1955. Retired to Campbell River, B.C.

Jim McDonald: Camp watchman in 1955

Dan McLeod: Camp cook assisted by two daughters, Rosa and Ellen

John McPhail: Steam jet operator for setting up power poles, from Hay River

Fred Norris: Owner of a 5-ton truck, D2 Cat, "Barbara Jean" tugboat and barge, taxi, a veritable DPW

Jake Peffer: First contractor at East 3 with Red Anders

Stan Peffer: Trader/Entrepreneur

Slim Semmler: Independent Trader

Gary Wagner: Contractor

Bruno Weidemann: Taxi, freighting, Bombardiers, with son John

Mike Zubko: Aklavik Flying Services

---

price of $5500 less depreciation. These cabins were small but were generally larger than the log cabins used in and around Aklavik. The main part of a 512 was the kitchen-dining-living area. At the rear were two small bedrooms. At the front was an indoor porch and a small honey-bucket room. By September 1956, eighty 512s were completed or at least roofed in, towards a pre-freezeup goal of 101 units.

Ten 512 cabins were constructed on a cul-de-sac near Boot Lake called Council Crescent, to provide accommodation for a meeting of the 11th session of NWT Council, August 23-31, 1956. The actual meeting was held in the newly completed government garage. This was the Council's first session held north of the Arctic Circle. The Council agreed that Curt Merrill would stay on as project manager until the end of the summer before transferring to Fort Smith. Afterwards the camp was turned over to Aklavik Contractors who were building the airport. The Gwich'in Tribal Council building is now located on this site.

In 1958 the new Federal Building opened on the corner of Mackenzie Road and Distributor Street containing the post office, administration offices for the Inuvik area and the Inuvik Region Indian Affairs offices, Department of Public Works Building Manager, NWT liquor store, Northwestel telephone exchange and court facilities. The Single Staff Quarters also opened in 1958 with 32 apartments for single teachers, stenographers and office help. It is now the McCauley Building operated by the Inuvik Native Band.

Accommodation for federal employees was provided in detached houses, row houses and single staff apartments. The plans for the three-bedroom and four-bedroom detached houses were said to be taken from a standard layout mainly used at military bases, a layout that was not particularly suitable for the Arctic. Several fourplex row houses were built along Mackenzie Road. All of the houses were painted in bright colours and were often called "Smartie" homes. Even the row houses were each painted in different colours. The colours were to brighten up the community especially through the dark winter period. Families were assigned houses randomly to purposely separate groups from various Departments. "An attempt has been made to prevent the personnel of different government agencies from forming enclaves, by assigning houses to them in different parts of the serviced area" (Lotz 1962).

In 1959 Dave and Mary Jones and Mike and Dawn Zubko started building their Inuvik houses on Spruce Hill Drive. For many years these two homes had the distinction of being the only private units amongst all the government accommodation.

The RCMP buildings on Distributor Street housed both the Western Arctic Subdivision

---

Inuvik Children Foiled

Inuvik visitors going through Inuvik's residential area often notice that several house windows are completely covered with aluminum foil as if the occupant had a photographic darkroom inside. They are told that the window covering is to "Foil children into sleeping at 'normal' evening time even though there is a 24-hour sun". The window foil is generally left on the windows all winter, as it doesn't make much difference when the days are mainly dark.

and Inuvik Community offices. There were barracks for eight single officers, a jail and a garage. The first RCMP constables came to Inuvik in 1957 and were housed in 512s. In 1958 they moved into new facilities and new houses. The first jail was a 512 building across the street. Fenced RCMP dog kennels were set up on East 3 Point.

Construction continued with the building of the school in 1959, and the hospital, office buildings and staff housing in 1960. The RCMP, CPC, NCPC, Transport, National Defense, National Health and Welfare, Citizenship and Immigration all had personnel living in Inuvik. The Federal Day School and hostels were to be opened in early September 1959.

The 740-square-metre government laundry building on Mackenzie Road, with 65 square metres of space for public showers, was completed in October 1959, and John Komaromi was hired as manager. It had shower facilities for local residents, and soap was provided for free as an educational measure.

Community Life

Just as quickly as the first buildings went up, the new town started to build its institutions, including schools, churches, medical facilities, and all manner of social clubs.

Schools

Formal education in Inuvik began in a tent school at East 3, which was organized during the winter of 1955-56 for the children of construction workers. East 3's first official school opened on September 10, 1956, with 46 pupils in a special 512 on Distributor Street, where the CFS Inuvik base was later located. Ella Shanahorn was the first teacher. She was soon joined by Connie Miller, wife of Dusty Miller, the vocational training instructor at the time. As there were 56 students and only 25 desks, a shift system was worked out with lower grades attending in the mornings and the upper grades in the afternoons (Brown 1996). An East 3 Parent-Teachers Association was formed in Fall 1956 with President Jim McDonald, Vice President Archie Lennie and Secretary Agnes Semmler. (The name was later changed to the Home and School Association.) The Association organized a Christmas party for the students (Brown 1996).

To accommodate additional students at the Distributor Street 512 school a second classroom was added in early 1957. A third classroom was added in September 1957 with Fred North as teacher. Mrs. Shanahorn left at Christmas 1957 and was replaced by Anton Solar. Mrs. Miller left in the summer of 1958 to go with her husband to Yellowknife. Her place was taken by Gladys Mackie. Ms Mackie returned to university for a year but returned to teach at the new Federal Day School which opened in October 1959.

When Inuvik was conceived it was decided that the residential school concept common on Indian Reserves would be replaced with a regular community day school, and that hostels would be provided for children from camps and distant settlements (Robertson 1959). This social innovation created a larger facility able to provide students with a wide range of learning opportunities, and allowed students from surrounding communities to mix with those from Inuvik. The Federal Day School facing Mackenzie Square opened in 1959, with

24 regular classrooms plus social studies, science, shop, home economics and library. Both primary and secondary classes were taught. It was built to accommodate 600 pupils but the 1962/63 enrollment exceeded 850. In 1961 its name was changed to Sir Alexander Mackenzie School, which everybody referred to as SAMS. Students were taught using the Alberta school curriculum until 1967, when the NWT Government moved to Yellowknife and established a northern curriculum.

Students from surrounding communities without schools, or where the senior grades were not taught, were accommodated in two hostels each housing up to 250 students. Stringer Hall was run by the Anglican church and the other, Grollier Hall, by the Roman Catholic church.

The CFS Inuvik presence was very positive for Inuvik education, as the military parents demanded quality and a national standard so their children could fit in when they arrived in Inuvik and be qualified to continue their education wherever they were posted after two or three years.

Notable early Inuvik school graduates were surgeon Noah Carpenter, engineer Frank Hansen, educator Larry Gordon and politician Bill Lyall.

SAMS school had a big auditorium-gymnasium with a stage and projection room, which was to double as a town social centre after hours. SAMS organized into three broad groups: regular grade system (students who have reached the normal grade for their age); preparatory classes (to assist young children who find it difficult to speak English to build them up to take their place in the regular curriculum); and opportunity classes (same kind of help for older children and young adults, with a view towards the job qualifications needed in the local economy).

In the early years, the SAMS school was the only education facility in the Western Arctic except for small schools at Aklavik and Tuktoyaktuk. Northerners living in other communities or "off the land" had the choice of sending their children to Inuvik or keeping them at home. Most Northerners readily agreed to send their children to Inuvik while efforts were continued to provide adequate schools in all the Inuvik region communities. But the Inuvik schools were criticized for taking away native culture and not teaching skills such as trapping.

A decision was made in March 1963 to construct a new Inuvik high school in the east half of Block 17 where the Rehab Centre was located.

Churches

Two East 3 church missions were set up in 1956 and 1957. Father Bern Will Brown operated a Roman Catholic mission in a small building along the river bank, and in July 1956 opened the first Roman Catholic church in a 512. Captain Ken Snider of the Anglican Church Army arrived in East 3 from Hay River in 1957 (*Aklavik Journal* Summer 1957). He opened up the Church of the Ascension in a 512 on Distributor Street. In 1959 the church moved to a large lot on Mackenzie Road that extended from the Town Square to Bompass Street, where a small parish hall and rectory were built. At the time there were plans for a new large church to occupy the property.

BUILDING THE IGLOO CHURCH

Inuvik's Igloo Church – officially known as Our Lady of Victory Church – is the community's major landmark. Construction was started in 1958. The building is 25 metres in diameter and the top of the 3-metre cross on a 6-metre diameter cupola is 21 metres above the ground. Visitors may ascend to the cupola to see the unique construction methods and observe a 360-degree view of downtown Inuvik.

The total cost of the building in 1958 was $70,000, less than $3/square metre. It was completed in 1960.

The Igloo Church is named the Lady of Victory Church, the same name as Notre Dame cathedral in Paris. The Blessing of the Church ceremony was performed by Bishop Piche on August 5, 1960. The Igloo Church replaced the 512 mission building which had opened in July 1956.

The architect and builder was Brother Maurice Larocque, an Oblate missionary who worked as a builder for his order all across the North. The entire concept was worked out and held in the minds of Brother Larocque and Father Joseph Adam.

Born in Quebec in 1908, Brother Larocque's formal education stopped at Grade 5. But in 1931 he joined the Oblate Fathers and was sent to Northern Canada, where he designed and built workshops, mission houses, hospitals, schools and churches.

In 1958, Brother Larocque arrived in Inuvik to consult with the Parish Priest, Father Adam, on the design of a new church. Father Adam was just one year older than Brother Larocque and had spent just about the same time in the North. He was fluent in Inuktitut and well versed in Northern cultures and beliefs.

Together, Father Adam and Brother Larocque worked to create a church that blended Catholic symbolism and local tradition. Their work was made especially difficult because in the Inuvik of 1958, machinery, labour and construction materials were all in constant demand. However, they worked out an ingenious design – which was only committed to paper years later – that met the challenges of building on permafrost, while also making use of recycled materials for major parts of the structure.

The Igloo Church is the only major building in Inuvik which is not built on piles. The Church is built instead on a cement raft foundation, separated from the upper church by an air space which prevents the building's heat from melting the permafrost.

The arches for the roof were built by Brother Larocque in the garage behind the church during the winter of 1958–59. The windows for the cupola came from another church which was being demolished. Metal sheathing on the outside was obtained at half price, and old hockey sticks were used for the grating in the false roof. Much of the other lumber was cut by Oblate Brothers at their Mission in Fort Smith, and barged to Inuvik on the Santa Anna. Parishioners included Bill Lawlor and Joe Pinsoneault built pews, the altar and other furnishings.

Much of the remarkable artistry in the church was produced on site. Father Adam himself carved the metal-embossed decorations of the altar rail and altar. Father Colas painted the windows of the porch. And the fourteen "Stations of the Cross" paintings were done by a young Inuit woman, Mona Thrasher, who had lost both her hearing and her powers of speech as the result of a childhood accident.

The Family Hall adjacent to the RC Rectory was started in May 1967 to provide a place for meetings, bingos, youth activities, dances and banquets. It accommodated 220 people and was well utilized until the 1990s when the regular monday evening bingo, which paid the hall's operating expenses, was stopped.

In 1957 Bishop Trocellier arrived at Inuvik for two-hour visit in a bright red Norseman. He inspected the new 512 church and directed Father Brown to start working on plans for new bigger church, plus a rectory and warehouse.

The Pentecostal Inuvik Christian Assembly was organized by Don Violet, Kayy Gordon and Terry Frith. Local church leaders were Charlie Smith, Bill Kikoak and Roland Shingatok.

The first East 3 marriage took place in August 1956 between John Pascal and Rosie Pokiak with Father Bern Will Brown officiating.

Baptist and Bahai congregations formed in the 1970s and a Muslim group started up in the 1990s.

Health Care

The community's first baby girl was born to Bertha Allen, when Victor and Bertha Allen were living in a tent at East 3 in the summer of 1956 (Brown 1999).

On December 10, 1957, Shirly Mason arrived as East 3's first nurse (Brown 1999, p 80). A Nursing Station was set up in 1957 in a 512. This was increased to a Double 512 in 1959 and remained in use until the new hospital opened in January 1961.

The original 1955 FENCO town plan had placed the hospital in the middle of the community just northwest of Mackenzie Square, where the Samuel Hearne Secondary School is now located. Against the wishes of most Inuvik residents at the time, an unknown Ottawa bureaucrat made the decision to locate the hospital at the east end of the community, far away from the Inuvik residents who would mainly use the facility.

The Inuvik General Hospital initially had 80 beds housed in three separate wards, plus a 53-apartment nurse's residence. The medical facilities were built along Mackenzie Road on a hill overlooking Boot Lake. The site included thirty acres of land to provide for future needs.

On Halloween night in November 1959 there was a serious setback when the almost finished Nurses Residence, including the pile foundation, burned to the ground. New piles were put in place, a metre off centre each way from the original piles, and the building was rebuilt by the contractor in time to coincide with the opening of the new hospital in January 1961.

On January 15, 1961, patients were moved from the Aklavik hospital to the new Inuvik facility. Ms Rivard and Agnes Walsh were in charge of the transfer under direction of the head doctor, Dr. Dale. After the official move of all hospital services a "Farewell Dance" was held for everyone in Aklavik. The last song played was "Save the Last Dance For Me" by the Drifters (Huskey 1994).

The first baby born at the new Inuvik General Hospital was Katherine May Edward to Mr. & Mrs. William Edward on January 23, 1961.

Fire Department

The Inuvik Fire Hall was built on Distributor Street with three bays for fire-fighting equipment, office and training rooms and accommodation for the fire chief. Mr. McDerby was Inuvik's first fire chief (*Nuna* Spring 1960). Later Len Adrian took over as the community's fire chief. When fire-fighting responsibilities were taken over by the new Inuvik Council in 1969, the office part of the building served as the Municipal Office.

Businesses

L. F. "Slim" Semmler started a store at East 3 in 1956, in a tent on the river bank above the town dock, but soon moved a building in from the Pokiak Channel near Aklavik. In 1957 L. F. Semmler's General Store became Inuvik's first commercial building. This facility was relocated in 1958 to a permanent site on Mackenzie Road, where the GNWT's Semmler Building is now located.

Also in 1957, the Hudson's Bay Company set up their first store beside Semmler's on the river bank. (This original Bay building is now at Ingamo Hall). Johnny Desrochers brought Stan Peffer's boat and barge with the store and stock from their Axel River post. This became Inuvik's third store.

Stan Peffer's first commercial building was erected in 1958, on Mackenzie Road across from the Bay store. It was known as the "Rec Hall" and contained a theatre, pool hall and cafe. A kitchen and bakery were in behind. This facility opened on September 15, 1958 with Cece McCauley as manager.

Joe Bourque cut lots all spring and built the first barber shop in East 3 in 1957 (*Aklavik Journal* Summer 1957). At least three residents of Aklavik asked for permission to open a licensed beer hall at East 3 (*Aklavik Journal* February 1957, Brown, 1996). Both Norris' and Weidemann's taxi first started in Aklavik but came to Inuvik when the Administration and RCMP headquarters moved over in 1959.

The first cafe in Inuvik was opened by Carl Gardlund in 1958 on the bank above the government dock. It was in a quonset-type building which later served as a bunk house, airline office and storeroom.

The offices and hanger of Aklavik Flying Services were moved over from Aklavik and

---

SLIM SEMMLER

One of Inuvik's most well-known businessmen was Lawrence Frederick Semmler, far better known by his nickname "Slim." He was born in 1900 in Oregon, but moved north in his early '20s, and kept moving until he reached the Arctic coast near Coppermine. It was in that area that he met his wife of 67 years, Agnes Norberg.

Slim was a skilled and successful trapper. But in 1945, the couple and their family travelled by dog-sled to the Mackenzie Delta, where he operated a trading post and a mink ranch. Ten years later, when construction began at East 3, they moved south and Semmler started trading at the new settlement. In 1957, L.F. Semmler's General Store became the town's first commercial building. Semmler's store remained an important local business until his retirement in 1984.

Slim Semmler died in 1998, at the age of 97, and was buried in the Inuvik graveyard under a stone with his chosen epitaph: "Slim Semmler. He was a dog musher."

located along East Channel below the power house. Later Arctic Wings and Rotors built a hanger in the same area. This building burned in 1964.

In 1958 Inuvik's first bank was opened by the Canadian Imperial Bank of Commerce in a 512 cabin on Mackenzie Road and was the most northerly branch on the continent. When the Bank of Commerce merged with the Imperial Bank of Canada in 1961 the name was changed to Canadian Imperial Bank of Commerce. Later a permanent bank facility was constructed on Mackenzie Road.

The new Mackenzie Hotel, built by Stan Peffer, opened in 1960 with 20 rooms. The hotel was completely booked from June to September each summer. The room rates in December 1963 were: Room without bath, $7.50, two in room, $5.00 each; with bath, $9.00, two in room $7.25 each. A standard complaint was that the cold water taps ran hot even when it was -40°C outside. The Mackenzie was home to the first licenced premises north of Yellowknife. The initial tavern was a relatively small area measuring only about 6 metres by 9 metres. However, as the only bar within "1000 miles" it was very popular with those attracted to it and became known as "The Zoo" from its many characters. There were regular tavern brawls amongst people unaccustomed to drinking spirits.

The Mackenzie Delta liquor store, which had opened in Aklavik in 1959, was transferred to Inuvik in 1960 where it operated initially in the Federal Building on Mackenzie Road at Distributor Street. Later the store was moved to the front of the new NWT Liquor Warehouse on what was later named Berger Street. With the privatization of the NWT liquor services the warehouse was transformed into the new Inuvik Centennial Library with a Mackenzie Road entrance.

Shell Oil opened an exploration camp in the summer of 1958 at Long Lake along Airport Road half way to the Inuvik Airport. Since then the lake has been called Shell Lake. As mussels are visible in the shallow water around the float plane docks, some people say this gives the lake its name.

The Northern Affairs boat building program started in Tuktoyaktuk in 1947 to build new boats and repair boats and was moved to Inuvik in 1961. A new boat shop at Boot Lake was begun in 1963 and completed in 1964.

Radio

During the initial construction period, 1957-1961, Inuvik's communication requirements were provided by a ham radio set operated by Northern Affairs and DPW. Later communications were handled by the Canadian Army's RCASC with transmitter-receivers in a small structure on Distributor Street where the government warehouses are now located.

The CBC's CHAK station on Distributor Street started broadcasting on November 26, 1960, with an output of 1000 watts, as the first CBC station in the Canadian North. CHAK is the call sign from the original broadcasting station which had been started by the Armed Forces at Aklavik in 1925. The first building was small with two rooms adjacent to CFS Inuvik. In 1969 the station moved to the old Mac's News Building on Mackenzie Road. In

1979 it transferred to its present home in the Mac Travel Building.

CHAK could be heard throughout the Western Arctic and provided essential communication with residents through a regular "news and messages" program. Berkeley Macmillan was the first station manager, from 1961 to 1963. Elijah Menarik from the Hudson's Bay area was the second manager from 1963 to 1969. Wally Firth was an announcer. Nellie Cournoyea was an announcer and later station manager.

Recreation

The Inuvik Community Association built a Butler type building for a two-sheet curling rink in 1960 on Distributor Street for the Inuvik Curling Club. A third sheet was added later. This building was sold and is now the Northern Metalic store.

The Inuvik Community Association (ICA) was formed in 1959 with a board of ten directors. Five directors were to be elected each year at the annual general meeting and serve for a two-year term. The Association was mainly responsible for community recreation, which had not been included in the mandate of any government department. The Association raised funds through membership charges, admittance tickets and raffles. It provided financial assistance to recreation groups, completed the first curling rink, and organized the annual Spring Carnival. In January 1963 the ICA organized regulation-sized hockey rinks in front of each hostel. There was always difficulty in maintaining full board membership as many of the elected directors would be transferred out before their term expired. However, the Community Association was an important first step for Inuvik's future responsible government.

In October 1961 the ICA Directors considered a new community centre with an arena and auditorium. The three-hectare open space behind the Mackenzie Hotel and the Navy Base was selected for the future site.

As a compromise in 1963 they proposed a two-story extension to the existing curling rink, which could serve as a community centre with space for committee rooms, a community library, offices, washrooms, kitchen and a dance floor. This project was submitted to the NWT Government for recreation funding but was rejected. At the annual general meeting on May 18, 1963, the organization then went ahead with the purchase of a Butler Building from Permasteel in Edmonton for the addition of two new rinks.

From June to August 1963 the curling club building was rented to British-American Oil Company for $150 month. In June 1963 the ICA Directors were Bob Baetz, Ron Lalonde, Fred North, Ron Hodgkinson, Ken Gerry, Agnes Semmler and Ken Walmsley. Lloyd Carrothers was ICA chairman in 1964 and 1965. Jim Maher was chairman in 1966.

The annual Spring Carnival is a regular event marking the return of Spring and Easter celebrations. The very first Spring Carnival at East 3 took place on April 23, 1957. A large igloo, 7.5 m in diameter and 3 m high, was built. Agnes Semmler was in charge of the northern food sales inside the igloo. Malcolm Firth was in charge of the snowshoe races. Reindeer from Reindeer Station were driven to Inuvik by Buster Kailik and Silas Kangegana. A dance and Carnival Queen activity was organized by Lee Post in the unheated 32´

STAN PEFFER – INDEPENDENT ENTREPRENEUR

Stan Peffer (1911-1999) was a self-made trader, manager, carpenter, architect, entrepreneur and promoter. During Inuvik's initial development he built most of Inuvik's non-government facilities including the Rec Hall, Mackenzie Hotel, Polaris Theatre and Bakery.

Stan arrived in Aklavik in 1930 with his father Harry and brother Jake after floating a large lumber raft down the Mackenzie from Fort Simpson with all their belongings, supplies and two horses. The Aklavik RCMP had set up a sawmill to provide lumber for their western Arctic posts, but after one summer the mill was put up for sale along with 1800 logs. The Peffers purchased it for $2,000. With the logs floated from Fort Simpson and the purchased logs, they had enough to last three summers. The horses were used to move the logs around. The horses caused quite a stir and the Indians and Eskimos had never seen a horse before. When they used their horses with a block and tackle to pull their scow out of the river in a short time, everyone with a scow, boat or barge wanted the Peffers to pull them out of the river. Previously they used a hand operated capstan which took at least half a day.

After erecting a trading post, the Peffers built a large two-storey rooming house with the main floor being a restaurant, a movie house and a dance floor. All of this was called Hotel Aklavik. Its six rooms were full all the time with four to six persons in each room.

The trading post dealing in Delta furs was the busiest part of the Peffer enterprises. As there was no bank and the businesses were always running out of coins, Stan manufactured his own coins, imprinted with "S.M. PEFFER YOUR HOME MERCHANT AND FUR DEALER", in denominations of 25 cents, 50 cents, one dollar and five dollars. In 1942 the Ottawa government ordered a stop to this independent currency

With the Federal Cabinet's December 1953 decision to move the Aklavik facilities to a new site, Stan actively pursued opportunities in the new community. He was given financial assistance for moving to East Three.

Next Stan bought a boat and barge at a bankruptcy sale and hired Johnny Desrochers to operate it. He hauled supplies from Hay River and Fort Liard as well as fuel oil from Norman Wells. To commute between Aklavik and East Three Stan bought the 'Time-Life' speed boat.

Although L. F. Semmler was the first trader to open in East Three from a 12′ × 14′ tent, Stan opened a temporary store and cafe in a Canol quonset hut with Karl Gardlund. Then came Peffer's 60′ × 120′ Rec Hall building on Mackenzie Road in August 1956 as a convenience store, cafe, pool hall, dance floor and movie house. Stan had Wien Alaska Airways land a C-46 on Aklavik's ice strip with 5 tons of fresh produce and a Beechcraft plane loaded with bananas for the store opening. Later he built the Mackenzie Hotel, the Polaris Theatre, a garage and a bakery.

Stan was famous for saving 'nickels' by being at the Edmonton airport and having travelers flying north bring in incidentals and supplies for his businesses as part of their luggage and carry-on allotments. Several of his employees became successful Inuvik business men such as Gary Wagner (Mackenzie Delta Construction) and Sig Gaida (Eskimo Inn).

Stan sold out his Inuvik investments in 1980 and moved to Edmonton. He married Elvina Cox in 1985 and died at age 87 in Edmonton.

× 100´ new liquor warehouse. Florence Hagen was the Carnival Queen. The events were patterned after Aklavik's traditional Muskrat Jamboree and were coordinated by Fr. Bern Will Brown.

Initially the activity was called an Ice Carnival. For several years the annual event was sponsored by the Inuvik Community Association. In 1965 the event was renamed the Muskrat Jamboree, coordinated by the Hunters and Trappers Association.

In 1957, the East 3 Home & School Association formed, and on February 14, 1957 the Association made $300 raffling off food baskets made by the women (*Aklavik Journal* Mar 57, Brown 1996).

Inuvik's Royal Canadian Legion Branch 220 opened in May 1957 with 15 members having moved over from Aklavik. The Legion had received its charter in Aklavik on February 24, 1947 with original members Jim Jones, Dave Jones, Nels Hvatum, Barney MacNeil, Clarence Bell and Bill Vehus. The Legion remains the most northerly branch in Canada. The organization took over the East 3 camp movie shows and raised the price from 25 cents to 50 cents (*Aklavik Journal* May 1957: Brown 1996). The Legion opened a new log building in 1962 as an upgrade from their original 512 building.

The Inuvik Lions Club started up in 1957 as the most northerly Lions club in the world.

The first East Channel ice "break up" pool was held in 1957. This allowed residents to bet on the date and time when the ice would start moving during the spring thaw. A rope was anchored on the ice and tied to a cord attached to an electric clock in Father Brown's shack. The tickets sold for 25 cents and earned Home & School Association over $300 (Brown 1999).

Inuvik and Western Arctic Development Association (WADA) was formed in 1961 with Mike Zubko as president. The association acted as a Chamber of Commerce to facilitate long term regional developments, and usually organized a barbeque for visiting groups with the opportunity for mixing with locals. Bob Baetz was elected WADA president in 1962.

In the winter of 1962-63 the Delta Women's League organized an ice rink in the unserviced area.

The Polaris Theatre building was erected by Stan Peffer in 1962, with several garages behind the theatre building. Later an apartment complex was built over the garages. Carol Bennett served as first theatre manager. In 1963 construction started for Peffer's Inuvik Bakery on Mackenzie Road beside the Bay store. It was completed in 1964 and is now the Phoenix Building.

The Ice Worms Association of hospital employees, mainly nurses, was organized in 1963 as a nonprofit charity. This group held an annual June 21 midnight trek to Mount Baldy north of the gravel pit, and participated in community parades carrying a large red papier-mâché ice worm.

On December 31, 1963, a New Years Eve drum dance was held in the conical dome of the new Inuvik Research Lab's neutron monitor building, before equipment was installed. An appropriate "igloo atmosphere" was provided with a single lamp at the top of the dome. This event was organized by David Sutherland.

Military, Police and other Government Activities

The Canadian Forces Station Inuvik was listed as a communications research facility. The station's operations base was at the end of Navy Road north of Inuvik. The military activities were top secret among station personnel but Inuvik civilians were aware that many of the operators spoke and understood Russian, and that the radio antennas were used to monitor Soviet public and military activities. It was joked in Inuvik that the only thing that moved at the CFS operations base was a directional antenna, which usually pointed North across the Pole to the Soviet region.

On 12 June 1957 the RC Signals Radio Station Aklavik-East Three was opened by Cpl Pete Grey. The activity increased, and a second operator could not be provided, so in a mistaken effort to ease Cpl Grey's plight, he was issued with a GI bicycle of uncertain vintage to expedite his deliveries. This monstrosity became the bane of Grey's existence as the townspeople saw him wandering about the site at all hours, carrying the bicycle more often than riding it.

The Aklavik communication facilities were transferred to the Department of Transport on August 9, 1958. At the same time CBC took over the broadcasting services as CHAK Aklavik (Vince 1960).

In November 1960, the Royal Canadian Navy took over from the contractors the complex of new buildings at Inuvik, including an administration/accommodation building located in Inuvik, an operations building eight kilometres to the north, a transmitter building 11 km to the south, a six-bay garage and an assortment of warehouse and storage facilities. During February and March of 1961 staff, equipment and supplies were moved over 120 km of frozen waterway from Aklavik by tractor-train, snowmobiles and sleds drawn by muskeg tractors. The RCAF used a Hercules aircraft to haul new supplies and equipment from the south. A jeep was also airlifted to provide much-needed wheeled transport for the Inuvik operations.

CFS military personnel were posted to Inuvik for three years, but often this posting was broken by a three- to six-month stay at CFS Alert. Although the armed forces personnel and dependents were less permanent than most Inuvik civilians, they were more than willing to support community efforts and participated actively in community organizations.

VEHICLES ON THE ROAD

Inuvik vehicle registration was started in 1961 when there were mainly trucks operating. In the next seven years the total number of vehicles more than doubled and there was a majority of automobiles over trucks.

INUVIK VEHICLE REGISTRATION 1961-68

	61/62	62/63	63/64	64/65	65/66	66/67	67/68
Automobiles	47	88	78	109	143	148	157
Trucks	89	87	93	108	110	126	136
Total	136	175	171	217	253	274	293

Source: Northern Information Note, 6 May 1968

Naval Radio Station Inuvik had four main components: 1) administration building with offices, stores, garage, galley, messes and living quarters for 43 men; (2) operations site north along Navy Road containing operational equipment to support communications research and SAR; (3) transmitter site on Airport Road south of Inuvik for military transmission and Department of Transport for air communications and aids to air navigation; (4) accommodation units for military personnel and families.

On September 10, 1963, NRS Inuvik became the land-based ship HMCS Inuvik, and on February 15, 1965, with the unification of the Canadian military, HMCS Inuvik became CFS Inuvik. The CFS Inuvik Station Badge had the motto of "Sannaiksemayot Sopayanon" ("Prepared for all things" in Inuvialuktun). Armed forces personnel participated with several sport teams including the CFS Blues hockey team and the CFS Cougars softball team. Many of the military facilities, including the gym and weight room, three messes, and station movies, were open for public involvement. Military personnel participated in church groups, education organizations, Inuvik's Spring Carnivals and Delta Daze parades.

The base later operated a CANEX store (Canadian Forces Exchange System), for groceries and some dry goods, that was not open to the public. CFS personnel were normally posted to Inuvik for a three year term but many requested extensions. Through the 1960s and 1970s military personnel and their dependents comprised at least 25% of Inuvik's population.

The RCMP G Division subdivision located in Inuvik in 1958 when it moved from Aklavik. It is headquarters for detachments in Aklavik, Fort McPherson, Fort Franklin, Fort Norman, Norman Wells, Sachs Harbour and Tuktoyaktuk. The duties include air detachment, boat patrol, ice road patrol, Dempster Highway patrol, search and rescue operations, sled dog inoculations, snowmobiles, and Inuvik policing, provided under a GNWT contract. They operate as a subdivision of the Yellowknife "G" Division headquarters.

The April 1961 RCMP detachment complement comprised Insp Ed Lysuk, Cst Bob Knights, Cst Lyle Trimble, Cpl Ed Boone, Sgt Scotty Steward, Cst Mert Mohr and Cst Laurie Jamont. The Inuvik quarters were constructed in 1963. The ancient cannon and stack of cannon balls in front of the detachment were originally from the RCMP's Herschel Island operations.

By 1983 the Inuvik RCMP had grown to 19 personnel plus eight support staff. Including the regional detachments in Aklavik, Fort McPherson, Fort Franklin, Fort Norman, Norman Wells, Sachs Harbour and Tuktoyaktuk there were 52 total personnel. An air detachment with a Twin Otter was based at the Inuvik airport. In the summer there were Mackenzie Delta boat and Dempster Highway camper patrols.

Ottawa's Interest in the North

Governor General Vincent Massey viewed the new East 3 townsite on March 30, 1956. He also traveled to Aklavik and Tuktoyaktuk. Frank Carmichael, NWT Councilor for Mackenzie Delta, addressed the regal visitor. Byron Riggan, a *Time-Life* correspondent, accompanied the Governor General as he toured East 3 on April 1, 1956. He reported, "Beginning soon the old town of Aklavik will be uprooted from its mud flats, and during the next four years, most of the permanent residents will move to a new government-selected site 35 miles to the east .... If the planned new town of Aklavik proves as successful as its designers hope, it may serve as a model for other new arctic communities" (*Time* 23 April 1956, *Aklavik Journal* May 1956).

The same year, a future prime minister also made a visit. From August 9 to September 5, 1956, Pierre Trudeau and Frank Scott paddled down the Mackenzie River and saw the East 3 construction activity (Christiano 1994).

When John Diefenbaker and the Progressive Conservatives came to power in July 1957, they did so with a "Northern Vision", a slogan coined by Alvin Hamilton who became the Minister of Northern Affairs and National Resources (NA&NR). Prime Minister Diefenbaker, speaking on his Northern Vision in Winnipeg on February 12, 1958 described "plans to increase self-government in the Yukon and Northwest Territories. We can see one or two provinces there." During the five years that followed, more was accomplished in the Canadian North than in any previous period of the nation's history. "According to a United Nations survey, Canada in 1959 was spending an estimated $2,300 a year per Eskimo in health and social costs – an amount equivalent to the theoretical cost of wintering Canada's entire Eskimo population at the Chateau Laurier hotel." "As the trouble was in the character of the North itself political rhetoric could work little magic in that inhospitable barren land" (Newman 1963).

Governor General Georges Vanier and party visited Inuvik on June 26, 1961, shortly before Prime Minister John Diefenbaker's visit (see page 76).

NWT Council

The NWT Council held an official meeting at East 3 on August 23, 1956, the first Council meeting north of the Arctic Circle. It was held in the partially built DPW garage on Distributor Street. The Council discussed liquor problems in the North including objections to opening the Aklavik liquor store the previous October. Also, Councilor T. A. Crerar opposed the move of the Aklavik Liquor store to East 3.

The NWT Council and staff were accommodated in ten newly built 512s located above Boot Lake on what became known as Council Crescent. Subsequently the camp was turned over to the Airport Contractor. In the 1960s the Yellow staff apartments were built here. The Gwich'in Tribal Council took over this building in the 1990s.

In 1957 Eddie Cook was posted to a new Indian Affairs agency at East 3. This was the first time that a native of the country was appointed an Official Agent. Eddie was originally from Fort Good Hope and was a college graduate fluent in English and French as well as his native Hareskin dialect. He served in Inuvik for a short time before Al Cottrel moved from Fort Norman to East 3 to take over. His assistant was Dan Norris (*Aklavik Journal* Summer 1957).

An NWT Council election for the Mackenzie Delta seat was called to replace Frank

Carmichael, who had resigned in March 1957 to take over the new Aklavik liquor store (*Aklavik Journal* February 1957; Brown 1996). In May George White, Mike Kozial and Abe Allen considered running but for the August 19, 1957, vote Knut Lang, Stan Mackie, Thomas Njootli and George White were on the ballot. The returning officer was Bill Strong. Knut Lang won the election (*Aklavik Journal* Summer 1957; Brown 1996).

Knut Lang (1895-1964) was born in Norway and traveled to the North via England and New Zealand. He arrived in Aklavik in 1928 and trapped, traded and cut wood for the Mackenzie sternwheelers. He was involved in Aklavik's Mad Trapper chase. He was actively involved in the selection of the East 3 townsite and the naming of Inuvik.

In a letter dated January 11, 1963 to MLA Knute Lang, concerning a petition to restrict sales at the Inuvik Liquor Store, Slim Semmler stated that Inuvik had a population of 250 preschoolers, 843 children in school, 60 young adults between 15 and 19, 30 nurses, 15 RCMP and wives, 100 Naval personnel including wives, and 300 other Civil Servants totaling approximately 1600 residents. In the unserviced area there were 90 dwellings with an adult population of around 200 people.

Research Activities

The establishment of a new planned town in the arctic was fertile ground for study, and from the first years there were researchers in areas as diverse as agronomy, astronomy, geology, and social sciences.

Canada Agriculture set up the East 3 experimental plots in June 1956 to explore the possibilities of growing lawns and raising hardy, short-season crops on permafrost in the Mackenzie Delta. A well drained one-acre site on a hillside facing southwest behind Stringer Hall was selected (Harris 1966). The project was coordinated with the Fort Simpson experimental plots and managed by the Canada Agriculture Experimental Farm at Beaverlodge, Alberta.

In 1956, Frank Nowasad of the Department of Agriculture started the experiments with vegetable crops. The area was cleared and vegetation cover was bulldozed off. On June 15 the soil could be loosened by disking to a depth of 3″. On August 29 the permafrost had receded to 24″. A few vegetable seeds were sown but these barely germinated.

In 1957 the garden was seeded earlier with beets, carrots, lettuce, radish, peas, turnips and potatoes. By fall the frost line had receded to 48″ below the surface.

In 1958, the frost receded to a depth of 58″, while in an adjacent undisturbed area, the frost depth was only 13 inches. In 1959 the frostline went down to 62″ by August 12 (*Whitehorse Star*, 5 May 1960).

In 1960 the Dept of Agriculture conducted a soil survey of the Inuvik townsite.

The National Research Council's Division of Building Research started northern engineering and permafrost studies at East 3 in 1956, and in 1957 installed several thermocouples to determine the subsurface temperature effects of buildings and disturbed areas. Elevation reference points were established on the pile foundations for major structures.

In addition three bench markers were installed in drilled holes to a depth of 15 metres to serve as reliable permanent datum points. The DBR ground temperature measurements were taken on thermocouple cables where most other ground study projects used direct reading transistors.

Two thermocouples were installed to a depth of 30 metres for assessing long-term permafrost changes in 1959. Also, measurements were taken on refreezing characteristics of piles placed in steamed holes. Most of the permafrost installations were completed in 1960 and arrangements were made for year-round observations. These were conducted by the Inuvik Research Laboratory after it opened in 1964.

In 1959, Walter and Jean Boek of Albany, New York, studied the resettlement of Indian and Eskimo groups from Aklavik and Inuvik. The aim was to determine the factors influencing the decision on the part of these people whether to move or not, and to suggest methods of gaining their cooperation in the move. They reported that around 300 people of native descent had settled in Inuvik by 1959. Of these new arrivals 55 were Indian, 110 were Eskimos and 120 were of mixed native-white descent (Boek 1960).

In 1959, an area economic survey for the Mackenzie Delta region was initiated by the NA&NR Industrial Division. It was coordinated with the Geographical Branch of the Dept. of Mines and Technical Surveys (Mackay 1963).

The Canadian Wildlife Services based two researchers in Inuvik during the 1960s, Tom Berry working on migratory waterfowl and Vern Hawley conducting Mackenzie Delta muskrat studies.

The Fisheries Research Board from Montreal conducted a Mackenzie Delta and Beaufort Sea fisheries inventory study from the MV Salvelinus in the summers of 1960 and 1961.

Jim Lotz of IAND's Northern Research and Coordination Centre visited Inuvik in the summer of 1961 to carry out a review of Inuvik's social planning problems (Lotz 1962). His recommendations for Inuvik included:

- a year-round waterline to the West End
- a bag system for sewage disposal
- use Rehab Centre as a small hostel/hotel that would provide both training and accommodation
- needs a tent campground for visitors
- greatest need is for adult education in its widest sense
- a community greeter is needed to provide practical information to visitors
- the Mackenzie Hotel needed to be enlarged.

Also, Lotz commented that:
- it was "gratifying to see so many women keeping their homes and families so clean"
- hotel and RCN flew food in from Fairbanks
- a road-air link in Fall 1961 hauled fresh food to Whitehorse and chartered a plane to Inuvik from there

- little use was made of the public showers in the NANR laundry building
- Mackenzie Hotel accommodated 25 people in double and single rooms, cold water is hot
- Navy personnel seemed to settle down well in Inuvik despite the shortness of their stay
- there is both horizontal and vertical social stratification in government departments.

Lotz concluded that "Inuvik has excellent potential, both in the local people and the administration. The development of a new town into a real community is a long, hard process but the potential does exist, despite the problems."

The Inuvik Research Lab was built by Poole Construction of Edmonton for $292,000. Pilings were placed in the summer of 1962, with construction completed in November 1963. A northern report at the time said "its facilities will be available for scientists from all government departments, universities and private research agencies. An annex will house the National Research Council's cosmic ray laboratory. It forms part of the Canadian program for the International Year of the Quiet Sun" (*Nuna* Spring 1963). Dick Hill, the Lab's first director, arrived in December 1963.

"East 3" becomes "Inuvik"

When the East 3 site was chosen in August 1956 there were no arrangements to provide an official community name and, as the new community was not scheduled to be operational until 1959, there was no rush to decide on a designation. The Department of Northern Affairs and National Resources proposed that the new settlement would be named "Aklavik" and the original community "Old Aklavik", but this was dropped due to strong local opposition and potential mail sorting problems. However, due to the large amount of mail being shipped to the new site the Post Office Department could not wait and a post office at the site was opened as "New Aklavik" on May 19, 1958 (O'Reilly 1987).

As the name "New Aklavik" still created considerable confusion with mail and communications, a new name was needed for the opening of a post office at the new construction camp. Local residents were asked to choose a designation. John Keevik proposed the name "Kegeatuk" meaning place of the beaver, which the Twin Lakes area was known as for many years. Several other names were put forward including Arctic Circle, Nanuk and Camsell.

The name "Inuvik" was the result of rumination by Graham Rowley before his shaving mirror (Robertson 2000). On April 16, 1958 Rowley wrote to Knut Lang and suggested Inuvik as "It is a short simple name, easy to pronounce and spell, and sufficiently different from Aklavik to ensure there would be no confusion." At the 1957 summer meeting of NWT Council in Frobisher Bay, Knute Lang recommended East 3 be named Inuvik – "Place Of Man" or "Where People Live". At the next NWT Council meeting in July 1958 Knut Lang, the elected MLA for Mackenzie Delta, proposed the name "Inuvik" as the Eskimo word meaning "the place of man" or "the place where man is" and which was comparable to the name of Aklavik translated as "the place of the brown bear".

The name Inuvik was officially accepted by the NWT Council and proclaimed by Commissioner R. G. Robertson on July 18, 1958, at the Fifteenth Session of the Council of the Northwest Territories meeting in Ottawa. The official Reference For Advice was in Sessional Paper No. 9. The Proclamation of the name Inuvik was covered in Sessional Paper No. 11, dated July 18, 1958. A week later the post office changed the name to "Inuvik" effective September 2, 1958.

Many people disagreed with the name change at the time but it was generally accepted as it was easy to say, related to Aklavik, and was northern. Billy Day in the September 5, 1996 *Inuvik Drum* stated that "Inuvik" does not really mean "the place of man" but should be translated as the gender-neutral "living place".

The Oblate Fathers Bulletin had this to say about the name: "Inuvik is now a well known settlement but the word itself doesn't mean anything to the Eskimos. Anyway it can't be translated 'the place of man' as many writers are doing even in the most authoritative articles on the North. True the civil authorities wanted it that way, but 'the place of man' could be INORVIK in the Western Eskimo, or INULIK in Copper Eskimo. INUVIK means 'time of birth' or 'birthday' in Copper Eskimo, and 'the happy man' in the Western dialect" (*Nuna*, Winter 1961).

The town's dedication

Northern Canada development, particularly the creation of Inuvik, was of particular interest to Prime Minister John Diefenbaker, and he was asked to come to Inuvik for its official dedication ceremony on July 21, 1961. Diefenbaker was the first Prime Minister to travel North of 60 degrees latitude. At the time, "Inuvik was raw and unfinished, with trucks stirring up clouds of gravel and dust as they hauled lumber and other freight from the dock to the building sites (Robertson 2000).

The Diefenbakers stayed in the new Stringer Hall. Mr. Diefenbaker and his party also attended sessions of the NWT Council which was meeting in Inuvik at the time. The last day of the Council session was special for Mr. Diefenbaker as Mrs. Diefenbaker was presented with the three best white-fox skins that Knut Lang could find to make a stole.

In the ceremony Mr. Diefenbaker unveiled Inuvik's official monument in Mackenzie Square, symbolizing the races of Indians, Eskimos and others living and working together in Inuvik. A plaque on the base reads:

> This was the first community north of the Arctic Circle built to provide the normal facilities of a Canadian town. It was designed not only as a base for development and administration but as a centre to bring education, medical care and new opportunity to the people of the Western Arctic.

The monument, sculptured by Art Price of Ottawa, has three bronze arches curving upwards to support a shining sphere. The design represents the friendship and mutual aid of the three races living in the Mackenzie Delta area and coming together in Inuvik. Mr.

Diefenbaker described it as a "symbol of racial unity, yet at the same time its sphere is the contour of the world." The sculpture was cast in bronze and nickel-plated. Its natural stone base was constructed of local rocks from Campbell Lake by a crew under the supervision of Rudy Tornow and Adolph Koziesak. Embedded within the monument is a three-inch steel pipe containing a newspaper, a dollar bill, some coins, blueprint of the cairn and a list of names who helped build it. In 1976 vandals removed the sphere but it was replaced.

In his speech at the dedication ceremonies Mr. Diefenbaker spoke extensively on the Federal government's decision to build Inuvik, construction difficulties with permafrost, the cooperation of northern residents with Southerners, the education and training facilities, the centre for arctic research and the spirit of circumpolar cooperation. He said that "Man's confidence in the northern future has made Inuvik necessary" and listed four community objectives that Inuvik was to provide:

1. "the normal facilities of a Canadian town"
2. "a base for development and administration"
3. "a centre for education and medical care"
4. "new opportunities to the people of the Western Arctic"

The full text of Diefenbaker's speech is included in Appendix A.

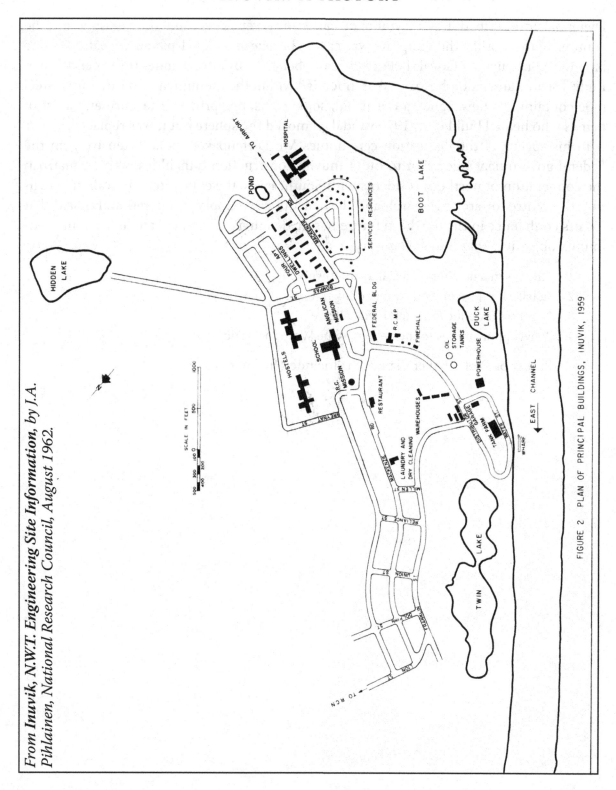

From Inuvik, N.W.T. Engineering Site Information, by J.A. Pihlainen, National Research Council, August 1962.

FIGURE 2   PLAN OF PRINCIPAL BUILDINGS, INUVIK, 1959

Aerial photograph taken in spring of 1959, with ice-clogged East Channel in lower right corner, Hidden Lake at upper left.

Aerial photo of Inuvik, 1964
This photo from August of 1964 shows most of the street network of Inuvik completed, although Bypass Road was still to be built. (Composite of photos # A18646- 51 & -52, Natural Resources Canada)

Hidden Lake

Airport Road

Boot Lake

Navy Road

East Channel

Twin Lakes

Inuvik Time Line 1964-1970

1964 Jan 1 — Inuvik Research Laboratory opens, Dick Hill director

Feb 19 — Inuit Cooperative Housing Association formed with Charlie Smith as president

Mar 28 — Great Alaska earthquake tremors felt in Inuvik

Mar 31 — Lyle Trimble elected to NWT Council representing the Mackenzie Delta riding

Apr 13 — Knut Lang, NWT Mackenzie Delta Council Member, died at age of 68

May — Inuvik Chamber of Commerce formed, Bob Baetz president

Aug 8–9 — Point Barrow Chamber of Commerce visits Inuvik

Aug 24–25 — Northern Affairs Minister Arthur Laing and Parliamentary Secretary John Turner visit

Nov 6-7 — NWT Council visit to Inuvik, Commissioner B. G. Sivertz

Nov — Peffer's Bakery building opens on Mackenzie Road with apartments above

Nov — Cross country skiing introduced for youth by Jacques Van Pelt & Father Mouchet

1965 Jan — First election for Inuvik Advisory Committee

Feb — Inuvik Ski Club formed with 100 members and rope tow on Mount Baldy

Mar — First 'Delta' oil well drilled on Richards Island

May 15 — First Science Fair north of the Arctic Circle held at the Inuvik Research Lab

Aug 22 & 23 — Carrothers Commission Inuvik hearings at Legion

Aug 24–25 — NA&NR Minister Arthur Laing tour to Inuvik

Oct — Pat Barry opened a West End kindergarten in her Kingmingya Road home

Dec 16 — Inuvik newspaper, *The Drum*, founded by Tom Butters

1966 Jan 6 — First issue of the *Inuvik Drum*, Tom Butters editor

Feb 15 — HMCS Inuvik Designated as Canadian Forces Station Inuvik

Mar 21 — 2nd Inuvik Science Fair held at Inuvik Research Laboratory

Apr 1 — Inuvik proclaimed as a NWT Local Improvement District by NWT Council

Apr — First jet aircraft lands at Inuvik airport, Patricia Silver Mines Lear Jet

Aug 2 — Telephone link to 'outside' established on CN line along Mackenzie from Hay River

Aug 23 — Northern Affairs Minister Arthur Laing visits Inuvik with Economic Council of Canada

Aug — Farley Mowat and Pete Murdock travel across the North in a Single Otter and visit Inuvik

Sep 15 — Inuvik Community Association vote for Inuvik's 1967 Centennial Project

Nov 30 — Sachs Harbour Conference at Inuvik Research Lab

Dec 5–6 — Northern Affairs & National Resources Dep't changed to Indian Affairs & Northern Dev.

1967 Jan 15 — Opening of new Inuvik Centennial Library on Mackenzie Road

Feb — Village Council's Recreation Board takes over Inuvik Community Association

Mar — Inuvik designated Regional Centre for communities from Fort Norman to Sachs Harbour

Apr 1 — Inuvik proclaimed an Incorporated Community with an advisory Council

May 6 — Soviet Gostroy northern construction delegation visit and Village Council dinner

May — Family Hall construction started

Jun — Inuvik Recreation Centre construction started (Dave Jones Arena)

Jun — Territorial Experimental Ski Training (TEST) program started

Jun — Anne Murray performs at SAMS as part of Centennial culture series

Jun 6–7 — Inuvik Regional Conference held at Research Lab with Dr John Honigman

Jul 14–19 — Professors Melnikov and Vyslov of Siberian Permafrost Institute tour Inuvik and area

Jul 23–24 — Arctic Institute of North America tour of Inuvik facilities

Aug — Imperial Oil experimental pipeline laid along Airport Road by CBC tower

Sep 1-2 — International Symposium of the Devonian System visits Inuvik

	Nov 1	Victor Allen addresses Northern National Development Conference in Edmonton
1968	Mar 2	NWT Council visits Inuvik with a public meeting
	May 25	4th Inuvik Science Fair
	May 25	First airplane lands at new Inuvik Intown Airport
	Jun 11	Progressive Conservative meeting at SAMS with Hon Walter Dinsdale
	Jun 27	Dr. Cam Sproule illustrated show at Research Lab on Arctic Resource Development
	Jun	First summer swimming pool opens in back of old Curling Rink on Distributor Street
	Jul 16	Royal Commission on Northern Transportation meets in Inuvik
	Jul 22	Prime Minister Trudeau and party visit Inuvik
	Jul 23	Mackenzie Forest Development Rangers program begins under Wilf Taylor
	Jul 30	Fisheries Research Board party under Wyb Hoek start beluga whale tagging program
	Aug 5	Northern Affairs Minister Jean Chrétien and party meet with Inuvik Council
	Aug 8–16	Inuvik forest fire burns around Inuvik in hot weather
	Aug	Eskimo Inn addition erected
	Aug	Ian and Sylvia Concert at SAMS
	Dec	NWT Power Corp building burns
1969	Mar 29	First Inuvik RCMP Ball
	Apr 1	Inuvik achieves Village status with fully elected eight-member council
	Jun	Federal government's new statement on Indian Policy presented by Jean Chrétien
	Jul 4	Energy Mines & Resources Minister Otto Lang reviews Prudhoe pipeline proposal
	Jul 19	Amoco spuds an oil well off Navy Road within town limits
	Aug 11	James Richardson, Minister of Transport visits Inuvik and pipeline research site
	Sep 24	Northern Affairs Minister Arthur Laing reviews Prudhoe oil pipeline proposal
	Sep	Samuel Hearne High School opened by Hon Jean Chrétien
	Sep	CBC Frontier Television starts with two hours of two-week-old programs
	Sep	Mackenzie Valley Pipeline Research project built along Navy Road
1970	Jan 1	Inuvik proclaimed full status Town with a Mayor and elected eight-member Council
	Jan 28	Committee for Original Peoples Entitlement (COPE) formed
	Mar 19	COPE certified by NWT Societies Ordinance
	Apr 23	Re-enactment of historic dogsled mail run from Dawson arrives in Inuvik
	Jun 14	Survey '70 tour visits Inuvik, briefing by Dick Hill and Mush Mersereau
	Jul 6-7	Queen Elizabeth, Prince Philip, Prince Charles and Princess Anne visited Inuvik
	Jul 17–19	First Northern Games at Inuvik
	Jul 28	Sir Alexander Mackenzie Canoe Race arrives in Inuvik after paddling 1100 miles
	Aug 16	US Secretary of the Interior Walter Hickel visits Inuvik, community dinner at Eskimo Inn
	Aug 17	Gov Gen Roland Michener and wife visit Inuvik, community dinner at Stringer Hall
	Aug	NWT 1970 Centennial barge arrives at Inuvik
	Sep 25	COPE officially incorporated
	Oct	Environment Canada offices open in Inuvik
	Nov 18–21	Man In The North Conference on Community Development
	Dec 19	Inuvik Aviation Council banquet and dance, Eskimo Inn

CHAPTER FOUR

Adjustment, 1964 – 1970

After Inuvik's construction, there was an adjustment period when new residents from the North and from the South consolidated their lives towards becoming a "normal Canadian community". Northerners accustomed to small town or bush life adapted to the wage economy, new services and amenities offered by Inuvik. Southerners, new to the North, had to adapt to the extreme temperatures, extended light and darkness variations, great distances to home communities and living with indigenous groups.

There are many myths about the Canadian North including natural purity, open spaces and wholesome aboriginals. However, the realities of life in Inuvik often confound both visitors and new residents. Edward McCourt commented after his August 1968 visit to Inuvik that it was the most scientifically planned town in Canada:

> Inuvik is a government-created community designed to overcome the frightful building problems caused by an unstable ground surface .... There is nothing Topsy-like about Inuvik, and nothing to reflect the personalities of the people who live in it. And because the town is so obviously a plan translated from the architect's drawing board into a full-blown reality, because there is no evidence of growth in the normal way (no old town, no new town, hardly any vacant lots), it is extraordinarily difficult for the casual visitor to adjust ... to an environment so wholly at odds with everything he has hitherto identified with life in the far north.... I found Inuvik a depressing place.... The population turnover of Inuvik is high.... (McCourt 1969)

Among the very real problems Inuvik faced was inadequate housing for non-government staff or people.

Inuvik started off as a government town for Federal offices and staff. Initially in Inuvik everything was paid for by the Federal government. There was little or no provision for services to non-government people due to the financial restrictions on the government budget process. Had government funds been diverted to "private" interests, the many political critics would have been up in arms. All non-government staff, whether Northerners or Southerners, had to fend for themselves.

Ironically, federal housing policy provided native housing in surrounding communities, where there was little employment, but no native housing for Inuvik, which offered considerable employment opportunities. There was no northern housing program when Inuvik was being built and the Ottawa politics would not allow it, although it was traditional for housing to be provided on military bases. Hence the perceived discrimination.

These conditions gave rise to heavy media and activist criticism about natives living in squalor while whites had everything.

83

But the designation of West Inuvik as an "unserviced" area during the 1960s was misleading. Although piped water and sewer services were not available, there was trucked water and sewage pickup plus electricity, telephones and roads. It was more appropriate to refer to the area as non-government.

The Innuit Co-op Housing Association was organized by local residents to address the housing shortage. Charlie Smith was the first Cooperative president. At the first meeting on February 19, 1964, members included Billy Day, Roland Shingatok, Joe Teddy, Victor Allen, and Dave Sutherland.

Lots were laid out, and future lots were requested for the opening of a Cooperative store. The group operated under the NWT Cooperative legislation and arranged to bring in precut houses from Edmonton. Through combined efforts, the houses were built. This group were a little ahead of their times, as the Federal Northern Housing Program later brought many low rental units into Inuvik providing the occupants with very low operating costs, whereas the Housing Co-op members were saddled with mortgages and full rates for services.

Another much-publicized problem was alcohol abuse. This was actually comparable to alcohol abuse in other Canadian communities of comparable size, but it was more visible in Inuvik. Inuvik's reputation for native drinking problems was seldom seen in context. The large majority of natives and others experienced normal family situations, but they were not visible to visiting journalists and researchers, who tended to concentrate on Inuvik's only public bar.

It was also unfair to blame all the acohol abuse on Inuvik residents, as many visitors and people from other Delta communities contributed to the problem. Inuvik had the only liquor store and bar in a 500-mile radius, and people from the surrounding area who were attracted to alcohol came to Inuvik.

Lack of local control

In the early years, Inuvik also had to cope with the fact that important decisions were made in far-away centres of power.

During the 1960s and 1970s much general knowledge about Inuvik's operations was monopolized by distant bureaucrats, remote academics and southern activists, who tended to "solve" Inuvik's community problems by writing long reports and holding conferences rather than working with the Inuvik Council which was responsible for community management and governance.

For example, in 1970 the NWT Government built a territorial campground beside Airport Road across from Twin Lakes without asking the Town Council for a building permit. The project was initiated by an NWT Tourism decision in Yellowknife without community input. The development was first noticed by Town Council when a gravel road was laid in an undisturbed area without a required Council planning approval. The short gravel road led though willow patch to a small pad with spaces for 12 very small camping sites.

The project was an expensive disaster, as the campsite was surrounded by mosquito-attracting willows, had no view, inadequate parking and was never used. Had Inuvik residents been consulted the location and layout could have been useful. By 1980 the site was completely grown over and hard to find.

The move to local government

Local government came about in stages over a full decade. As there had been no democratically elected government in Aklavik to represent the common welfare of all residents, there was no local authority to transfer over to Inuvik. Inuvik residents were certainly consulted on all issues and changes, but there was no official body to make community decisions and handle disagreements.

In spite of the problems, there was a steady move through the 1960s and 1970s towards more effective and responsible government in the north, on a territorial as well as municipal scale. The Carrothers Commission played an important part in this development.

The Advisory Commission on the Development of Government in the Northwest Territories, chaired by A.W.R. Carrothers, was appointed on June 3, 1965, to investigate and report on northern constitutional development. The Carrothers Commission held hearings throughout the Territories beginning August 1, 1965.

A public hearing was held in Inuvik at the Legion Hall on August 22 and 23, 1965. Official presentations were made by Tom Elanik, Larry Mann, Fr Jean Franche, Charlie Smith, Grace Menarik, Agnes Semmler, F. P. Jordan, Tom Butters, Tom Barry and Pat Barry. Speakers at the public meetings included Fr Joseph Adam, Owen Allen, Pat Barry, Nellie Cournoyea, Victor Ekutuk, Tom Elanik, Rev Terry Frith, Fr Jean Franche, Cynthia Hill, Dave Jones, Jim Koe, Larry Mann, Elijah Menarik, Jackie Norris, Fred North, Abe Okpik, Orville Radcliffe, Dr John Rookes, Agnes Semmler, Charlie Smith, Wes Smith, Lyle Trimble, Tom Yate and Mike Zubko. Owen Allen made an impassioned speech on the opportunities for effective democratic government in the Mackenzie Delta and the need for unity across the North (Carrothers 1966).

The Carrothers Commission reported on August 30, 1966. The report recommended against dividing the NWT, and suggested the territorial government should be transferred to a permanent northern capital. Based on the Carrothers Commission's findings, the NWT government was moved to Yellowknife in 1967, and in 1974 the NWT Council became a fully elected 15-member body with the Commissioner withdrawing from the law-making process.

Inuvik Community Association

The Inuvik Community Association was formed in 1959. The association was responsible mainly for community recreation, which had not been included in the mandate of the government departments. The Community Association was an important first step for Inuvik's future responsible government. In additional to deciding on a Museum and Library as Inuvik's Centennial Project for 1967, the Association had paid out over $25,000 towards the construction of the new arena.

Inuvik Community Councils

The Association's last Annual Meeting was held on 22 November 1967. At this meeting, it was decided that the assets and responsibilities would be turned over to the newly formed Recreation Board under the Inuvik Village Council. This transfer became effective on April 1, 1968.

The Inuvik Advisory Committee (IAC) was formed in 1964 by Northern Affairs Regional Director Tom Butters as a step towards community self-government. The West End was divided into seven electoral wards. The East End was divided into three electoral wards. In one of the West wards there was a tie vote for two candidates, so they were both given committee seats. Henry Rivet was appointed to represent Tent Town because it was thought impossible to hold a valid vote there as the residents were very mobile. In each area the runner-up was considered an alternate representative. In effect, all of the non-elected candidates were considered as alternate members. Due to the newness, or innocence, of the democratic process in Inuvik at the time there was initially very little community awareness of the Advisory Committee's presence. It served solely in an advisory capacity.

The committee started off with Tom Butters, chair, Agnes Semmler, Deputy Chair, Jackie Norris, secretary, Fred Beaulieu, Stephen Firth, and Henry Rivet. Later it was expanded to include Bob Baetz, Dave Jones, Gary Wagner, Vern Opel, Billy Day, Cliff Moore and George Castle. Alternates for the Committee were George Norris, Len Adrian, Bob Hunter, Dick Bullock, Gwen Walmsley, Victor Allen and Bill Starling. The IAC served as an embryo local government body for residents to be informed of Federal and Territorial government programs and through which any local concerns could be heard.

On November 8, 1965 the NWT Commissioner proclaimed Inuvik as a Local Improvement District as of April 1, 1966. The LID was managed by a six-member Advisory Council with a NWT-appointed Reeve, two NWT-appointed Councilors and three elected Councilors.

In December 1965 there was a community movement requesting the Commissioner to rescind this LID order, as local property taxes would be imposed without representation,

LID COUNCILS 1965–1968				
	Appointed Reeve	Deputy Reeve	Councilors	
1965	Tom Butters*	Robert Baetz	Ellen Binder	Dave Jones
	Sid Hancock		Ken Look	Barney MacNeil
1966	Sid Hancock	Robert Baetz	Ellen Binder	Dave Jones
			Ken Look	Barney MacNeil
1967	Sid Hancock*	Robert Baetz	Ellen Binder	Dave Jones
	George Thompson		Ken Look	Barney MacNeil
1968	George Thompson	Robert Baetz	Ellen Binder	Dave Jones
			Elijah Menarik	Barney MacNeil
	* Served part year			

since there was no provision for an elected council to decide how the taxes would be spent. Also there was concern over the possibility of a poll tax on non-property owners and no provision for grants-in-lieu of taxes for government properties. At a Committee meeting on January 11, 1966 there was a motion passed in support of proceeding with Village status for Inuvik.

With the resignation of Tom Butters as Regional Administrator in November, 1965, Sid Hancock took his position and became chairman of the Inuvik Advisory Council.

Village Status

On April 1, 1969 Inuvik was incorporated as the Village of Inuvik with the Northern Affairs Regional Administrator, Sid Hancock, designated as Village Reeve. Inuvik was the first incorporated municipality north of the Arctic Circle. Later George Thompson, who replaced Sid Hancock as Regional Administrator, became the Village Reeve.

At the first meeting of the new 1969 Inuvik Village Council a program was initiated which would provide piped water and sewer services to all the present and future Inuvik lots (Mackenzie Institute June 1969). The Village Council also banned the use of DDT insecticide, which had been widely used each summer to control mosquitoes, and initiated a program of draining all mosquito breeding areas in the community. This environmental action happened long before communities in the South did the same thing.

At the end of 1968, the Advisory Council had met with town planner Danny Makale. They accepted Makale's plan, delivered in November 1968, and instructed him to draw up an Inuvik Zoning Bylaw.

In 1969 Doug Bailey, in defiance of Town zoning regulations, erected a building on Airport Road across from Shell Lake for "agricultural" purposes. The Town office assumed that the real purpose of the building was to be a base for Bailey's electrical business, and this was contrary to town planning policy which at the time was to keep all businesses and housing within the town limits. However, when the Town's Secretary-Manager inspected the building, he was surprised to find it full of chickens.

Town Status

Inuvik officially became a town under the NWT Municipal Act on January 1, 1970 with Mayor Dick Hill and Councilors Tom Butters, Gordon Campbell, Frank Hansen, Barney MacNeil, Jim Robertson, Agnes Semmler, Gary Wagner, and Tom Yate.

The first priority of the new Council was to complete the servicing of the utilidor water and sewer services throughout the community. The five-year project was budgeted at $1,000,000. Also, the Council planned to introduce a zoning bylaw providing industrial land for the anticipated development connected with the discovery of oil in the region. Councilors were concerned that at least half of the Council meetings were taken up with complaints about taxi and dog bylaw issues.

The Council's administration office was set up in the Old Fire Hall on Distributor Street in 1970, and Council meetings were held in the Inuvik Research Laboratory's conference room. In August 1971 Councilor Tom Butters proposed the introduction of a ward voting system for an elected representative from each Inuvik area. As community wards were not permitted under the NWT Municipal Act, Council voted to request a change in the Act allowing wards. The motion was defeated.

Inuvik's official logo design involves an Indian teepee representing the Gwich'in, an Inuit igloo representing the Inuvialuit and a house representing the non-native residents. The logo was initially used in 1965 on drawings for the decorations for the front of the Inuvik Centennial Library. In 1967 this logo was officially adopted by the Inuvik Council. Later the logo was was embellished with a setting sun behind the buildings. The Inuvik Council commissioned an Inuvik pin and town flag using the three-building symbol.

A centre for Arctic research

At Inuvik's dedication ceremony on July 21, 1961, Prime Minister John Diefenbaker had stated:

> the government is building a centre here for Arctic research – for research into resources, into a wide range of problems and possibilities common to an Arctic environment. Its facilities are not limited to government scientists but are to be available to industry and the universities too, research is yet another field where Canada takes her northern responsibilities seriously. It is teamed with what we have done with roads, communications, mining, agriculture, surveying and community development.

Construction of the first research facility in the Canadian North started in the summer of 1962 and was completed by the end of 1963. The Inuvik Research Laboratory opened on January 1, 1964 as a regional scientific facility to support permanent research activities and temporary projects. Government agencies and visiting scientists from universities and industries had a supportive facility in a cold climate, to encourage their projects and make them more productive through the provision of local technicians, communications, appropriate equipment, modern laboratory space, workshop, library, offices and accommodation.

The research facility was administered by Northern Affairs' Northern Coordination and Research Centre (NCRC) in Ottawa and was initially designated as the Inuvik Scientific Research Laboratory. The name was later shortened to Inuvik Research Laboratory (IRL). In 1962 NA&NR initiated a grants program to stimulate research in the North by Canadian universities and other interested bodies such as the AINA, (Baird 1969). Many of the projects supported by these grants were carried out at the Lab.

Six abandoned DEWline intermediate sites (I-sites) were acquired by the Inuvik Research Lab to serve as field stations for scientific work. Edward McCourt visited Inuvik in 1966 and wrote that "A scientific centre has been established in Inuvik in the Mackenzie River Delta as a base for investigation of every kind" (McCourt 1969). The Lab provided technical and logistic support for long term, year round, data collection and research assistance. It was associated with the Polar Continental Shelf Project (PCSP) under the Department of Energy, Mines and Resources, which operated satellite facilities at Tuktoyaktuk and Resolute.

During Inuvik's "Adjustment Period" from 1964 to 1970, hordes of investigators from government, universities, activist groups and industry, studied all aspects of Inuvik activities. Like migratory birds, they generally arrived in the spring and were gone by autumn. They asked endless questions and took boundless observations and went back South.

Mountains of research reports in all disciplines from "anthropology to zoology" were produced. Arctic technology studies included construction on permafrost, arctic sewage lagoon performance, northern social issues, aboriginal archaeology, and cold weather equipment testing. A bibliography of research supported by the lab in its first 20 years had 658 entries (Castonguay and Sherestone 1985). Inuvik residents did not see the written reports for most of the investigations, although there was a justifiable suspicion that these studies affected southern decisions on Inuvik's development.

From its beginning the Lab played a significant part in Inuvik's overall development. It facilitated strong community liaison through use of its specialized equipment, northern library, photography darkroom and large conference room by individuals and community groups. Starting in 1969, the Lab conference room served as the Inuvik Council Chambers. The Friday evening "Northern" movie program, showing classics such as "Nanook of the North" and "Building in the North", was well attended by locals and visitors.

As part of its role to keep the public informed on northern studies Northern Science Notes were prepared for distribution to the CBC, the *Inuvik Drum* and local administrators. These contained local technical information and "outside" developments affecting Inuvik. SAMS students were often at the Lab preparing projects for the annual Inuvik Science Fair.

Field reconnaissance and drilling were carried out around Inuvik to survey the extent of permafrost beneath Mackenzie Delta lakes and rivers. NCR-DBR set up thermocouple stacks at Inuvik sites to evaluate the effect of community construction on permafrost temperatures, in disturbed areas under buildings, roads, airstrip and utilidors as well as in undisturbed natural areas for comparison. IRL staff took monthly observations.

Canadian Reindeer Project

Starting in 1964 the Inuvik Research Lab cooperated extensively with the Canadian Reindeer Project by providing operating space and assistance in range studies and product research. Dick Hill published four significant reports on the reindeer operations (Hill 1966, 1967). Starting in 1966, George Scotter, with the Canadian Wildlife Service in Edmonton, carried out several studies on the reindeer range and project management. He found 186 lichen varieties on the Reindeer Preserve (Scotter 1968, 1969, 1971, 1972). Two recent books have been written on the Mackenzie reindeer: *Reindeer Days Remembered* (Hart 2001) and *Reindeer Herders of the Mackenzie Delta* (Conaty 2003).

Mackenzie Delta Research Project

In response to Inuvik social adjustment concerns, Northern Affairs commissioned the Mackenzie Delta Research Project, including twelve research studies, with the field work carried out in 1965 and 1966 mainly in Inuvik. A Mackenzie Delta Conference was held in Ottawa on December 5, 1964, to review research needs for the project. In attendance at this conference were Jim Maher, John Wolforth, Derek Smith, and Joe Lubart. Mr. Maher commented about grade school students that "children from town have less on the ball than bush children despite their initial language difficulty" (RMH diary 5 December 1964).

The studies were coordinated by the Northern Science Research Group under the supervision of A. J. "Moose" Kerr, a former Aklavik school principal. The project was an attempt to describe and analyze the social and economic factors related to development in the Mackenzie Delta, with particular emphasis on the participation of the native people in the area, and the extent to which they are making effective adjustments to the changes brought about by government and commercial expansion in the North. The individual research studies and the conclusions arising from them were published in a series of reports.

1. *The Mackenzie Delta – Its Economic Base and Development*, J. R. Wolforth, 1965
2. *The Mackenzie Delta – Technology*, P .F. Cooper, Jr., 1967
3. *The Mackenzie Delta – Domestic Economy of the Native Peoples*, D. G. Smith, 1967
4. *Inuvik Community Structure – Summer 1965*, Jose Mailhot, 1968
5. *New Northern Townsmen in Inuvik*, A.M. Irvin, 1968
6. *Mackenzie Delta Bibliography*, M. J. Jones, ed, 1969
7. *Psychodynamic Problems of Adaptation – Mackenzie Delta Eskimos*, J. M. Lubart, 1971
8. *Arctic Suburb: A Look at the North's Newcomers*, G. F. Parsons, 1970
9. *The Tchiglit Eskimos by Emile Petitot*, D. Savoie, ed, 1971
10. *The Loucheux Indians by Emile Petitot*, D. Savoie, ed, 1971
11. *The Evolution and Economy of the Delta Community*, J. R. Wolforth, 1971
12. *Natives and Outsiders – Pluralism in the Mackenzie River Delta*, NWT, D. G. Smith, 1975

Neutron Monitor

From the beginning, one of the areas of research was astrophysics. The Inuvik neutron monitor operates in a specially designed cone-shaped building adjacent to the Inuvik Research Laboratory. The project was was funded by Atomic Energy of Canada Ltd. (AECL) and the National Research Council (NRC) as part of a worldwide effort to measure and understand particles coming from outer space. Twenty tons (about 20,000 kg) of lead and electrical equipment, which make up the monitor, were shipped from Ottawa and barged to Inuvik during the summer of 1963.

Electronic recording tubes, surrounded by a thick lead shield, count the number and source direction of the neutrons. The data is collected continuously and is used to measure and predict solar flares and their effects on communications. In recent years the data has been useful in understanding particle effects on astronauts and satellites. The monitoring equipment and lead shields were moved into the building and set up by Dick Hill and Ernie Moore by hand in January 1964. Neutron data collection started in February 1964 and has operated continuously since then (Houseman 1996).

In the 1980s the operation of the neutron monitor was taken over by the National Research Council's Herzberg Institute of Astrophysics (HIA). In 1995 the Bartol Research Institute of the University of Delaware contracted to continue operating the monitor under a US National Science Foundation grant.

Todd Mountain Mine: A silver-lead-zinc mining prospect in Cambrian outcrops north of Campbell Lake and 16 km southeast of Inuvik was drilled by Todd Exploration of Vancouver during the 1968 summer. The company held 80 mineral exploration claims and carried out an electromagnetic survey. The site was locally referred to as the "Todd Mountain Mine". No commercial mineralization was found.

Inuvik Seismograph: The Geological Survey of Canada constructed a seismograph vault along the road to the airport quarry in 1969, as part of the Canadian National Seismograph Network. The three component broadband instrumentation was upgraded in 1992. A geodetic station designated INVK was added in July 2001 as part of the worldwide global positioning system (GPS). The reference marker consists of a brass plate with a stainless steel bolt embedded on top of a 2 m high, 40 cm diameter concrete pier, anchored to exposed bedrock to a depth of 1.5 m by four steel reinforcing rods. Its coordinates are 68.3067 × 133.5200 and elevation is 46.36 m.

Beluga Whales Trapped in Eskimo Lakes: On November 6, 1966 Mike Zubko, flying between Tuktoyaktuk and Inuvik, reported seeing several beluga whales stranded in the Eskimo Lakes. Thick ice had formed in the narrow sections between the lakes cutting off access to the Beaufort Sea. The Inuvik Research Laboratory organized a project to observe the whales. Many Inuvik residents flew out to see the spectacle of at least 50 whales regularly surfacing in three breathing holes. The Inuvik Lions Club organized a "Save The Whales" project to provide food and try to keep the breathing holes from closing in. Observations were continued until the last breathing hole closed over at the end of January (*Toronto Star Weekly* 4 February 1967) (*Globe and Mail* 16 January 1967) (Hill 1968).

Beluga Whale Tagging: A crew of Eskimo cowboys riding outboard powered canoes rounded up a herd of beluga whales near Richard's Island during July and August 1968. The research project, coordinated by Wyb Hoek of the Fisheries Research Board in Montreal, was to tag the whales so their movements along the Arctic Coast could be followed by scientists. A similar program had been carried out on Hudson's Bay near Churchill.

Task Force on Northern Ecology: In May 1970 Northern Affairs Minister Jean Chrétien appointed a Task Force on Northern Ecology to determine what, if any, damage was being done to the northern ecology by oil company operations. The eight-man task force was a mixture of academics, conservationists, oil men and public servants, and concentrated on the Mackenzie Delta and Beaufort Coast region. A report was due within one month in time to have some influence on new land use regulations. Task force members, all with extensive northern experience, were:

Dr. J. C. Ritchie, Botany Professor, Dalhousie University

Dr. J. D. H. Lambert, Biology Professor, Carleton University

Dr. William Fuller, Zoology Professor, University of Alberta

Gavin Henderson, Director, National and Provincial Parks Association of Canada

R. C. Passmore, Executive Director, Canadian Wildlife Federation

J. T. Wopnford, Shell Oil

E.M. Lakusta, Gulf Oil

Gerry Remple, Imperial Oil

Government representatives were F. A. McCall, Northern Affairs Regional Director of Resources in Yellowknife, and Dick Hill, who primarily took on an advisory and logistics role.

Miscellaneous Research Projects

A variety of studies were conducted in social sciences, agronomy and forestry.

In a study on the *Drinking Behaviour of Eskimos and Indians in the Aklavik area*, Donald Claremont claimed that the native people were growing increasingly similar to other Canadians. He noted problems of deviant behaviour for people acquiring cultural goals while not having the means to achieve these goals (Claremont 1977).

Charles Hobart studied children living in Stringer Hall in 1967 and wrote a report, *Some Consequences of Residential Schooling*, which claimed the children had abnormal bed-wetting problems (Hobart 1968). The hostel administrators were incensed with the publicity given to this report and the lack of comparative evidence for the problem. It was claimed that any hostel bed-wetting was not excessive and was comparable to that for children of the same age in Inuvik homes or anywhere in Canada.

Potato farm feasibility was studied by Bob Hunter in summer 1967. The study looked at conditions in the alluvial silt along Delta waterways, particularly the banks exposed after spring floods.

During April and May 1968, 2 × 6 boards of Mackenzie Delta white spruce (*Picea glauca*) were tested at the Inuvik Research Lab by Forestry Officer Wilf Taylor. The strength, elasticity and density tests were within the Canadian Standards for white spruce joists. The Canada Forests Research Laboratory Ottawa commented that the lumber would be suitable for general construction purposes including dwelling construction. In 1969, Wilf Taylor estimated that forest resources between Fort Good Hope and the Beaufort coast totaled 760 MM board feet of potential lumber. He studied species including white spruce, black spruce, birch and alder.

During the winter of 1966-67 a severe frost buildup was noted under the roofs of the DPW row houses. The Lab cooperated with DBR and DPW to study the temperature and humidity conditions in relation to outside temperatures. This data indicated that larger roof vents were required for the houses.

Jim Ritchie, a paleoecolgist doing quaternary research at the University of Toronto wrote "I spent a summer in the late 1960s being flown around in a Cessna by Tommy Gordon, first-ever Inuit pilot, absorbing the landscape and vegetation of that treeless region, collecting a suite of modern lake sediment samples, and selecting lake sites for future winter coring expeditions" (Cwynar 1999).

Environment Canada operated an Upper Air Site at the Inuvik Airport. The rawinsonde balloon system and particle measuring system contributed to national and world weather monitoring.

Petroleum Exploration

Oil companies had arrived in the Western Arctic in the late 1950s. The first Mackenzie Delta well drilled was Richfield's Point Separation No 1. at 67°34′ × 134°00′. It was spudded on July 31, 1960 and completed on October 16, 1960.

In June 1969, Pan American Oil considered several possible drilling locations near Inuvik. They chose a site along Navy Road. This was discussed with Inuvik Council for permission to use the site, and the company agreed to build a road that could be used later by the community. Al Sharp, rig foreman, ordered thousands of dollars of gravel on his own initiative; this was amazing to government administrators accustomed to bureaucracy. Amoco spudded the Inuvik D-54 well on July 19, 1969 and drilled until 12 September 1969. The target depth was 5126 feet with an 8 3/4" pipe. The location later became the site of the present-day Inuvik Gun Club range.

However, these drilling projects were just two examples of a much wider pattern of oil exploration, which stretched across the entire western arctic. Although actual drilling operations were still rare in the Inuvik region in the 1960s, extensive prospecting work preceded the drilling. A major part of this was the seismic exploration. Long line corridors were cleared, allowing truck-mounted drills to be moved in. A series of holes were drilled to specified depths, dynamite charges were placed in the holes, the charges were exploded in sequence, and the reflected sound waves were recorded. When analysed using computer software, the sound wave patterns could tell petroleum geologists much about subsurface conditions and the probability of finding oil or gas.

As a regional centre, Inuvik played an important staging role for seismic exploration. The petroleum exploration activities had several significant benefits for local trappers, for whom the seismic lines sometimes offered much easier access to distant areas. The cleared areas also promoted new vegetation and the regeneration of small animal foods. Also, many trappers working for oil companies were more successful trappers than others who theoretically trapped full time. This was because workers on two-weeks-on and two-weeks-off had more interest and energy and were able to purchase good equipment such as snowmobiles and camp supplies.

During the period of high activity there was considerable income for local businesses providing services to the oil patch. One vehicle service company even charged an oil company $25 for each time a garage door was opened to compensate for the hot air that was lost.

By the late 1960s, it was clear that there was strong potential for commercially exploitable oil and gas finds in the region. But along with the efforts to locate promising drilling sites, the question of getting these potential reserves to market was a major subject of research.

In preparation for moving oil and gas reserves from the Mackenzie Delta, several pipeline research projects were initiated. Several small oil pipelines were built at Arctic Coast DEWline sites from the shore to the base. Two experimental pipelines in permafrost conditions were built at Inuvik.

The first of these lines, the IOL Pipeline Loop, was built in August 1976. The IOL was a 520-metre experimental pipeline alongside and underneath Airport Road, close to the CBC tower. The purpose was to investigate pipeline laying and operating techniques in permafrost soils under Arctic conditions. The Imperial Oil Limited Producing Department was in charge. The site was selected to represent all types of Arctic terrain. It began on a dry hillside with clay soils, passed under the corner of a lake, crossed a peat area with high ice content, and ended in a gravel hillside. Various pipeline diameters, depth of burial and insulation types were used to evaluate the effects of temperature and strain on the pipeline. Temperature and strain measurements were made every two weeks by the Inuvik Research Laboratory. The project was followed closely for three years, so that obvious pipeline problems could be avoided should a full-scale Arctic pipeline evolve.

The second experimental pipeline was built in response to developments in Alaska. The Prudhoe Bay field on Alaska's North Slope, with estimated reserves of 10 billion barrels of oil and 30 trillion cubic feet of natural gas, was discovered in 1967 and confirmed on February 16, 1968. It was the largest oilfield in North America. As the most direct route for a

---

TELEPHONE SERVICE

Local residents, government operations and businesses of every sort welcomed the establishment of telephone services between Inuvik and the outside world. On August 2, 1966, Prime Minister Mike Pearson officially opened the new Mackenzie Valley telephone link when NWT Commissioner Ben Sivertz phoned him from Inuvik.

The Canadian National Telecommunications line involved 3050 kilometres of wire strung along 55,000 tripod poles. The line was completed to Fort Simpson in 1964, and was extended to Norman Wells in 1965. The CN telephone land line from Hay River was completed to Inuvik in July 1966. It was a single wire strung along tripods on a 16-foot right of way for 1600 km (1040 miles). The project was started in 1962 to connect the Mackenzie River communities. Its construction contrasted with the Mackenzie Highway project along the same route which was blocked near Fort Simpson over native land claim issues.

pipeline to central United States markets was along the Beaufort coast and south along the Mackenzie Valley, a consortium of 15 Canadian and US oil and pipeline firms proposed in early 1969 that a major oil pipeline be built for this route. The Canadian route was 1300 km long from the Delta to Northern Alberta, and 2800 km from Prudhoe Bay to Alberta; the Alaska route through Yukon and BC to the US Midwest was 5000 km.

Mackenzie Valley Pipeline Research Ltd. built an experimental pipeline along Inuvik's Navy Road in September 1969 with actual testing underway in February 1970. The site was selected because it was representative of soil and climatic conditions that would be encountered by a pipeline running from Prudhoe Bay to Alberta. The test line was to determine the environmental effects of operating a warm oil pipeline in permafrost conditions. The test facilities included a 600-metre closed loop of 48-inch steel pipe, a crude oil heating system, oil storage and an instrumentation network. Hot oil ranging from 70°C to 82°C was circulated through the pipe under Arctic conditions. Half the loop was straight with the pipe laid in a gravel berm on the surface of the ground. The depth of gravel below the pipe varied from two feet to five feet to evaluate bearing and insulating characteristics. The other half

EARLY INUVIK COMPANIES

Early Businesses	Manager/Owner
Aklavik Flying Services	Mike Zubko
Arctic Wings & Rotars	George Clark
Baetz Trucking	Bob Baetz
Campbell Construction	Gord Campbell
CIBC	John Comeau 1964
CN Telecommunications	Don Yamkowy 1964
Connelly Dawson Airways	Trevor Burroughs
Cox Contracting	Ray Cox
Hudsons Bay Company	A. Stadler 1964
Imperial Oil Agency	R. Hewitt, Dave Jones 1964, Frank Hansen
Inuvik Barbershop	P. Joseph
Inuvik Drum	Tom Butters 1965, Dan Holman 1975
Mackenzie Hotel	Stan Peffer, John Greekas 1964, Lou Bassinet 1967
Mack Travel	Jim Robertson
Norm's Hardware	Norm Street, later Doug Billingsley
Norris Contracting	Fred Norris
Pluim Contractors	Al Pluim
Polaris Theatre	Cece McCauley
Semmler's Store	Slim Semmler
Territorial Liquor Store	Mac McInnes
Tuk Traders	George Clark
Wagner Construction	Gary Wagner

of the closed loop was supported above ground on 16-inch diameter wooden piles inserted 5 metres into the permafrost and 21 metres apart in a zigzag pattern. Sliding plates on the piles permitted horizontal movement of the pipe due to thermal expansion and contraction. Several types of insulating materials were attached to the pipe in both the buried and aboveground sections. These construction methods provided optimum pipe security with minimum permafrost disturbance.

This pipeline research project cost an estimated $500,000, and served to establish Canadian skills in northern pipeline construction. It attracted many visitors from government and industry, including Queen Elizabeth, Alaska Governor Walter Hickel and Governor General Roland Michener.

This pipeline project was phased out in September 1973 when the test program was completed and the Canadian option to move Prudhoe Bay crude oil was lost. United States business interests built the the Trans Alaska oil pipeline extending 1270 km from Prudhoe Bay to Valdez, at an estimated cost of $3.5 billion plus an estimated $2 billion for tankers to California, totaling $5.5 billion. The proposed Canadian pipeline system to move Prudhoe Bay oil would have extended to the US heartland at an estimated cost of only $5 billion. The Mackenzie Valley route was more economical and more environmentally acceptable, as later confirmed by the massive Valdez marine oil spill in March 1989.

The supertanker option for shipping oil also received attention in the Canadian Arctic. In 1969 the supertanker SS Manhattan traversed the Northwest Passage to promote tanker movement of Prudhoe Bay oil.

During this period, the federal government also initiated research into the feasibility of a deep-water port at Herschel Island.

A Growing Local Business Sector

In 1967, the Inuvik Village office issued 51 business licences. In 1970, the number had nearly doubled to 98 licences.

Many of the businesses featured distinctively northern names: Polar TV, Arctic Plumbing, Eskimo Inn, Raven's Nest, Polaris Theatre, Mackenzie Hotel, Arctic Wings & Rotors, Aklavik Flying Services, and Boreal Books.

The Inuvik and District Chamber of Commerce was formed in 1964 with Bob Baetz the

CHAMBER PRESIDENTS 1964-1970		INUVIK BUSINESS LICENCES	
1964	Bob Baetz	1967	51
1965	Tom Butters	1968	52
1966	Jack Heath	1969	75
1967	Jack Heath	1970	98
1968	Jack Heath		
1969	Ray Berube		
1970	Ray Anderson		

first president. Special low-priced memberships were available for businesses in surrounding communities. The Chamber's guiding principle was to be independent, representing only business interests and not taking any operating or grant funds from government. The Inuvik Chamber was an active member of the NWT Chamber of Commerce. Later when a Tuktoyaktuk Chamber and a business group formed in Aklavik, the name was changed to the Inuvik Chamber of Commerce, with special memberships for businesses in surrounding communities.

Transportation

On December 11, 1965 Larry Mann and Dick Hill drove an International Scout from Inuvik to Aklavik and back over smooth and relatively snow-free ice. This was the first wheeled vehicle to cross over from Inuvik to Aklavik on the Delta ice since Inuvik was founded, but their feat had first been accomplished in a Jeep almost 10 years earlier by Dr. Ian Black and RCMP Inspector Huget from Aklavik to East 3 and back on November 4, 1956.

One day in August 1966 there were three new Twin Otters parked by the Inuvik airport terminal. By coincidence these modern bush planes were the first Dehavilland production units 1, 2 and 3. The Twin Otter was first flown in 1965 and initial deliveries were made in 1966 with a total of 844 produced. These versatile aircraft were used extensively throughout the North for passenger, freight, exploration and government services.

During the late 1960's there was a surge in demand for charter air services from Inuvik to the communities of Aklavik, Fort McPherson and Tuktoyaktuk. Aklavik Flying Serves, operated by Mike Zubko, and Reindeer Air Services, operated by Fred Carmichael, expanded with more aircraft mainly operating off the East Branch, using float planes in the summer and ski planes in the winter. The Inuvik Aviation Council was formed to provide improved local facilities for both commercial and private aircraft operators.

In May 1968 the Inuvik Aviation Council constructed a 60 metre by 600 metre landing strip, by bulldozing willows off the river bank between the sewage lagoon and the East Branch. Provision was made for hangers and for float plane operations off the East Branch. There had been pressure from the MOT to move all float plane operations to Shell Lake and to use the lake as an ice strip. The Aviation Council under its president Ron Williams took responsibility for the construction and maintenance of the Intown Airport. Strong community support developed for the intown airstrip when the Inuvik taxi fares to the main airport were increased to $10 per passenger. At the time, the charter air fare between Inuvik and Aklavik amounted to only $10 per passenger.

The Inuvik Council gave approval for operation of the new strip at a meeting on May 13, 1968. On May 25, the first aircraft to land on the strip was a Piper Cub piloted by Sven Johansson of Reindeer Station.

In January 1965 Earl Harcourt of Yellowknife Transportation Ltd. proposed the construction of an 80 metre by 12 metre pleasure ship, to carry 120 passengers and a crew of 40, that would operate between the Great Slave Lake and Inuvik. The ship, costing $1.5 million,

THE MACKENZIE BEER BARGE

Pat Berry's 1964 song about the Mackenzie Beer Barge captured much of Inuvik's social spirit in the 1960s.

I went down the Mackenzie on a barge load of beer
Got to the Delta – heard a big cheer
All them folks was standing about
They saw that beer and they start to shout

The whole town shoving and pushing on the dock
And that old dock began to roll and rock
They jumped on board as we got near
Ready to help unload the beer.

There were Linklaters, Smiths and Father Adam
Agnes Semmler and Nels Vatum
Bruno's Taxi was packed inside
With Fred Jacobson's whole tribe
There was Tim Timmons, his wife Jean
Cece McCauley and Carl Franzin
Jack Wainwright, Moose and Knut
The Gordons and the Norrises ready for a toot
There were Zubkos, Holmans and Davy Jones
The Mountie detachment – dry as a bone
Oblate fathers and nursing mothers
Fishermen, whalers and a few others.

Cat drivers, bushed trappers
Mines and Tech Survey mappers
Auditors of government books
Stan Peffer's last two cooks.

Gold seekers without hope
Peddlers of mosquito dope
Indian agents, T.B. detectors
Licensed beverage tax collectors.

Ottawa types and M.P.s
Refugees from the D.T.s
Bishops, nurses and weathermen
Smugglers disguised as customs men.

Muskox hunters from southern zoos
CBC with canned news
Game wardens, fur buyers
Bottled propane gas suppliers.

Glacier experts from McGill
Americans seeking an Arctic thrill
N.T. and Y.T.
Carpenters and royalty
Churchwork volunteers.

Monitors of Russian Stations
Distributors of welfare rations
Electricians
Dieticians
Britain's barmiest physicians
Analyzers of housing cost
Probers of permafrost
Men sampling oil
Air and soil
Conmen seeking north spoil
Estimators
Regulators
Economic stimulators
A faith healer
A Banksland sealer
The nearest authorized kicker dealer.

Professors from the U of T
Bird-watchers and the DOT
Field men from the Lions Club
The Governor General and the General Crud

And when that barge wouldn't hold no more
They shout and ramble along the shore
Till the captain yells "You're out of luck,
This here beer is going to Tuk."
Tuk-toy-ak-tuk, tuk-tuk.

P.S. Barry, *Edge*, Autumn 1964

was to be christened the Arctic Dawn and would introduce luxury tourism to communities along the Mackenzie River. Unfortunately, this project did not get off the drawing boards (*Financial Post* 23 Jan 1965).

Community Activities

1967 Canada Centennial Celebrations: When Canadians' thoughts were turning to Canada's 100th birthday in 1967, funding for NWT community Centennial projects was announced in 1965. The Inuvik Advisory Committee requested that the Inuvik Community Association assume responsibility for coordinating project selection. The ICA held a public meeting on July 21, 1966 where several proposals were considered including:

1. Curling rink addition
2. Curling rink addition with community centre
3. Community arena with swimming pool
4. Skating arena and community centre
5. Native meeting house
6. Museum and Library

At this meeting the projects were narrowed down to the community centre with swimming pool, the native meeting house and the museum and library. A public meeting for further presentations and detail was scheduled at SAMS auditorium. The museum and library was promoted by the Inuvik Museum and Library Society, chaired by Cynthia Hill. The native meeting house was promoted as a Friendship Centre by the Ingamo Association under Bill Enge. The community arena with swimming pool promoters did not organize and their project was left off the ballot. A public vote on the projects was held on September 15, 1965 with 250 votes cast for the library and 217 for the native friendship centre. This total of 467 votes was comparable to the 483 votes cast by Inuvik residents in the preceding Inuvik election for a NWT Council member. The friendship centre had its day a few years later, when Ingamo Hall was constructed on Mackenzie Road a couple blocks west of the Centennial Library.

For Canada's 1967 celebrations in Inuvik, several prominent musicians performed including Anne Murray, Ian and Sylvia, and the Irish Rovers. Astronaut James Lovell made a public appearance. Readings by Canadian poets and authors at Inuvik Centennial Library included Al Purdy, Matt Cohen, Victor Coleman, Dave McFadden, Frank Davey, Daphne Marlatt, George Bowering, Michael Ondaatje, Margaret Atwood and B. P. Nichol.

Inuvik Centennial Library

The books in the Aklavik public library were transferred over to Inuvik in 1959 when the new Inuvik Federal School opened. This library was sponsored by the Home and School Association and opened once a week from a small room beside the stage in SAMS. Annette Shaw and several volunteers organized the collection. Ellen Binder was the first local librarian. This was Inuvik's only library service until the Centennial Library opened.

The Inuvik Museum and Library Society was registered in May 1965, prior to the Centennial vote, and was not involved in the operation of the library although it obviously had full support of the librarian, library patrons and the Inuvik Community Association. The original Society members were: Mary Darkes, with northern library experience while she lived in Fort Smith, who served as the first chair of the Society; Flora Neave, RCMP wife; Larry Mann, RCN Lieutenant-Commander of CFS Inuvik; Donetta Stewart, wife of the Inuvik Region Social Services Superintendent; Cynthia Hill, Inuvik Preschool Association and long-term supporter of libraries for community education. When proposals for 1967 Centennial projects were advertised, the Society decided to enter the Inuvik competition for a construction grant. The library building project won the community vote on September 15, 1965 and the commitment for the $75,000 grant.

Library building designs and construction drawings were prepared by student architects Walter Wright and Clarence Aasen, who were working on a community planning project at the Inuvik Research Laboratory. Gary Wagner of Mackenzie Delta Construction bid on the work at a very low price per square metre. In effect, he proposed the largest building possible with the available funds as a community gesture. The Mackenzie Road "main street" site was purposely chosen to establish the new library as an essential part of Inuvik living.

There was considerable volunteer effort by members of the Inuvik Museum and Library Society getting things organized, arranging for book donations, financial donations and responding to normal "political" interference mainly from the new NWT Public Library director in Hay River. The new building was to have shelves for 10,000 books, space for children's books, study carrels for students, current newspaper and magazine files plus special spaces for Inuvik "museum" items. Donations for the library came mainly from Inuvik residents but also from across Canada. There was a funding project to buy a shelf for $10 and have a brass plaque put on it. (Jim Birch made all the library shelving at just the cost of the boards.) The Society directors and members purchased a Mona Thrasher painting of the Inuvik library and gave it to the Hills at the opening in recognition of their support for the project. Thousands of books were collected and donated by many southern organizations. PWA both advertised this promotion and gave free transportation of the books to Inuvik.

The Inuvik Centennial Library was ready for occupancy in November 1966 and its official opening was on January 15, 1967 as the only public library within the Arctic Circle, and the only separate library building in the Northwest Territories. The library was the only NWT Centennial building project completed in time for the start of the 1967 Centennial. Ellen Binder, as an Inuvik Councilor, cut the opening ribbon. No outside dignitaries were present for the opening.

Louise Hunter was selected as the first Centennial librarian. She was an RCMP wife with library experience. Ellen Binder asked that she not be considered for the position as she was busy on the community council. Ellen did accept the position in December 1967 when Louise was transferred out of the community. The Library's logo was designed by Inuvik student artist Heidi Willkomm.

Sociologists John and Irma Honigman lived in Inuvik during 1967 and commented on the Inuvik Centennial Library activities in their book *Arctic Townsmen* (Honigman 1970).

Samuel Hearne Secondary School

Construction of Inuvik's Samuel Hearne Secondary School began in the 1966 spring with the setting of 400 piles in Lot 17, which was the original location of the Rehab centre. The construction commencement ceremony was held on June 28, 1967, with the cutting of the first pile top with a power saw in place of the usual turning of sod. Bob Baetz represented the Inuvik Village Council, and commented at the ceremony that it was 10 years earlier that construction had started on Inuvik's first school. Yukon Construction of Edmonton were the building contractors for the $1.7 million building.

There was considerable effort made by the Inuvik Council and community groups to have the school named "Anisaluk" after Charlie Smith, a community leader who died in 1967, rather than having it named after an English explorer who had never traveled near the Mackenzie Delta. However, the NWT government decreed that the high school be named after a foreigner as had the Sir John Franklin High School in Yellowknife. The new facility served grades 7 to 12, with 14 classrooms, science room, and art room. Also, there was a chemistry lab, a physics lab, home economics room, industrial arts and a gymnasium with a folding door across the middle.

The Samuel Hearne Secondary School was officially opened in September 1969 by Hon. Jean Chrétien, Minister of Indian and Northern Affairs. At the time there were 212 students in Junior High, 90 in Senior High and 33 in Occupational for a total of 335.

Stefansson Science Club

The Stefansson Science Club was founded in January 1964 by Willie Ho, SAMS science teacher, and Dick Hill. The club sponsored the first Inuvik Science Fair at the Inuvik Research Laboratory on May 15, 1965. A compact transistorized radio receiver for arctic pilots, made by Grade 8 student Tom Zubko, was judged the winning exhibit. Second prize was won by Dave Wilderspin for his rock mineral analysis. Third prize was won by Norbert Vollmers for his living cell exhibit. There was a group exhibit on pingos.

Dave Jones Community Centre

In 1967 the Inuvik Community Association initiated a project for construction of a community centre complex including a regulation ice rink, curling rink and a community banquet room with a kitchen. Construction began in early 1968. The centre's core area was completed in 1969 with funds borrowed from the Town of Inuvik. The total project was budgeted to cost $694,000. There was considerable fund-raising, NWT Recreation grants, volunteer labour and contributions from the Village Council. But by September 1970, the budgeted funds were used up but the project was only half finished, and any completion date appeared very distant. However, after a regular military inspection of CFS Inuvik operations in October 1970, and a fortunate meeting of Inuvik's Mayor and Brigadier General Mussels at a social function, the Community Centre problems were considered. Since the Armed Forces personnel would be major users of the ice rink and curling facilities, the visiting General suggested that a non-interest-bearing loan from the National Defence Central Fund be made for materials, and that military trades specialists be assigned to work on the project until it was finished. Arrangements were made for Military Construction Engineering to supply a projects officer and 12 tradesmen plus Armed Forces airlift support. In January 1971 project materials were airlifted from Edmonton in 11 Hercules flights. Off-duty military volunteers helped the specialist tradesmen. Major J. C. "Tug" Wilson tasked each CFS officer and man to provide four hours of work each week in teams to supplement the town's project crew. Hence, Inuvik's first community centre was completed in 1973.

The finished complex consisted of a hockey arena and a six-sheet curling rink. There was a snack bar, changing rooms and comprehensive banquet facilities. The arena was used extensively for hockey, broom ball and figure skating. In 1975, Inuvik Mayor Jim Robertson proposed that the centre be renamed the Dave Jones Community Centre after the long-time Inuvik resident, town councilor and sports enthusiast.

Mackenzie Institute

The Mackenzie Institute was formed in 1968 by Agnes Semmler, Victor Allen, and Dick Hill. Its purpose was to provide local input into the social and technical research programs and to provide local education, culture and development activities for residents. The organization held its first official meeting on 23 October 1968, with Chair Elijah Menarik, Vice Chair John Pascal, Secretary Agnes Semmler, Admin Board-President Dick Hill, Vice President Victor Allen, Treasurer Tom Butters, Director of Research Elijah Menarik.

The Institute sponsored the "Man In The North" Conference on Community Development with AINA, held on November 18-21, 1970 in Inuvik (Helen Murphy, editor). Victor Allan as eskimology Professor gave lectures on the Eskimo language and culture. Rose Mary Thrasher carried out studies on the effects of Delta seismic lines. Local names were provided to the petroleum industry for appropriate names for exploration grid and well locations.

Rosemary Thrasher, Project Leader, stated, "I am willing, with the Mackenzie Institute, which is independent of government and oil companies, to help you bring your messages across to them, and also to bring you up-to-date news on what is happening. The Mackenzie Delta Environment Project is a communications program to keep in touch with residents of the Mackenzie Delta about present government and petroleum activities so that they can be more involved in the 'action'. The main emphasis of the project is on the petroleum programs and how it affects the land, wildlife and Delta residents" (Mackenzie Institute, *Delta Newsletter*, Aug 1970.)

During the 1970 summer the Mackenzie Institute and the University of Western Ontario operated a teletype connection at the Inuvik Research Laboratory to the Althouse College of Education. A group of Inuvik students and elders used the system to study simple arithmetic and sophisticated cultural problems. Computer Assisted Instruction allowed each student to master the problems at each student's own rate of learning. The students couldn't "fail" in the conventional sense as the system adjusted to the level of difficulty where the student can operate best. This Computer Assisted Instruction program, co-ordinated by Valerie Maguire, was a pioneering effort, about 15 years ahead of widespread use of computers in classrooms.

There was considerable opposition to the Mackenzie Institute from NWT Education authorities in Yellowknife. The Mackenzie Institute ceased operating in 1971 when COPE and other groups took on most of its responsibilities.

Committee for Original Peoples Entitlement

The Committee for Original Peoples Entitlement (COPE) formed on January 28, 1970 and was incorporated on March 19, 1970. COPE was initially directed by Nellie Cournoyea, Agnes Semmler and Sam Raddi. "Its membership is limited to nonwhites, and its aims are to get compensation for aboriginal rights and for damage being done to the environment and its inhabitants by oil exploration" (Lotz 1970).

COPE started off speaking for all Inuvik natives – Indians, Eskimo and Métis. However, with the formation of the NWT Indian Brotherhood in 1970, the Inuvik Indian and Métis were attracted to join and the Inuvialuit decided to go on their own.

Ingamo Hall

The origin of Ingamo Hall dates back to 1965 when Inuvik's Indian and Eskimo Association was formed. The HBC donated their original Inuvik store which was located by the riverbank at East Three Point. It was moved to a temporary lot beside Grollier Hall and then again to Ingamo's present site on Mackenzie Road. The Ingamo Hall Native Friendship Centre was funded under a Northern Affairs program involving a three-way partnership of the federal government, the local community council and local native organizations. Visits were made to the Friendship Centres in Calgary and Edmonton which had active municipal participation. The Inuvik Council turned over the large lot at the corner of Mackenzie Road and Dolphin Street, which had been reserved as a public park/playground, for the Ingamo building. Although the Inuvik Council was most supportive of the proposed friendship centre and offered to budget for one third of its operating costs, the group organizing it wanted to be independent without involvement of the Inuvik municipal government. This was a missed opportunity for ethnic cooperation in Inuvik. Many times Ingamo Hall projects were short of funds and could have used municipal assistance. In January 1966 the

INDAMO HALL, NOT INGAMO

Fred Beaulieu was one of the founding members of the Indian and Eskimo Association in Inuvik. As an Indian married to an Eskimo, he referred to his children as "Indamos". At one of the initial meetings Fred proposed that the organization be called "Indamo". It was agreed that membership cards would be obtained. However, there was a printing error and the cards came back with "Ingamo Association". Rather than return the cards the directors agreed to call it Ingamo.

Ingamo Association directors were Bill Enge, Ann Enge, Elijah Menarik, Victor Allen, Jim Koe, Bill English, Bob Hunter, and Ed Lennie (RMH diary 4 Jan 1966).

The new Ingamo Hall Friendship Centre was built with 1000 large white spruce logs from the Liard River, which were rafted down the Mackenzie River to Inuvik in 1975. The building was constructed from 1976 to 1977 almost single-handedly by Allan Crich, a Swiss-Canadian builder who has been referred to as the "Father of Canadian log building".

Company of Young Canadians

The Company of Young Canadians (CYC) under George Erasmus operated in Inuvik during the late 1960s. They rented an east end house and operated casually. They refused to discuss their activities with the Town Council. An *Edmonton Journal* report on June 24, 1969 was titled "Mackenzie Too Hot For The CYC", as the Carrother's Commission stated that the CYC would be wise to stay out of the Mackenzie region communities until it had experience and reputation to cope with the problems due to the "turmoil, conflicts and difficulties there".

1970 NWT Centennial Activities

Throughout 1970 there was a flurry of celebrations for the 100th Anniversary of the Northwest Territories. The Inuvik activities included an April 23 enactment of the historic western dogsled mail run; the Top of the World Ski Championships in April; an International Fly-in, hosted by Inuvik Aviation Council, at the Intown Airstrip; July 1st Northern Games; and an NWT Centennial barge, with farm animals, and a ferris wheel on top. Gina Blondin was NWT Queen. Nellie Cournoyea was chair of the 1970 Centennial Organizing Committee.

The Sir Alexander Mackenzie Canoe Race, part of the Centennial celebrations, began at Fort Providence on July 9th, 1970 with the starting gun fired by the Duke of Edinburgh. The race was restricted to six-man voyager-type eight-metre canoes, with one entry from each of the Mackenzie River settlements. The race ended in Inuvik on July 28th with the presentation of a $10,000 prize to the winners from Aklavik.

A highlight of the NWT Centennial in Inuvik was the visit by the Royal Family on July 7 & 8, 1970. A community lunch was held, with Mayor Dick Hill and his wife Cynthia seated at a 22-person head table alongside the Queen and the Duke of Edinburgh.

A GIFT FOR THE QUEEN

Garret Ruben, chairman of the Paulatuk Council, had been invited to the dinner celebrating the Royal Family's visit. He brought a "regal" gift from his community – a superb white fox pelt. Inuvik's Mayor, as Master of Ceremonies for the occasion, was aware of Garret's intent to present the fox pelt, but he wasn't told that the "handlers" at the back of the hall had refused to allow the gift to be presented because the skin was not tanned. Hence, when Garret was called to come forward nothing happened. The thought was that he was too shy to come forward. On further encouragement, Garret finally broke away from the officials and elegantly made his presentation to the Queen; she gracefully accepted.

Notable Visitors

Other notable visitors during this period included a USSR Delegation, August 24, 1965. The reception and dinner was sponsored by the Inuvik Advisory Committee. A six-member Soviet delegation specializing in northern development and construction toured the Canadian North and arrived in Inuvik on August 24th. This was a return visit from Northern Affairs Minister Arthur Laing's visit to the USSR in May and June. John Turner, MP, Parliamentary Secretary to the Minister of Northern Affairs, accompanied the group.

Northern Affairs Minister Arthur Laing visited Inuvik on August 22-25, 1966, accompanied by six foreign ambassadors based in Ottawa, seven members of the business community, and three members of the Parliamentary Press Gallery (Charles Lynch, Southam, Blair Fraser, *Macleans*, and Maurice Western). Laing's Special Assistant, Jack Austin, liked to promote the analogy the north is like a crawling baby. It needs its mother (Southern Canada) before it can walk (Reguly, 1963c).

In the summer of 1967 Toronto Symphony Orchestra members played in the Igloo church and commented on the acoustic quality.

On May 22, 1969, Ross Munroe, publisher of the *Edmonton Journal*, and Bill Heine, editor of the *London Free Press*, made a tour of Inuvik. Heine officially staked out a mining claim, called "Heine's Folly Claim", along Airport Road, using markers he had picked up at the Mining Recorder's office in Yellowknife.

Inuvik residents not only hosted visitors, but were invited to conferences elsewhere. Victor Allen was a featured speaker, along with Northern Affairs Minister Arthur Laing and Newfoundland Premier Joey Smallwood, at the the National Northern Development Conference in Edmonton on November 1, 1967. He was well received as he spoke on the situation of the Eskimo and Indian in the areas of language, education and development and the need for all groups to work together.

Miscellaneous Activities

Gardening has been practiced in Inuvik from the start. There can be 50 growing days each summer. The 24-hour daylight creates gigantic vegetables. Some plants don't grow well in the continuous daylight as they need some rest to thrive.

Father Adam's garden measured 50 × 100 foot. The garden produced radishes as big as tangerines and because of their quick growth they were neither hollow or hot. Fr Adam used cold frames for starting flowers, and lettuce, carrots and radishes for early use. He planted several rows of carrots in the fall, giving them a head start in the spring. As Inuvik is practically a desert during the summer months with little or no rain, Fr Adam used large barrels filled with water, and put fertilizer into the water so that one application does two jobs. He used superphosphates, and found that small quantities go a long way. He also used his own potatoes for seed.

Drum Dancing: Starting in March 1964 Eskimo Drummers and Dancers held weekly sessions mainly to provide traditional arts training for Inuvik youth. The participating Inuvik elders were Tom Goose, Kenneth and Rosie Peelooluk, Tom Kalinek, Tom Kimiksana, Sydney Ayuluk and Erastus Oliver. The program was organized by Dave Sutherland and Dick Hill. Nightly sessions were held at the old Hudson's Bay Company store. Margo Kasook Hill remembers the good times at these sessions as a young girl.

Inuvik Drum: Tom Butters organized the *Inuvik Drum* newspaper on December 16, 1965. The first issue was published on January 6, 1966 using an ancient 1928 multilith press. It had a paid subscription base of 1500. (The *Drum* was sold to Dan Holman in 1978, and sold again to Northern News Service of Yellowknife, publishers of *News North*, in February 1988.)

Butters resigned from the NWT Government as Inuvik Regional Administrator effective October 8, 1965. A farewell reception was held on October 15th. Sid Hancock took over as Regional Administrator.

During the Mackenzie River breakup in the spring of 1964, there was concern for serious flooding of Aklavik and Delta camps. Regional Director Tom Butters organized several reconnaissance flights from Inuvik to check the flooding risks. He made several CBC community announcement reports on the water levels at the Main Branch "doughnut" due West of Inuvik, where the river had broken through a turn to form an island. For some time this feature was known as the "Buttered Doughnut".

Territorial Experimental Ski Training (TEST)

In 1964 Jacques Van Pelt of the NWT Recreation Department invited Father J. M. Mouchet, OMI, of Old Crow to visit the Northwest Territories to advise on the suitability of introducing cross-country skiing for young Northerners. He recommended that an outdoor education program be initiated with the Inuvik hostels as there were:

1. Excellent trail possibilities with rolling hills within the treeline;
2. Good weather conditions for skiing from mid-October to the end of May;
3. Students who could readily relate to cross-country skiing activities.

Ski training was led by Fr Mouchet for 10 days in the Spring of 1964.

Spring ski clinics were held in Inuvik in 1965 and 1966 under Bjorger Petterson, a certified cross-country ski instructor from British Columbia with considerable Scandinavian skiing experience.

Time Magazine noted, "even in Inuvik, inside the Arctic Circle, 100 skiers have formed a new club" (19 February 1965, "The Swinging Slopes").

In 1967 the Territorial Experimental Ski Training (TEST) program was formed by Peggy Curtis, Dave Sutherland and Dick Hill to apply for a National Fitness Council grant. When the grant came through, Bjorger Petterson was appointed as coach and arrangements were made for Father Mouchet to assist with the program. A TEST Trustee Board was established to oversee the program and assist with the skiing activities. The initial Board members were:

Dick Hill	Chairman, Director, Inuvik Research Laboratory
Dave Sutherland	Sec-Treas, Craft Officer, Inuvik
Jim Maher	Principal, Samuel Hearne Secondary School, Inuvik
Beth-Ann Exham	Community Teacher, Old Crow
Peggy Curtis	School Councilor, Inuvik
Dave Jones	Chairman, Inuvik Village Council
Fred North	Principal, Sir Alexander Mackenzie School, Inuvik

Petterson remained as TEST coach until 1971 when he became coach of the Canadian National Cross Country Ski Team. He was replaced by Hans Skinstead. Dick Hill was chair of the TEST board until 1971. Jarl Omholt Jensen was a CBC Inuvik announcer and an avid cross country skier who helped with TEST communications and spirit.

The skiing activities were based out of Grollier Hall with the enthusiastic support of the hostel supervisor, Father Max Ruyant, who was looking for creative sports for the student residents.

The Inuvik Top of the World Ski Championship was organized to provide TEST skiers and other racers in northern communities with a chance for friendly competition and sport socializing. It became an international event with participants from Alaska and Europe as well as several provinces. The 1970 Top of the World Ski Championship involved 12 Canadian teams, nine American teams and world class competitors from Sweden, Norway and Switzerland.

During the winter of 1967-68 TEST skiers skied more than 20,000 miles in training and competed in 45 races. Significant cross-country races for the TEST skiers were in the 1968 Canadian Championships, the 1969 American Championships, the 1970, 1974, 1978, and 1982 World Ski Championships and the 1972, 1976, 1980 and 1984 Winter Olympics.

In the late 1960s TEST skiers dominated Canadian Junior Championships, and the Firth sisters beat top American skiers in North American competitions. In 1969 a national women's cross-country ski team was formed with the Firth sisters, Sharon and Shirley, as the first members. The Firths went on to compete at the Olympics in Sapporo in 1972, Innsbruk in 1976, Lake Placid in 1980 and Sarejevo in 1984. Sharon quit in 1978 but came back in 1979. Shirley retired in 1984. Sharon continued for one more year. Sharon received the Order of Canada. She worked briefly at the NWT Pavilion at Expo '86 in Vancouver. She now works in Yellowknife. Shirley married a Swede and moved to the French Riviera (Holmes 1989).

TEST skiers also participated in the 1970 World Championship. The NWT ski team at the 1972 Arctic Winter Games in Whitehorse was organized by TEST skiers Kane Tologanak as coach and Margaret Steen as manager. Roger Allen retired from TEST in 1972 at age of 19 and became Assistant Coach. He became a successful northern politician and served as Minister of several departments.

In 1975 industry (Shell, Gulf and Imperial Oil) built a large culvert under the Bypass Road for cross-country skiers. DPW had refused to accommodate the skiers when the road was planned. The Inuvik Ski Club aided in developing 8 km of groomed ski trails through the hills north of Inuvik.

The TEST program operated until 1984 when its Federal operating grant was no longer available.

A research report evaluating the effectiveness of the TEST program was prepared by a team of University of Alberta researchers under Dr. R. G. Glassford. The program's effectiveness for northern youth was confirmed in developing personality and achievement, suitability of cross-country skiing as a meaningful athletic endeavour, and development of excellence. TEST skiers were found to be self-assured by their accomplishments and at the same time humble and unwilling to be above their peers. Any pride from skiing accomplishments was shared with family and community (Glassford 1973).

A comparable program operated out of Old Crow and Whitehorse with Father Mouchet's involvement.

At about the same time the TEST program was beginning, another winter sport also got its start in Inuvik. In October 1964, a group of skiing enthusiasts cleared brush on the Mount Baldy slopes for downhill runs, and a portable rope tow was loaned by the NWT Recreation Department. This group formed the Inuvik Ski Club in January 1965. At the Inuvik Ski Club meeting on January 17, 1968, members elected Kane Tologanak, President; Dick Hill, Vice President; Margaret Steen, Secretary; Anita Allen, Treasurer; Harold Cook, Racing Director; Peggy Curtis, Touring Director; Sister Biellka, Membership; Bjorger Petterson, Certified Ski Instructor. However, downhill skiing was found to be very limited due to the winter darkness and extreme cold temperatures, causing an uncomfortable wind chill for the skiers.

Fire and Ice

Two other events hold strong memories for Invuik residents during the 1960s.

Around noon on August 8, 1968, two youngsters started a small campfire between the Twin Lakes along Airport Road west of the CBC radio tower. A strong breeze developed and the campfire spread into the surrounding dry brush. This fire was reported to the Inuvik Fire Department at 2:05 pm. When the Inuvik Fire Brigade and the Inuvik Forestry Officer arrived the fire was approximately 15 metres in diameter. Water pumps were operated from one of the lakes. However, a southeast wind pushed the fire onto the hillside behind the lakes, where it traveled rapidly through the tinder-dry underbrush faster than the fire-fighters could lay hose. (There had been no significant rainfall in the area since May 13th.) By 6:30 pm the fire had reached Boot Creek Valley, and at 9:00 pm it was threatening Inuvik's Hidden Lake water facilities. Bulldozers cut lines to protect Inuvik and around 150 volunteers assisted the operations.

The following day an Emergency Measures Centre was set up with the NA&NR Forestry Officer, Wilf Taylor, in charge. On August 10th, the NWT Commissioner closed all Inuvik liquor outlets to free more people for fire-fighting. The town proper was protected, but the fire passed around the community sweeping down on the Canadian Forces operations facilities, burning the antenna posts and toppling the communications towers. Most of the power posts along Navy Road were toppled, cutting off power to the base. The bar at the Mackenzie Hotel was closed and all patrons were put on the fire lines. Additional crews and equipment were brought in from the surrounding communities.

A total of 450 people were involved in the fire-fighting. All of the Inuvik townsite buildings were protected and suffered no damage. On August 18th, there were cooler temperatures and some rainfall which held the fire dormant around Inuvik, although the fire continued to burn for several weeks to the north of Inuvik along the Caribou Hills.

"Visitors who drive along the Airport Road toward the Town of Inuvik may not notice a grown-over fireguard that runs eastward and up the hill across from the Juk Campground. To residents of Inuvik who were in town during the month of August in 1968, this cutline has a special meaning. On hot days in summer when smoke drifts into town from distant fires, these people remember that the fire guard was built to protect the Town from a fire that broke out on August 8 and burned for 10 long days..." (Wein, 2002)

At the other extreme, Inuvik experienced a cold spell in February 1965 with a minimum temperature -62° F, and warming to not above -8° F for the entire month. The monthly average minimum was -44.4° F, average maximum was -23.8° F, and the mean monthly average was -34.1° F. For early Inuvik residents who experienced this long cold period, it has always been pleasantly warm in the following years.

Three images from Northern Games in Inuvik, early 1970s.

Above, a drum dance at Ingamo Hall, 1975. Below, showing off one of the locally made parkas at Northern Images, 1970.

Inuvik Time Line 1971-1982

1971	Jun 10	Federal Joint Committee on Constitution hearing
	Jul 11-30	Arctic Summer School (ASS) 1st session at Grollier Hall, U. of Alberta Extension
	Nov 19-22	University of Canada North founding meeting
	Dec 18	Alaska land claim passed, with over 1000 Western Arctic beneficiaries
1972	Mar 10	National Defence College tour and dinner
	Apr 8-9	5th Annual Top of the World ski meet
	May	First Pacific Western Airlines B-737 jet flights to Inuvik Airport
	Jun	Major natural gas discovery at Parson's Lake north of Inuvik by Gulf Canada
	Jun 9	Samuel Hearne 1972 Graduation with 28 graduates
	Jul 10	Total solar eclipse at Inuvik viewed by locals and world observers
	Aug	Electrical power line constructed on poles between Inuvik and Tuktoyaktuk
	Nov 3	CFS Inuvik Fall Ball
1973	Mar	CBC live television broadcasts using the Anik satellite
	Jun 2	Gulf Oil announces more natural gas discovered at the Parsons Lake field
	Mar 31	3rd Annual Ice Review, Inuvik Figure Skating Club
	Apr 13	RCMP Centennial Ball at CFS Inuvik
1974	Feb 10-15	Building In Northern Communities, AINA conference/workshop
	Mar 15	Mikel Pulk receives Commissioner's Award for Public Service at Eskimo Inn banquet
	Apr 24	Berger Inquiry at Family Hall, Inuvik Chamber of Commerce & COPE presentations
	Aug	Plans for addition to Inuvik General Hospital
1975	Mar29-Apr 1	Top of the World Ski Championships
	May 26	Poet Al Purdy at Inuvik Centennial Library
	Jun	Stringer Hall student residence closed
	Jun 12-13	Chinese Permafrost Delegation visits Inuvik, Chinese Civil Engineering Society
	Sep 21-22	Northern Roads Fact-Finding Committee meetings in Inuvik
	Sep 22	Margaret Atwood visits Inuvik and holds a reading at the Inuvik Centennial Library
	Oct	Forestry complex completed at Shell Lake
1976	Jan 20-30	Berger Inquiry for producing companies and community presentations
	Feb 12-15	Berger community hearings in Inuvik
	Jun	Ed Broadbent, leader of the New Democratic Party, visits Inuvik
	Jul 30	Science Council of Canada Seminar on Northern Development
	Aug	Inuvik airport runway paved
	Oct	New Town Council chamber, administrative office and fire department opened
	Nov	Finto Motel opened
1977	May 9	Berger Inquiry report conclusions via TV at Family Hall
	May 18	NWT Commissioner's tour to Inuvik
	Jul 22-23	Conservative Caucus Northern Energy Group visits Inuvik
	Jul	Mini-pipeline for natural gas transmission proposed from Parson's Lake to Inuvik
	Sep	Petition for closure of the Inuvik Liquor Store
	Oct 25	New Minister of Northern Affairs, Hugh Faulkner held an open house
	Nov 14	Committee of the Concerned petition for closure of Inuvik Liquor Store

1978	Apr 15	Berger Report's 10-year moratorium on Mackenzie Valley development announced
	Mar	Major Inuvik road paving program launched
	May 28	Inuvik TV's Northern Access Network on the air
	Jun	Dan Holman purchases *Inuvik Drum* from Tom Butters
	Jul	Wooden plank boardwalk along Mackenzie Road replaced with a cement sidewalk
	Oct 78	COPE land claims Agreement In Principle signed
	Oct	Tom Butters returned as Inuvik MLA
1979	Apr 3	First edition of *Mackenzie Drift* newspaper published by Marius Dakin
	Apr 17	'Northern lights' from Fairbanks lithium rocket flare seen in area
	Aug 18	Official opening of Dempster Highway at Flat Creek by Hon Jake Epp, Minister IAND
	Aug	Jack London's Klondike movie filmed out of Inuvik
	Oct	Herschel Island photo exhibit at Town Council Chambers
	Nov	Power brownout as main NCPC generator broke down; town relied on standby units
	Nov	New Ingamo Hall log building opens
1980	May	Arctic Circle Press Club formed with special meeting table in Mad Trapper
	May 5	Armed Forces sky diving with landing in front of SAMS school
	Jun	Western Arctic Visitors Association formed, Larry Springay, president
	Jul 15	Gov General Ed Schreyer and party visit with community dinner at Eskimo Inn
	Jul 16	Alberta Government Ministers Tour to the North hold public meeting
	Aug	Diplomatic Missions Northern Tour to Inuvik
1981	Jul	Town boundaries extended from 45 square miles to 200 square miles
	Sep	Delta House opened in old YMCA building
	Nov 20	Beaufort Sea Environmental Assessment Panel Draft Guideline Meeting
	Oct	Polaris Theatre closed
1982	Jan 25	Robbie Burns Society formed; 1st annual Burns Night with haggis, Scottish dancing
	Feb 18	Inuvik Council officially twins with Barrow, Alaska
	Mar	Inuvik Native Band organized by Cece McCauley
	Apr	Plebiscite on Division of the NWT
	Nov	NCPC plant fire

CHAPTER FIVE

Resource Support, 1971–1982

The hope of petroleum extraction in the far north had been a major impetus for the construction of Inuvik, and during the 1970s it appeared that this industrial destiny was close to being realized.

Many factors, including dramatic rises in oil and gas prices, and a federal government push to increase domestic oil production, contributed to a sharp upturn in exploration activity around Inuvik. At the same time, other social trends, including new attention to unsettled native land claims, and fervent if not always well-informed emphasis on ecological concerns, complicated the plot line of the decade.

Resource Potential

The Beaufort-Mackenzie Basin is a geological province which contains large volumes of discovered oil and natural gas resources, and has high potential for future discoveries. An exploration success ratio of near 30%, which is quite high by frontier basin standards, attests to the basin's resource richness.

In geological terms, the Basin is "a rifted continental margin and foreland basin containing a depth of up to 15 km of Mesozoic-Cenozoic clastic sedimentary strata" (Dietrich & Dixon, Geological Survey of Canada, 2000). In simpler terms, the Basin encompasses a deep depression in the continental crust, as well as a break in the edge of the continent. This low area has been filled quickly, in geological terms, by sediments and the resulting sedimentary stone. The sedimentary stone dates from the Mesozoic era – which spanned from 250 million years ago to 65 million years ago, an era which had an exceptionally warm climate – as well as from the Cenozoic era, which began 65 million years ago and continues to the present.

Within this Basin, "The combination of thick and widespread reservoir intervals, abundant structures, and multiple phases of hydrocarbon generation provide the conditions for formation of abundant oil and gas accumulations" (Dietrich & Dixon, 2000).

Estimates of the total petroleum resource potential, discovered and undiscovered, in the Beaufort-Mackenzie Basin are 7 billion barrels of recoverable oil, and 67 trillion cubic feet (tcf) of recoverable gas (Dixon et al., 1992, 1994). Basin-wide appraisals indicate high potential for undiscovered petroleum resources, including the likelihood that several major fields with recoverable volumes of greater than 100 million barrels of oil or 1 tcf of gas remain to be discovered. The most promising areas appear to be in the shallow-shelf areas offshore of the Mackenzie Delta, and the relatively little-explored strata in the southern Mackenzie Delta area.

These Beaufort-Mackenzie Basin resources represent about 25% of the total oil and 20% of the total gas resource potential in Canadian frontier basins. The Delta-Beaufort basin is comparable in size to the Alberta basin.

Another potential resource is also abundant in the area. Methane hydrates, which lie buried beneath the sea floor, are solid compounds which expand 164 times in volume when extracted. Methane hydrates in the Arctic are estimated at 300,000 tcf, or ten times present known hydrocarbon resources. Although research continues into this possible resource, methods have not yet been developed to safely and economically extract methane hydrates.

Inuvik's Preparations for Petroleum Exploration

As planned, Inuvik was ready for intensive resource activity, socially, environmentally and technically. Petroleum exploration and industry support was Inuvik's main activity from 1971 to 1975. There was adequate infrastructure, an established government presence, and a trained, competent workforce with strong representation by locally owned businesses.

In 1972, the town of Inuvik issued 149 business licences, and Inuvik also became the site of major offices for Esso, Gulf and Dome. Over 50% of non-government employees were native. At the beginning of the decade, the overwhelming dominance of government in the local economy also diminished rapidly; by 1970, the non-government sector accounted for 31% of full-time jobs, and 41% of part-time jobs.

Most of Inuvik's exploration action took place on the Mackenzie River or at the Inuvik airport. The oil companies agreed with the requests of the Inuvik Council, the NWT Government and Federal Departments to minimize any social and economic problems from their activities. Hence, Inuvik benefitted greatly from the exploration without overloading town facilities.

During the petroleum exploration boom there were three operating airports, and Inuvik was the smallest multi-airport community in the world. In addition to the main airport 12 kilometres south of town, there was an in-town airport for small planes, and a float plane airport on Shell Lake. At one point there were 18 Twin Otters based in Inuvik, with only one of them available for charter. The others belonged to industry or government or were tied up in long-term lease arrangements.

Inuvik's main airport provided daily connections to Edmonton via Yellowknife and to Vancouver via Whitehorse. For a time, this airport was the busiest uncontrolled airport in Canada, until a control tower was built in 1972, and it was designated as a Class 1 facility. Also in 1972, Pacific Western Airlines established Boeing 737 jet service to Inuvik.

INUVIK EMPLOYMENT 1966 & 1970			
Year		Permanent	Part Time
1966	Government	79%	
	Non-government	21%	
1970	Government	69%	59%
	Non-government	31%	41%

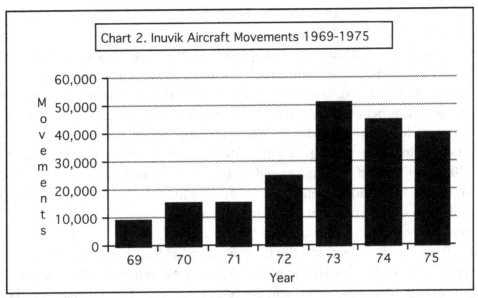

Chart 2. Inuvik Aircraft Movements 1969-1975

Activity at the Inuvik airport was one obvious indicator of the pace of exploration activity. Aircraft movements were logged at 9,000 in 1969, rose to about 14,000 in each of 1970 and 1971, and then jumped to about 25,000 in 1972 and over 50,000 in 1973 (MOT Aircraft Movements).

The rapid growth seemed likely to continue and possibly accelerate. There was a caution that expansion should be tamed and not allowed to move too fast. A new general plan for the Town of Inuvik was prepared by Makale, Holloway & Associates of Edmonton and presented to the Town Council in September 1973, to prepare the town for an "impending boom". This study projected Inuvik's population would increase to 4351 in 1976, 5682 in 1978 and 7000 in 1981.

In July 1981 the Inuvik Council passed a motion requesting that the NWT Government extend the town boundaries to approximately a 24-km radius from the town centre. This motion expanded the Town's area from approximately 115 square km to 510 square km.

Exploration Activities

For several decades, there had been awareness of possible petroleum resources in the arctic and subarctic. As early as 1957, Shell had a lease and was exploring an area west of Aklavik. But petroleum exploration in the area began in earnest in the mid-1960s, with the bulk of exploration drilling activity occurring in the 1970s and 1980s. There were many reasons for increased interest by oil companies and governments alike.

CHAMBER OF COMMERCE PRESIDENTS 1971-1982	
1971	George Clark
1972	Jim Robertson
1973	Dick Hill
1974	Lin Stewart
1975	Lin Stewart
1976	Peter Clarke
1977	Lin Stewart
1978	Bill Farmer
1979	Doug Billingsley
1980	Doug Billingsley
1981	Al Pluim
1982	Al Pluim

One major impetus was the massive Prudhoe Bay development in Alaska during the late 1960s. Also, as both the US and Canada looked to the future of the North in 1969, Humble Oil's supertanker, SS Manhattan, escorted by the United States Coast Guard, sailed through the Northwest Passage, while refusing to acknowledge Canadian sovereignty.

In 1973, with the OPEC-created oil shortage, world oil prices jumped from $2 to $35 a barrel. Although it was believed that Arctic oil would be expensive to extract, the huge price jump suddenly made northern oil development an economically attractive proposition.

The first oil well in the Inuvik region was in 1969. The first natural gas well was at Parsons Lake in 1970. By 1972, Gulf had discovered 14 billion cubic feet of gas at Parsons Lake. To date, a total of 183 exploration wells (and 66 development wells) have been drilled in the region, resulting in the discovery of 53 oil and/or gas fields.

The largest onshore discoveries include the Taglu field, with estimated recoverable gas reserves of 2.0 trillion cubic feet, and the Parsons Lake field, with gas reserves of 1.2 tcf (National Energy Board, 1998). The largest offshore field is Amauligak, with estimated recoverable oil reserves of 235 million barrels and gas reserves of 1.3 tcf. Total discovered resources in this field are estimated at 9 tcf of recoverable gas and 1 billion barrels of recoverable oil.

There were several players in the exploration, but the most agressive exploration program was run by Dome Petroleum. Under the leadership of Jack Gallagher, Dome argued against importing oil on the grounds that exploration would spur the country's economy. In 1976, Dome started drilling in the Beaufort Sea. In the same year, the Federal government provided a "super depletion" incentive for exploration wells costing more than $5 million. This arrangement provided a write-off of 120% of well-drilling expenses. With these generous tax incentives Dome built up an extensive offshore drilling fleet for working in the ice-congested Beaufort Sea.

Dome was a world leader, drilling the first well in the Arctic Ocean, operating the first commercial Canadian icebreaker, the Kigoriak, and being first to hire women on offshore drillships.

Dome initiated many Northern-involvement programs, including the Beaufort Sea Community Advisory Committee, a Tuktoyaktuk bank during the drilling season, community visits to its Tuk Base and offshore drilling units, and the offering of shares of Dome Petroleum in the North.

Dome headed up a number of training programs for Northerners. One program became known as the University of Tuktoyaktuk, or "Tuk U", and was a major program to train local people in the skills needed by oil companies. "It was very exciting for the people who were working on the project and I think it was exciting for the local people too," said Murray Todd, referring to the personal exchange at the time between the Northerners and the workers from the south.

National politics, and the international economy, played an equal part in both the upturn and the downturn in Dome's activities.

In 1980 the National Energy Program was introduced; it greatly benefitted Canadian oil companies operating in the North but was a serious irritation to Alberta oil exploration. Dome Petroleum expanded greatly to take advantage of this program for their northern exploration activities.

But the National Energy Program remained deeply unpopular in Alberta. When the Conservative government of Brian Mulroney was elected in 1984, the NEP was cancelled. At the same time, world oil prices also dropped drastically.

That was the beginning of the end for Dome. Calgary oil consultant Doug Matthews commented, "After the price of oil tanked in the early '80s, combined with the conservative government getting elected and the end of the National Energy Program, the exploration in the Beaufort came to a screeching halt. The companies that were left exploring up there found they had no money of their own left because they were strictly creatures of the government purse" (CBC 14 October 2007).

Dome kept offshore exploration going on a limited scale even after the Mackenzie Valley Pipeline interest went dormant. In 1988 Amoco Canada acquired Dome.

Environmental and Social Issues

The 1970s was a decade of increasing environmental consciousness, and the far north received a great deal of attention. Unfortunately, there were many extreme statements about the Arctic environment in relation to the Beaufort-Delta petroleum exploration programs, such as the permafrost is melting, the ice has disappeared from the North Pole and wildlife is disappearing.

In some cases, federal government grant money seemed to work at cross-purposes to local self-government. For example, the University of British Columbia Department of Regional and Community Planning was given a $250,000 grant to study Inuvik's planning while the Inuvik Council had no funds to do the actual planning. Also, the Company of Young Canadians were funded to set up an Inuvik operation, but they refused to communicate with the Inuvik Council.

The Canadian Arctic Resources Committee was formed in the 1970s to oppose the original Mackenzie Valley gas pipeline proposal. Dene Nation and Committee for Original Peoples Entitlement (COPE) utilized generous federal funding to argue that oil exploration and pipeline construction would have damaging environmental effects.

Southern environmentalist Gary Gallon wrote about Inuvik in 1974:

> Inuvik is located in the centre of the North's oil and gas exploration activities. It has become a boomtown. The rutted dirt roads, the old board sidewalks, and the excitement of money-to-be-made gives the community the air of a Klondike gold mining town. Inuvik, like most other Canadian towns, creates environmental damage. The town's raw sewage is dumped into two small lakes north of the town. The lakes empty into the Mackenzie River East Channel and are flushed once a year into the river by spring floods. Toxic chemicals from the town's budding secondary industry are being discharged to the lakes through the

sewage system. The electric generating plant is fired with Bunker C oil. Harmful contaminants such as sulfur dioxide, nitrogen oxides and unburned hydrocarbons are emitted from the plant smoke stacks. A growing internal combustion engine population is also adding a significant number of the same contaminants to the air. During the hot summer months Inuvik's dirt roads are repeatedly oiled for dust control. Summer rains and spring runoff waters leach the oil from the roads and carry it into small creeks which carry it into the Mackenzie River. Persistent toxic and carcinogenic hydrocarbon compounds present a chronic sub lethal danger to the waterway's aquatic life" (Gallon 1974).

Sensational and one-sided statements captured the attention of the media and affected distant political decisions. But reporting with balance and perspective was absent. Over the millenia, the Mackenzie River system has quietly carried millions of barrels of oil from the Athabaska oil sands into the Arctic Ocean without adverse effect. During World War II, 64 oil tankers were sunk in the Gulf of St. Lawrence and the area survived.

Oil drilling in the Arctic takes place in what is essentially a frozen desert and in the end will have affected less than 1/100th of 1% of the region. The biggest danger of melting the North might come from all the hot air talked about it.

Don Gill, a University of Alberta geography professor, stated that the modern industrial activities of oil exploration, with the safeguards now practiced, will not damage the Arctic environment beyond repair. Natural physical disturbances such as fire and floods have been affecting the North for centuries. Yet the North bounces back and in many cases is improved by the disturbances. An overland trail made during the Klondike gold rush has brought about the growth of shrubs and willows which are a helpful habitat for wildlife like caribou, small animals and ptarmigan (*Edmonton Journal* 6 February 1975).

Tracked vehicles do disturb lichen ecology, but lichens are a climax vegetation and when disturbed are replaced very rapidly by a grass ecology which is much more luxuriant.

Len Cardinal, an Inuvik native contractor, said too many northern natives have been spoiled by the government and should get off welfare because they feel the country owes them a living without having to work for it. He pointed out that there was little concern about the land until the pipeline proposals arrived. He noted the mythology about the delicate Arctic ecology and environment and "it can generally look after itself in competition with people" (*Oilweek* 1 August 1977).

Environmental regulations which were enacted with the best of intentions sometimes had unfortunate consequences. For example, Federal government regulations required the petroleum industry to completely clean rig camps. Hence much usable matter, which could have been used by local residents, was buried or burned. The same thing happened with the Canol pipeline project when the US Army pulled out.

ALURE (Arctic Land Use Research Program) was sponsored one third by the federal government, one third by universities and one third by industry, to carry out extensive environmental studies beginning in 1971. One result of this and many other programs was that the people are consulted to the point of boredom about trivial details at endless meetings.

Nevertheless, education was recognized as a key factor of sustainable development in the north. This blended well with the traditional Eskimo theory of total education, "Illihavik", where teaching involves all life skills and is a family responsibility. This concept anticipated the words of the Bruntland Commission on the Environment and Development, convened by the United Nations in 1987. The Commission introduced sustainable development for growth with a human face, citing education as the most significant activity to assist a people to become viable and independent.

University of Canada North

One major education venture was University of Canada North. This started when Toronto lawyer Richard Rohmer became interested in the North during the 1967 Mid-Canada Corridor Program. After reading Jim Lotz' book *Northern Realities*, which proposed a northern university, he visited Inuvik on July 6, 1970 and met with community leaders to discuss the possibilities for higher education opportunities for Northerners to take part in their region's development.

Rohmer met with Tom Butters, Nellie Cournoyea, Wally Firth, Victor Allen, Dick Hill and Agnes Semmler, and they agreed to form the University of Canada North (UCN). The UCN administrative headquarters were to be located in Inuvik. On July 10, 1970 the Inuvik Council set aside a large land block on the ridge between Hidden Lake and Boot Creek for a university site; this land initially had been reserved for Mackenzie Institute activities.

Yukoners were involved at another meeting held in Whitehorse to consider a northern university in partnership with NWT residents.

The University of Canada North received Federal letters of patent on June 15, 1971. There were 15 directors from the NWT and 15 from Yukon, with Richard Rohmer as the 31st.

A University of Canada North concepts conference was held in Inuvik at the Family Hall on November 19-22, 1971, with Dick Hill as moderator. The 112 participants were from Canada, USA, Sweden and Norway. One third were natives from the NWT, Yukon, southern Canada, Alaska and Arizona. The conference was structured as a weekend of panel-type workshops and plenary discussions intended to clarify the role of a new northern university. The proceedings were broadcast live by CBC throughout the Mackenzie Valley.

After Nellie Cournoyea welcomed the participants at the opening ceremonies, George Erasmus, the Company of Young Canadians agent in Inuvik at the time, took the microphone and said that everybody was out of step but him. He asked who had invited the delegates and said "I'm between you and the rest of the Indian people of the Northwest Territories." The conference moderator responded that most of the northern delegates were natives who had an interest in improving northern education opportunities, and had volunteered their time to attend without representing any special interest group or government department.

Many delegates thought the UCN had the potential to be an indigenous cultural institution along the lines of the Navajo College in Arizona. The need for vocational training was emphasized by many. Noah Carpenter spoke to the delegates in Eskimo, saying "Time is running out. We must get our families together and also our spirit. And we must work hard to save our land. Today lots of white men say we have to be smart and they want to make a university to make people better where Indians, Whites and Eskimos can work together so that this land will be better. It's up to the young people to study hard. Don't drink too much. Learning is better. And learn English well but don't forget your own language. Don't go on welfare. Help each other like in the old days. In this way we can help the country."

Three themes evolved during the conference deliberations:

1. The North needed its own university for social and political development, responding to northern needs and free of governmental and southern influence.
2. There was a need for access to higher education for Northerners in the North with opportunity to stay at home and learn about the North in the North.
3. There was dissatisfaction with current northern research programs initiated in the South, funded in the South, employing Southerners to study the North and reporting back to the South.

The UCN conference gave northern people a chance to have their concerns aired. It was the kind of discussion the founders hoped would become a permanent fixture of any University of Canada North. Their efforts were a rejection of the colonialism that the founders believed limited northern social and political independence and growth.

NWT and Yukon divisions of the UCN operated to promote college opportunities in each Territory. Some UCN-sponsored classes were held in Inuvik and Yellowknife. The directors of the NWT UCN division met regularly and organized an October 1973 Annual General Meeting in Yellowknife.

Stan Dodman, a former Inuvik student, spent the 1973 summer visiting communities to prepare a report on current feelings for a northern university or college. Dodman's College North Report (Dodman 1973) was presented to the UCN NWT Division. It recommended a community college model for the NWT. The NWT directors supported this concept and proposed NWT Government financing. As no support or funding was available, the NWT Division slowly faded.

The UCN Yukon Division remained active until 1985 with the support of the Yukon Government, Yukon Indian Brotherhood and companies proposing the Alaska Highway Gas Pipeline Project. Its activities became the foundation for Yukon College in Whitehorse.

Amanda Graham of Yukon College studied the University of Canada North programs and wrote:

Despite the founders' desire to remedy the near total lack of northern post-secondary education opportunities, The University of Canada North must not be interpreted solely as an educational venture. It should also be viewed as an expression of social consciousness, that is, of a recognition by northern residents that their part of Canada was worthy of closer scrutiny by its inhabitants and not solely by outside experts and researchers. The creation of The University of Canada North demonstrates that at least a small group of northern residents thought there were important issues that needed examination and vital questions that needed answering."

The creation of the University of Canada North is an important event in the history of education in the Canadian North. Yet, practically from its inception, UCN was beset by problems serious enough to first stunt its growth and eventually to suffocate it entirely. Those problems were rooted in philosophical and conceptual differences about the institution, and exacerbated by financial and administrative difficulties.

(Graham 1994)

Arctic Summer School

During the same period, an annual Arctic Summer School was organized by the University of Alberta's Boreal Institute and Extension Department, in cooperation with the Inuvik Research Laboratory. The first session was in July 1971 and the school operated until 1981. The purpose of the school was to provide people from private industry and government an opportunity to become familiar with the developments and problems in northern Canada. With the increased northern development activities, and concern for the environment, it was thought that the mainly southern groups providing inputs into the decision-making processes affecting the North should have an understanding of the conditions there and the problems that changes may create. The program was a two-week total immersion course based at Grollier Hall, and involved knowledgeable instructors who were researching, operating and resident in the area. There were lectures, social sessions and field trips. Community leaders including Nellie Cournoyea, Agnes Semmler, Victor Allen and Dick Hill led discussions on local issues. Later sessions involved Yellowknife and Whitehorse activities.

There was ample opportunity for cross exchange of ideas with local and visiting specialists, as well as between the participants themselves who brought their own expertise into the courses. In its six years of operation, there were over 500 ASS graduates who moved into management positions with industry and government, making more informed decisions which affected Northerners and northern development. The success of the Arctic Summer School also carried a message to those resident Northerners who often aren't too interested, or don't have the opportunity, to learn about the North and the many points of view on northern development. Northerners would benefit from attending courses along with interested Southerners to understand the complexities of development and optimum regional assistance programs.

Mackenzie Valley Gas Pipeline proposals

In addition to the difficulties of finding and extracting petroleum in the Arctic environment, there was the obvious challenge of getting oil and gas to southern markets. Throughout the 1970s, proposed pipelines were the subject of not only industry research but environmental concern.

The possible pipeline routes under discussion included:

- an NWT pipeline from Inuvik to Northern Alberta – 1300 km
- a route from Prudhoe Bay, through Yukon Territory, BC & Alberta, to the US Midwest – 5000 km
- an "over the top" alternate from Prudhoe Bay, along the Beaufort Coast, to the Mackenzie Delta, to Edmonton – 2700 km

Canadian Arctic Gas Pipeline Ltd (CAGPL) went before the National Energy Board (NEB) in 1975. The Inuvik Town Council on September 13, 1976 supported the Canadian Arctic Gas Ltd. proposal to construct a gas pipeline down the Mackenzie Valley. Later, on July 8, 1977 the Town Council endorsed the immediate construction of a Mackenzie Valley Pipeline, under strict control and without prejudice to native land claims.

However, the Canadian Wildlife Federation in 1973 called for a railway down the Mackenzie Valley, claiming a railway would have less environmental impact than a pipeline. The railway study referred to calls for a double-track railway, requiring millions of yards of scarce gravel, and involving trains three kilometres long traveling at 100 kph and passing a given point every 25 minutes. The Federation said it was more economical than a pipeline, without providing any justification.

Berger Inquiry

Northerners were well aware of ecological concerns and unsettled land claims as they related to pipeline construction. But in the Berger Inquiry, which ran from 1974 to 1978, these concerns came together with the power of a far-away central government, and changed the course of Inuvik development for a generation.

The inquiry began because the proposal to build a gas pipeline through the Mackenzie Valley had aroused national controversy. Jean Chrétien, then Minister of Indian Affairs and Northern Development, turned to British Columbia Supreme Court Justice Thomas Berger, a prominent native rights lawyer and former leader of the BC New Democratic Party. Berger's task was to head a public inquiry into the potential impacts of gas pipeline.

Berger took his inquiry to 35 communities, traveling the vast expanse of the Mackenzie Valley and the Western Arctic. He heard from nearly one thousand northerners, speaking in seven different languages.

Berger held hearings in Inuvik in January and February of 1976. The testimony reflected some of the division of opinion about the whole project:

Jim Robertson, then the mayor of Inuvik, commented to the Inquiry that the "the uncertainty created by the Inquiry was hurting the economy and community planning. He wanted to know if northern development could take place expeditiously. The Inquiry was a 'difficult' time for Inuvik because it was hijacked by special interests" (CBC Inuvik).

Claire Barnaby, who had been a GNWT Inuvik Region Director, challenged the Inquiry at the Norman Wells hearing saying that "life was better for aboriginal people than it had been and that nothing was stopping people from living traditional lives" (CBC Inuvik).

But Peter Usher, a geographer working with COPE, criticized the "myth" of cooperation between races to develop the North. He said, "The white man made the town, made the rules, set the priorities and that was not co-operation with aboriginal people" (CBC North July 2003).

Fr. Bern Will Brown later wrote about the hearings at Colville Lake. With the press in attendance, he said, native speakers used this opportunity to air grievances that had nothing to do with the pipeline. The fact that their statements were similar to what he had heard before prompted Berger to conclude that the natives of the NWT were of one mind in their opposition to the building of a pipeline. In fact, Brown wrote, the speakers had been well coached in advance of what to say. Many people expressed the opinion that nothing to date had done more to drive a wedge between natives and whites (Brown 1999).

Three years after he was asked to look into the pipeline proposal, Berger handed down his final report.

Berger's main recommendation was a ten-year moratorium on building a pipeline down the Mackenzie Valley. He concluded that while it was environmentally feasible to go ahead with a pipeline in 1977, it would be better to wait. Berger advised that the project should go ahead only under careful planning and strict regulation. He said that planning could only come about after native land claims had been settled. He also concluded no pipeline should ever be built across the north Yukon.

Residents of Canada's North were bitterly polarized over the death of the pipeline. As some Native leaders celebrated the Berger Report as a vindication of their rights, many community leaders, both native and non-native, were dismayed and outraged by the decision to delay construction of a pipeline. They watched years of investment and employment opportunities go down the river.

Inuvik had all the infrastructure buildup for a Mackenzie Valley gas pipeline. But after the Berger Report, Inuvik was left with the operating costs of infrastructure such as the Carn Road industrial area, Navy Road industrial area, NTCL facilities, and Marine Bypass Road, which little or no income to cover them.

Native Land Claims

Although unsettled land claims came into sharp focus during the Berger Inquiry, these issues had been prominent throughout Inuvik's history, and most land claims in the Mackenzie Valley were not settled for another 15 or 20 years. In Inuvik, major land claims were finalized in 1984 and 1992.

Indian Treaty No. 11 had been signed on June 27, 1921, and it extended along the Mackenzie Valley from the Alberta border through to the Arctic Coast and included the Inuvik townsite. This agreement followed the discovery of petroleum at Norman Wells in 1920.

The treaty was ratified in Arctic Red River on July 26, 1921, and in Fort McPherson on July 28. The agreement provided for native reserves, among other things, but this provision was never fulfilled as the Indian leaders did not want reserves or did not understand the reserve concept.

More than three decades later the Nelson Commission was set up, on June 25, 1959, with Jim Koe as a commissioner. Jim Koe, an Aklavik resident at the time, was listed as a member of the Fort McPherson Band. The purpose of the Commission was to investigate the unfulfilled provisions of Indian Treaties 8 and 11 as they apply to the Indians of the Mackenzie District, and to make recommendations on the finalization of the Mackenzie District treaty obligations as "there is doubt whether it is in the interests of the Indians to have reserves set aside for them in the NWT in the proportions provided for by the treaties and informal discussions with the Indians have indicated that they have no firm opinion on the matter and might be prepared to consider renegotiating the treaties on some different basis" (Nelson 1959).

The Commission found no consensus on handling the unfulfilled claims. Several years later in 1974, the Hay River Band settled for a 135-square-mile reserve which is the only NWT reserve.

In June 1969 the Federal government issued a White Paper Statement On Indian Policy which recommended repeal of the Indian Act and abolition of all legal distinctions between natives and non-natives. At the time, there was general unrest amongst Indians across Canada against the injustices of the Indian Act and many unsettled grievances. Aboriginal people in Inuvik were generally supportive of the White Paper concepts as it supported their aspirations for land claims and direct control of their resources.

In addition to the public attention to land claims across Canada, land claim settlements in Alaska provided a strong impetus to negotiations in the Inuvik region. During the run-up to the construction of an Alaskan pipeline from Prudhoe Bay, land claims were finalized in 1971 with Gwich'in and Inupiat (Eskimo) groups in Alaska. These groups had close cultural, linguistic and even family ties to the Gwich'in and Inuvialuit in Canada.

Of the two native groups in the Inuvik region, the Inuvialuit made the most rapid progress towards their land claim settlement. Negotiations were led by the Committee for Original Peoples Entitlement, founded in September of 1970, and led by Nellie Cournoyea, Agnes Semmler, and Sam Raddi. In January of 1972, the Inuvik and District Chamber of Commerce unanimously passed a motion to the Federal government "in favour of a just and early settlement of legitimate native claims in the Northwest Territories." Even so, it was eight years before the federal government and Inuvialuit representatives signed an Agreement in Principle, and another six years elapsed before the Inuvialuit Final Agreement was signed in Inuvik on June 5, 1984. At that time, only one other comprehensive land claim agreement had been concluded in Canada.

The Gwich'in Comprehensive Land Claim began as an integral part of the Dene/Metis Comprehensive Land Claim, involving the Treaty 11 part of the Northwest Territories. In 1970, the Indian Brotherhood of the Northwest Territories was founded, later to be renamed the Dene Nation. Efforts were made for the Federal government to negotiate a comprehensive land claim with the Dene Nation and the Métis Association of the Northwest Territories. Frustration with the negotiating process led to the formation of the Mackenzie Delta Tribal Council to consider a regional land claim.

The Dempster Highway and the Growth of Tourism

Throughout the 1970s, a road network was being constructed in the Inuvik region. Some of the roads were winter roads only, on the Mackenzie River ice to Aklavik and Tuktoyaktuk, but the biggest project, one that had been forseen for decades, was the Dempster Highway, a gravel ribbon linking Inuvik with Dawson City, Yukon.

Another route to Inuvik, the Mackenzie Highway, was also much discussed. This road from Hay River to Inuvik was proposed along with the first Mackenzie Valley pipeline project, but was stalled by groups not wanting it to proceed through their region. Hence, the Dempster Highway alternate was promoted by government and industry.

The Dempster Highway had been planned as a "road to resources", but ironically, in the late seventies, when the Dempster was nearing completion, petroleum industries had just been dealt a blow from the Berger Inquiry. By the time the Dempster was completed, in August of 1979, petroleum companies were beginning their generation-long retreat from the Western Arctic.

Construction had begun in 1959, at the south end of the highway, but progress was so slow that in 1961 only 115 kilometres had been built. The project was then dormant until 1968, when the Prudhoe Bay oil finds in Alaska created renewed interest in, and renewed funding for, exploration work in the Canadian Arctic.

During the 1970s, work proceeded from both the south and the north. Thus, long before the highway's completion in 1979, the road was open between Inuvik, Arctic Red River (now Tsiigehtchic) and Fort McPherson.

This all-weather road was a major boon to travel within the region, and was complemented in winter by an extensive network of Mackenzie Delta ice roads, opened up each winter by the petroleum exploration industry. As a courtesy the industry extended the roads to delta communities. From Inuvik the ice road distance to Aklavik was 112 km and to Tuktoyaktuk was 194 km. With ice thickness of over 1 metre for most of the winter, large 20-ton,18-wheeler trucks were common. These ice roads were generally plowed to a width of at least four traffic lanes to facilitate thicker ice and to minimize problems from snow drifting. Later the Mackenzie Delta ice roads to Aklavik and Tuktoyaktuk were taken over by NWT Transportation.

But when the Dempster was finally completed, it was possible to drive all the way from southern Canada to Inuvik, and vice versa. This gave more substance to the phrase "If you don't like it, leave!"

Although the petroleum industry was already pulling back, the Dempster had obvious benefits for Inuvik in many other ways. Freight of many sorts could now be transferred to Inuvik more cheaply, at almost any time of the year. (There were a few weeks in the spring and fall when the unbridged river crossings at the Arctic Red River and the Peel River were not open either to ferries or to crossings by vehicles over the ice.) Construction goods, consumer goods, and fresh fruits and vegetables could now be transported to Inuvik without the long transit times of barges or the exorbitant costs of air freight.

If a region has no economic resource base the usual alternate is tourism. Inuvik was rich in tourism opportunities – ecological, nature, aboriginal – both nearby and in more remote areas which are most easily reached by small-plane flights from Inuvik. Tourism received a major boost from the Dempster.

As the most northerly point in Canada that can be reached by all-weather roads, Inuvik quickly became a popular destination for vacationing motorists. Even bikers, both motor- and foot-powered, came from across the continent to bike the Dempster to Inuvik. To cite one example, Frank McCall brought a Vancouver group of mainly 80-year-olds on bicycles to Inuvik. (McCall was the Game Warden in Aklavik in the early 1960s, and had a continuing role with Inuvik as an Administration Officer in Fort Smith and the Area Administrator in Yellowknife.)

Inuvik was also a popular destination for expense account tourists from government, universities and industry. For the most part these visitors did not stay in campgrounds, and the demand for hotel rooms continued to grow. A significant addition during the 70s was the Finto Hotel, opened in 1971 by Tony Scheiweiller and Harold Wulf, originally in abandoned oil camp trailers. Tony's model railway served drinks at the bar and ran extensive trackage in the crawl space under the hotel.

FINTO?

After 1976 the Finto Motel between the Airport and Bypass Roads was the first building seen by visitors coming into Inuvik during the 1980s and 1990s. The initial structure built and operated by Tony Scheiwiller and Harold Wulf was connected oil exploration trailers. But, how did it get its name?

Finn Volke and Tony Scheiwiller came to Inuvik in 1970 to operate the Eskimo Inn restaurant. This business was called "Finto" and the name stuck even though Finn departed after six months.

Another little known feature of the Finto Motel is its "vertical pipeline" which is used as a flagpole. Two 45-foot lengths of surplus petroleum pipe were welded together. During Inuvik's resource support and Berger era, Inuvik residents and visitors recognized it as a symbolic statement as the Delta's only visible petroleum pipeline.

Even the cruise ship sector was represented in Inuvik. MS Norweta made its inaugural run to Inuvik from Hay River in July 1971. This was the first tourism vessel on the Mackenzie River, and was organized by Captain Don Tetrault of Hay River. At 103 feet long, with 10 cabins, the ship made one-week trips, up and down the Mackenzie. The Norweta operated as a cruise ship until 1975, when it switched to working as a standby vessel for Dome's drillships. The Norweta was rebuilt in 1991 and started runs to Inuvik from Yellowknife.

Inuvik has always been a snowmobiler's heaven, with 10,000 km of Delta channels to explore over powder snow, as well as tundra trails north to the Beaufort Sea coast and west to the Richardson Mountains.

Inuvik Media

In 1976 the Federal Department of Communications initiated a satellite TV experiment in Inuvik involving a low-power transmitter and a small 1.5-metre dish on the roof of the Inuvik Research Laboratory. The remote community project was based on the Canadian-built high-power Hermes satellite designed to make all Canadian homes accessible with a small receiving dish. The system worked well and Inuvik residents were quite pleased to be receiving live TV rather than the "canned" programming with two-week-old CBC shows. However, after a year the test was cancelled as this government-sponsored technological breakthrough was not picked up by commercial television interests.

In May 1978 David Brough came to Inuvik to promote his mini-TV system. This was operating in small northern Ontario communities where Brough was known as the "picture pirate of Pickle Lake". There was considerable interest for a new television service as at the time Inuvik only had one hour a night of two-week-old taped CBC programs. A public meeting was held at the Small Family Hall where Mr. Brough said he could put a mini 100 watt TV station on the air in only half an hour. When the CBC technicians attending the meeting said the proposed station wouldn't work, many at the meeting took up the challenge; that evening they set up the small transmitter which could reach all Inuvik homes. A local community television committee, with Dennis Cichely as chair, operated the system and broadcast six hours a day of programs taped by Mr. Brough and supplied by mail. This Inuvik TV station was illegal under the Canadian Radio and Telecommunication (CRTC) regulations but there was broad public support.

Inuvik TV was initially operated by the Inuvik Community Broadcasting Society on the second floor of the Rexal building, with volunteers changing the six hours of tapes provided by the Brough organization. There was a daily Inuvik Today show with special guest interviews and comment from visiting dignitaries The Mackenzie Road Show filled in any blank times by pointing a live camera out of the station window towards the entrance of the Mad Trapper Bar. Besides viewing the Mackenzie traffic, people could also check who was coming and going from the Trapper. Viewers were asked to contribute, but very little money was collected as everybody could view the shows for free. Sometimes the teenage operators would hold a party in the "studio". In 1984 the Society decided to turn Inuvik TV into a commercial operation with decoders in each home so only subscribers could receive the signals. Hence, Inuvik TV Ltd. was formed and a commercial broadcasting application made to the Canadian Radio & Telecommunications Commission. The CRTC granted an operating licence in June 1985.

As there were operating difficulties with the over-the-air decoders, and it was considered too expensive to run a television cable to every home, Inuvik TV was sold in July 1990 to Tom Zubko who proposed to improved the programming and to install a modern cable system throughout the community. During the 1990s the company expanded as New North Networks Ltd. and became a world leader in northern communications and high-speed internet services.

The *Mackenzie Drift* newspaper was started up by Editor Marius Dakin with its first issue on April 3, 1979. It operated for a little over one year.

The Arctic Circle Press Club was formed in May 1980 by John Stanton of CBC, Dick Hill of Inuvik TV, and Dan Holman of the *Inuvik Drum*. The group met regularly in the Mad Trapper with a special plaque attached to the club's table.

Several Canadian poets and writers toured northern communities in 1975. Over a four-month period, Inuvik received public readings by Al Purdy, Matt Cohen, Victor Coleman, Dave McFadden, Frank Davey, Daphne Marlatt, George Bowering, Michael Ondaatje, Margaret Atwood and B. P. Nichol.

Miscellaneous Activities

Norilsk in Soviet Siberia was proposed as a sister city to Inuvik during Minister of Northern Affairs Jean Chrétien's tour of the Russian North in July-August 1971. Both communities lie on the 69th parallel. Norilsk is a mining centre. Northern Affairs Minister Jean Chrétien traveled to Siberia and made the sister city proposal. Dick Hill accompanied the Chrétien party. The Mayor of Norilsk said the city was interested but would make a decision later. It never happened.

A Permafrost Research Chamber was proposed by Inuvik Research Laboratory in 1975. This facility would be located within a large ground ice lens in the river bank close to the town dock. It would allow investigators to sample and measure Inuvik permafrost ground details and be similar to the extensive permafrost chambers in Siberia. No funding was obtained for this project. COPE did spend most of a summer digging the ice pit but did not complete an entrance to make it useful.

Another development at mid-decade was of special significance to skiers. When plans were made for the construction of the Inuvik Bypass Road to accommodate the anticipated pipeline construction activities, it was noted that the main cross country ski trail would be blocked. When NWT Transportation ignored the Inuvik Ski Club's request for a large diameter culvert under the road to accommodate the ski trail, petroleum companies were contacted for assistance. In summer 1975 when the bypass road was built, industry came through, with Imperial Oil, Shell and Gulf splitting the $6640 cost to the Inuvik Ski Club of the three-metre diameter, 20-metre long culvert.

Finally, the sale and consumption of alcohol continued to arouse strong feelings. In 1977, the Committee of the Concerned was formed, to protest alcohol abuse and push for closure of the Inuvik Liquor Store. A petition presented to the Inuvik Council of November 14, 1977 was signed by 754 residents with a majority in favour keeping the liquor store open.

The Great Northern Arts Festival was founded in 1989, and quickly became a summer high-light for Inuvik residents, area artists, and visitors alike. Above, Deputy Mayor Cynthia Hill at the Festival entrance in 1990.

Another imaginative endeavour met a less happy fate. A set of wooden "caribou" was built in the early 1990s in front of Sir Alexander Mackenzie School for children to play on. But a safety inspector decided the creatures were hazardous and they were removed.

Inuvik Time Line 1983–1991

1983	May	EVTV local over-the-air television broadcasting opens
	Jun 23	Beaufort Delta Deveopment Impact Zone (DIZ) first meeting in Inuvik
	Jul 11-18	Inuvik's 25th Birthday celebrations
	August	NCPC Power Plant fire
	Oct	Inuvialuit Communications Society organized
	Nov 22	Beaufort Sea Environmental Assessment Review Panel hearings in Inuvik
	Dec	Inuvialuit Land Claims Settlement ratified
1984	Jun 17	Inuvialuit Final Agreement signed
	Jul	Beaufort Environmental Assessment Review Panel (BEARP) report published
1985	Apr 21	Dedication of new Inuvik Christian Assembly with Rev. Terry Frith
	May	National Defence announce closing of CFS Inuvik
	May 20	Doug and the Slugs performed at the Community Centre
	May 29-Jun 1	Beaufort Industry Group's BIG '85 Northern Energy Conference and Trade Show
	Jul	Traffic lights installed at junction of Mackenzie Road and Distributor Street
1986	Jun	Esso, Gulf and Dome Inuvik exploration offices closed
	Jul 20	Jeff MacInnes & Wade Rowland leave Inuvik on sailboat to the Northwest Passage
	Dec 1	CFS Inuvik closed
1987	Jan 6	First 'Return Of The Sun' festival on Twin Lakes
	May 25	Chamber briefing to National Defence on Forward Operating Location (FOL)
	May	Arctic College opened in former CFS Inuvik buildings
	Sep 19	Toronto Symphony Orchestra tour of north, performs at Igloo Church
1988	Feb	*Inuvik Drum* sold to Northern News Services of Yellowknife
	Jun	Inuvialuit Corporate Centre opens
	Jul	Proposal to open Lunar Links golf course in reclaimed gravel pit
	Sep 16	Pierre Berton launches his new book *The Arctic Grail* at Inuvik reception
1989	Mar 23-27	Muskrat Jamboree
	May 26-27	ICATS presents the musical 'The Butler Did It Singing'
	Jun 9	Jean Chrétien visited Inuvik and played baseball with residents
	Jul 21-30	First Great Northern Arts Festival
	Aug 6	Air Canada Directors visit Inuvik with NWT Air, dinner at Eskimo Inn
	Sep 24	World Energy Congress delegates visit Inuvik with community dinner
	Sep 29	Fairbanks Symphony Orchestra performs in SAMS auditorium
	Oct 18	Earthquake shock felt at 3 pm
1990	Mar 30-31	Inuvik Regional Science Fair
	April	Inuvik TV installs cable connections throughout Inuvik
	May	Ptarmigan Hill Subdivision 64 lots put on sale
	Jul 7	Inuvik hottest spot in Canada at 29 degrees, breaking the record of 28 degrees
	Jul 31	Gov Gen Ray Hnatyshyn visits Inuvik, community dinner
	Nov	Keith Spicer's Citizens Forum On Canada's Future held a public meeting
1991	Mar 22	Toronto's Tafelmusik Baroque Orchestra performs at Family Hall
	Apr 3	Open Citizen's Forum on Canada's Future in Council Chambers
	Jun 3-4	Governor General's Canadian Study Conference visit to Inuvik
	Jul	Travelling circus from Alberta set up in Hearne High ball park
	Aug 7-8	Inuvik Lion's Club hosted a circus
	Aug	First Demolition Derby organized by Brian McCarthy and Kurt Wainman

	Oct	Agnes and Slim Semmler celebrate 60th wedding anniversary at Ingamo Hall
	Nov 23-25	Alaska North Slope Group visits Inuvik
	Dec 15	ICATS present a Christmas Cantata at Igloo Church
1992	Apr 22	Gwich'in land claim settlement ratified
	Apr	Western Constitutional Forum (Bourque Commission) report tabled
	Jul 24	Inuvik Science Forum with theme "Speaking from the land, one arctic, one future"
	Jul 20-24	Inuit Circumpolar Conference
	Aug	Forward Operating Location (FOL) construction started at airport by DND

CHAPTER SIX

Local Control, 1983–1992

By 1983, Inuvik Council had been granted the same type of political powers exercised by other small towns, and it no longer had to defer to distant governments in Yellowknife and Ottawa to the same extent as in the town's early years. This move to local control took additional steps forward with the signing of comprehensive land claims agreements – for the Inuvialuit, in 1984, and for the Gwich'in, in 1992.

At the same time, external events buffeted the town, as falling oil prices led to a drastic drop in petroleum exploration, and the closure of the Canadian Forces Station cost Inuvik a sizeable portion of its population.

Land Claims

Inuvialuit Final Agreement

During the 1970s several native organizations formed to promote the settlement of native land claims, but it took two decades before the groups coalesced and signed agreements in their present configurations.

The Committee for Original Peoples Entitlement (COPE) had been founded in Inuvik in 1970. For a short time, it included not only Inuit but also Indians and Métis. However, around the same time the Indian Brotherhood of the Northwest Territories, later to be re-named the Dene Nation, was formed, and for two decades it formally represented the land claim interests of the Gwich'in and Métis residents of the Inuvik region.

The Inuvialuit of the Inuvik region had much stronger linguistic and cultural ties to the Inupiat of Alaska than to the Inuit of Canada's eastern Arctic (now Nunavut). Most of them also had close relatives in Alaska, due to the immigration from Alaska that had played such a major role in repopulating the Mackenzie Delta after the disease epidemics around the turn of the 20th century, and later movements for the Delta's lush trapping opportunities.

Therefore the signing of the Alaska Native Claims Settlement Act, in 1971, had strong repercussions in the Inuvik region. The Inuvialuit soon made the decision to negotiate their own land claim, separate from the claim that eventually led to the formation of Nunavut in 1999.

During the late 1970s, the negotiations were nearing completion with the signing of an Agreement In Principal in 1978. Six years later, on June 17, 1984, the Inuvialuit Final Agreement (IFA) was signed at Sachs Harbour. Billy Day and Sam Raddi signed for the Inuvik Inuvialuit.

On June 26, 1984 the IFA received three readings in the House of Commons in one session, and on July 25, 1984 it was proclaimed into legislation. With this event, the Inuvialuit became the first aboriginal Canadians from the Northwest Territories to negotiate a comprehensive land claims settlement with the Government of Canada.

135

NELLIE – BORN TO LEAD

Nellie Cournoyea is a dynamic leader known throughout the Western Arctic by her first name. Her hands-on, tundra-roots style has been effective in the social, economic and political life of the Inuvik region.

Nellie Cournoyea was the second child of Maggie and Nels Hvatum, who were married in 1936 and had 12 children. Maggie was from Herschel Island, the daughter of Mike Siberia from the Beaufort whaling days. Nels left Norway in 1923 and finally ended up in the Mackenzie Delta in the early 1930s. Nellie was born on March 4, 1940, and spent her early years at a Delta camp where as first daughter she had many family responsibilities.

Her father insisted that she learn to read and be aware of local plus worldly happenings. When her family moved into Aklavik she had the opportunity of attending school. At the age of 18, she met and married Russ Cournoyea with the Aklavik Canadian Forces. They had two children, John and Maureen, but divorced after five years.

While in Aklavik Nellie started working with local radio station CHAK as an announcer-operator. Upon returning to Inuvik after a family posting to Halifax and Ottawa, she worked for CBC Inuvik. In January 1970 she became the CBC station manager.

In 1969, Nellie co-founded COPE, the Committee for Original Peoples Entitlement, with Agnes Semmler and Sam Raddi. In 1974 she started working full time on native rights with the Inuit Tapirisat and later in 1976 for COPE. She played a critical role in settling the Inuvialuit land claim in the Western Arctic in 1984.

Nellie was first elected to the NWT Legislature in 1979 for the Nunakput riding. She held numerous cabinet portfolios between 1983 and her selection as government leader in November 1991. She was the first native woman to lead a provincial or territorial government in Canada. She retired from territorial politics in 1998 to successfully run for the chair of the Inuvialuit

Regional Corporation. She is now in her fifth term as IRC leader as she was returned by acclamation on January 16, 2008.

Nellie is an Inuvik role model confirming that the community has provided opportunities for resident betterment through hard work, skills and communications. Her live-and-learn leadership style is summarized in excerpts from an interview with Lauren McKeon in *Canadian Business*, May 12, 2008:

In the last 60 years there's been so much change. It's important that people adapt and have enough information so that they can move with these changes and not get lost.

Our economy is based on oil and gas. We don't have a lot of mining potential and the harvesting economy has been kicked to pieces by the protectionist organizations.

We have to understand the connection between everyday life and operating the bigger business. We make the bottom line attractive so we can do more things for the community.

The little gains you make in individual people and their understanding matter a lot to the success of the bigger business.

I've always been a person who likes to see things done. I've always been very inquisitive about how do you succeed and, no matter what it is, how do you do things better?

Survival is a business. If you didn't make enough from your own or your family's efforts, you would lose. That type of living teaches you the strength you need and to respect people around you who know better than you.

Failure is death. When people didn't pay due attention to what others could teach them and what they could learn, they didn't last long.

The IFA gave the estimated 2,500 Inuvialuit beneficiaries of the Mackenzie Delta and Beaufort area title to 91,000 square kilometres, including surface and subsurface rights to 11,000 square kilometres, plus another 78,000 square kilometres with full surface rights to sand and gravel. There were financial payments of $45 million in 1977 dollars over 14 years and $10 million to help pay for Inuvialuit participation in the Western Arctic economy, $7.5 million for a social development fund, and preferential and exclusive rights to harvesting in the settlement region.

To implement the settlement, the Inuvialuit Regional Corporation (IRC) was established, with its headquarters in Inuvik. The mission of the IRC includes:

- Preserve Inuvialuit cultural identity and values within a changing northern society;
- Enable Inuvialuit to be equal and meaningful participants in the northern and national economy and society;
- Protect and preserve the Arctic wildlife, environment, and biological productivity.

The IRC is directly controlled by the Inuvialuit population. Its subsidiaries include the Inuvialuit Development Corporation, which in turn owns many subsidiaries, including the Inuvialuit Petroleum Corporation. The Inuvialuit Corporate Centre, opened in 1988, is a state-of-the-art, three-story structure which serves as headquarters for the Inuvialuit group of companies.

A beneficiary of the IFA must be a Canadian citizen and:

1. On the official voters list used for approving the Final Agreement; or
2. Of Inuvialuit ancestry and, born in the Inuvialuit Settlement Region or Inuvik, or a resident of the ISR or Inuvik for a total of least ten years, or if under ten years of age, ordinarily residents in the ISR or Inuvik. A person may also be eligible if he or she:
3. Has Inuvialuit ancestry and is accepted by an Inuvialuit community corporation as a member; or,
4. Is an adopted child of a beneficiary.

Descendants of beneficiaries are also eligible to participate in the Settlement. A person may be enrolled in only one claim settlement in Canada. However, individuals who qualify for more than one settlement may choose which and, if enrolled in the IFA, may, within 10 years, transfer to another settlement for which they qualify.

Gwich'in Final Agreement

The Gwich'in of the Inuvik region had to wait another eight years before their land claim was finalized. The Gwich'in are the northernmost of all North American Indians, but they have close cultural and linguistic ties to the Athabaskan or Dene groups throughout the Mackenzie Valley. During the 1980s, the Gwich'in participated with the other Dene groups in combined land claim negotiations. However, these negotiations eventually failed, due in part to fundamental disagreements over the status of prior treaty and aboriginal rights if a new land claim were to be signed.

In April 1990, the Mackenzie Delta Tribal Council, which represented the Gwich'in and the Métis in the Inuvik region, took a stand against the position of the Dene Nation. In July 1990, the Dene Nation voted against an Agreement In Principle with the federal government, but the Gwich'in and the Sahtu Dene/Métis dissented. In November 1990, the federal government agreed to negotiate separate claims with groups in the five regions of the Mackenzie Valley. After that point, the Gwich'in made rapid progress, and in July 1991, they reached an Agreement In Principle, based substantially on the agreement which the Dene Nation had turned down a year earlier. In April 1992 the Gwich'in Final Agreement was signed in Fort McPherson, and in December 1992, the Gwich'in Comprehensive Land Claim Agreement was proclaimed into law.

The Agreement for 2,200 beneficiaries recognized Gwich'in title to approximately 23,000 square kilometres of land in the Northwest Territories and Yukon. This included subsurface rights to 6100 square kilometres, and surface rights of 1554 square kilometres in Yukon Territory. The agreement also provided for payment to the Gwich'in of $75 million in 1990 dollars, over a period of 15 years. Other provisions included wildlife harvesting rights, management provisions and resource royalties.

To be a beneficiary of the Agreement, a person must have resided in the Gwich'in Settlement Area before 1922, or be a descendant of such a person.

The Gwich'in Tribal Council (GTC) was recognized as the organization which represented all Gwich'in in implementing the Agreement. Similar to the IRC, the GTC established subsidiaries for educational and cultural purposes, for land administration, and to promote economic development. The latter branch was named the Gwich'in Development Corporation.

Land claims and the local economy

In Inuvik the land claim settlements are working well with extensive participation and benefits for the members. The Inuvialuit and Gwich'in organizations are as smart and aggressive as any national or international corporation, employee union, environmental or special interest group. The agreements give the indigenous residents "citizen plus" rights to look out for themselves and they are doing that.

The finalization of the land claims provided signifiant political and economic security plus an infusion of cash into the regional economy. Both Inuvialuit and Gwich'in organizations purchased business interests in areas as diverse as transportation, construction, and hotels. These organizations were ideally positioned to be full participants in the type of resource development industry that had originally been envisioned for Inuvik.

Ironically, though, the late 1980s and 1990s were years of a major economic slump for Inuvik, due to trends and policies set thousands of kilometres away.

The Closure of CFS Inuvik

In May 1985 the Federal Government announced the closing of the Canadian Forces base in Inuvik. The base was the North's largest military installation, staffed by 267 military personnel with around 800 dependents – a quarter of the community.

The Town Council felt that the military had made a mistake due to Inuvik's very strategic location at the Northwest air entrance into North America and the western entrance to the Northwest Passage. Pointing out the strategic value of Inuvik, the Inuvik Council and the Chamber of Commerce lobbied for a replacement for the base. As a result Inuvik was named as a Forward Operating Location for F18 fighter aircraft, and as the resupply base for the western portion of the North Warning System. The CFS administration buildings became the Inuvik Campus for Arctic College.

The Department of National Defence started construction of a Forward Operating Location (FOL) in 1992. This base, complete with living quarters and hangers, is in a state of readiness for immediate activation. But there was almost no local involvement or employment in the construction, and when the base is used for occasional military exercises, personnel and supplies are flown in, so the FOL has minimal impact on the local economy.

Petroleum Exploration

Inuvik during the 1980s saw a moderate level of resource exploration activity, and the town played an important logistical role for activities further north in the Mackenzie Delta and the Beaufort Sea. In 1985, the Beaufort Industry Group (BIG) was formed by the Inuvik Chamber of Commerce to coordinate local businesses with the Delta and Beaufort petroleum industry opportunities. The result was the BIG 85 conference and trade show, May 29 – June 1, 1985, with over 400 registrants, with booths in the AES and Aklak Air hangers at the Inuvik airport. Featured speakers at the conference included Pat Carney, Federal Ministry of Energy; Richard Nerysoo, NWT Government Leader; Tony Pennikett, Yukon Government Leader; Tagak Curley, NWT Minister of Economic Development and Energy; Mines and Resources, Billy Day, President COPE; Randal Pokiak, Inuvialuit Development Corporation; Maurice Tashereau, Administrator of the Canadian Oil and Gas Lands Administration.

A variety of other public sector and public-private agencies, set up to study the social,

CHAMBER OF COMMERCE PRESIDENTS 1983-1992	
1983	Al Pluim
1984	Doug Billingsley
1985	Doug billingsley
1986	Doug Billingsley
1987	Stu Coates
1988	Doug Billingsley
1989	Jane Gillman
1990	Malcolm Eyes
1991	Eileen Gour
1992	Allen Stanzell

environmental and economic impacts of resource extraction activity, also provided some ongoing economic stimulus through the 1980s. These programs not only provided some direct employment in the region, but also kept a stream of researchers flying in and out of Inuvik, and provided business for Inuvik's hotels and restaurants.

The Beaufort Environmental Assessment Review Panel (BEARP) was initiated in 1980, to look at the impact of hydrocarbon production and transportation. The panel members for this environmental review were John Tener, chairman, Titus Allooloo, Doug Craig, Knute Hansen, Allen Lueck, Ross Mackay and Mike Stutter. Public hearings were held in September to December 1983. There was a public hearing in Inuvik on 22 November 1983. The final report was published in July 1984 (Tener 1984).

The Northern Oil & Gas Action Program (NOGAP) was a multidisciplinary program initiated in 1983 by Northern Affairs, to investigate potential environmental and social problems. The program identified research and monitoring needs for future petroleum industry developments. It involved the Department of Environment, Department of Fisheries and the governments of the NWT and Yukon. The program involved research and planning to improve the Federal government's ability to respond to northern oil and gas development proposals. NOGAP funding initiated the Beaufort Environmental Monitoring Program (BEMP) in 1983, Mackenzie Environmental Monitoring Program (MEMP) in 1985, and Beaufort Region Environmental Assessment & Monitoring (BREAM) in 1991, to coordinate the BEMP and MEMP programs. (In the absence of any current development proposals for the Beaufort Sea, Mackenzie Delta and Mackenzie Valley areas the program was canceled in 1994.)

There was renewed exploration interest in 1989 when Esso, Shell and Gulf proposed a natural gas pipeline down the Mackenzie Valley to export natural gas mainly to the United States. In August 1989, the National Energy Board issued licences to Esso Resources, Shell Canada and Gulf Canada Resources for the export of 144 billion cubic meters (bcm) of natural gas from the Mackenzie Delta/Beaufort region. The exports via an anticipated Mackenzie Valley pipeline were to commence between 1996 and 2000 and continue for 20 years.

But with a worldwide oil price collapse in the early 1990s, the Mackenzie Delta area petroleum companies stopped exploring and pulled out.

LUNAR LINKS

In August 1988 plans were made to create an 18-hole golf course in a reclaimed section of the Inuvik gravel pit called the Lunar Links Municipal Golf Course. It was sponsored by the Arctic Circle Golf Assossoication (ACGA). Catchy names for each of the 18 holes were listed on the score cards including Dusty Drive, Campbell's Cut, Smith's Delight, Stringer's Peak, Koe's Caper, Rockey's Ridge, Mount Baldy, Semmler's Nook and the Bypass Junction.

Tourism and Parks

Tourism in the Inuvik region continued to grow during the 1980s, boosted not only by growth in eco-tourism, but also by the finalization of land claims. The Ivvavik National Park, on the Beaufort coast in northern Yukon, was the first National Park to be set up as part of the terms of a native land claim (the Inuvialuit Final Agreement).

In 1984, Inuvik became the administration base for National Parks in the Western Arctic. This office has responsibility for management of Ivvavik National Park, as well as Aulavik National Park, on Banks Island, and the Tuktut Nogait National Park, which contains the calving grounds of the Bluenose caribou heard. (National parks, which are co-managed by Parks Canada and Inuvialuit organizations, take up 18% of the the Inuvialuit Settlement Region.)

The Canadian Pingo Landmark Park, just outside Tuktoyaktuk, is also administered from Inuvik. In addition Herschel Island Yukon Territorial Park (Qikiqtaruk) has a park warden based out of Inuvik. It was founded in July 1987.

The Yukon First Nations Umbrella Final Agreement of 1993 created the Inuvik Gwich'in National Park, renamed the Vuntut Gwich'in Park in 1995.

Community & Cultural Activities

Although the 1980s were lean years for many Inuvik businesses, the town continued to grow culturally.

A highlight was the 25th Birthday Celebrations, July 11 – 18, 1983. Jim Robertson was Mayor, and Max Elanik the co-ordinator of the celebration. Prime Minister Pierre Elliott Trudeau was present. In his speech, he reflected that he had first been to Inuvik in 1957 (when he camped at East Three during a canoe trip down the Mackenzie River), and the town had changed considerably. Shirley and Sharon Firth were presented with medals by Trudeau. Many old time residents returned, for activities including Northern games, a fashion show and a trade show.

A popular annual celebration, the "Return of the Sun" festival, was held for the first time on January 6, 1987. The event was organized by Inuvik Fire Chief Bernie Campbell. Because fireworks would be pale and unexciting during the constant daylight of an Inuvik summer, Inuvik decided to hold fireworks in the middle of winter instead. The timing is the night before the sun first peeks above the horizon, after an absence of 30 days. In addition to fireworks, the Return of the Sun festival featured a large bonfire of Christmas trees and scrap lumber, usually on the ice of Twin Lakes.

On the cultural front, Strings Across The Sky (SATS) was an important initiative. It was formed by Andrea Hansen of Toronto and Frank Hansen of Inuvik, during the Inuvik stop of the September 1987 Toronto Symphony Orchestra tour. Andrea is a violinist who played with the Toronto Symphony until 1999, and Frank is a well known Delta fiddler and guitarist. They are not related although both have a Danish background.

Strings Across the Sky operates as a nonprofit foundation. Summer fiddle schools were

141

started in Inuvik, and the SATS performers played in Toronto at Roy Thompson Hall in June 1997. On April 15, 1999 Andrea was awarded the Order of Canada for her work with Arctic youth. She says that at least 100 donated violins had been left in 12 communities across the NWT.

Great Northern Arts Festival

Inuvik artists Charlene Alexander and Sue Rose got together to plan an arts Festival in the late 1980s. At first they envisioned bringing together just a few dozen artists from the Inuvik region. But they soon found that artists throughout the Northwest Territories were eager to find ways of connecting with each other.

When the first Great Northern Arts Festival was held in July 1989, in the Inuvialuit Corporate Centre, there was representation from carvers, printmakers, fibre artists, and many more disciplines, from throughout the Territory. They were able to meet, share techniques, learn about marketing practices, and inspire each other.

The response from the public was equally enthusiastic. The reputation of the Festival soon spread to places as far as Germany and Japan. Since the first Festival in 1989, the GNAF has become the premier cultural event in the NWT. Visitors can attend and participate in workshops, and browse the extensive galleries, which sell up to 1000 works of art for exhibiting artists each year.

The Festival has received funding and support in kind from many government departments, corporations and businesses, and from volunteers in the town of Inuvik.

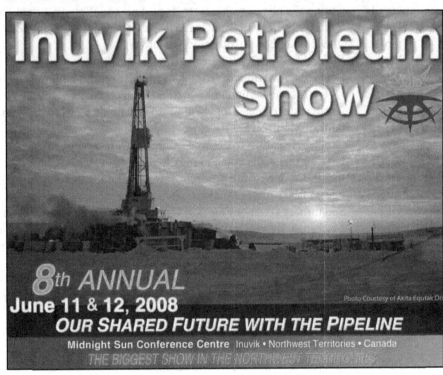

Inuvik plays host to petroleum industry trade shows, in 1985 (top) and 2008 (at right).

Inuvik Time Line 1993-2008

1993 Jan 13   Town Council moved to take over the Inuvik utilidor system from the GNWT
      Apr 2-3   9th Inuvik Regional Science Fair
      Apr 15   Actor Eric Thrasher Schweig visited Inuvik relatives
      Apr 16   Beaufort Delta self government agreement in principle signed
      May 22   Gum Boots singing group from Yellowknife performs at Ingamo Hall
      Sep   Inuvik Laundry closes after operating 30 years

1994 Apr 28   Edmonton Symphony Orchestra perform in SAMS auditorium
      Jun 5   Inuvialuit Final Agreement 10th Anniversary celebration
      Jun   Alex Moses Greenland building opens as office for Gwich'in Tribal Council, Nihtat Gwich'in Council

1995 Apr 12   Susan Aglukark concert at SAMS
      Jul 2   Wind Chill play performed by ICATS, written by Rod Hunchak
      Jul 8   Taste of the Arctic Banquet at Family Hall with buffet, slide show, drummers and reelers
      Aug 7   Inuvik Airport name changed to Mike Zubko Airport
      Aug   Western Arctic Visitors Centre opened

1996 Mar   Arctic Environmental Strategy Committee meeting in Inuvik
      Jun 20   New Inuvik Centennial Library opened in former NWT Liquor warehouse
      Jun 21   First Annual Aboriginal Day celebrations in Jim Koe Park
      Jun 30   Grollier Hall closes
      Jul   Northwestel's Inuvik office closes
      Aug 5   Convoy of 13 Volkswagen Vans arrives from the South
      Aug   Holy Cross Lutheran Church merges with Anglican Church
      Oct   Optimism Club formed to support Inuvik developments and counter pessimism
      Oct   Beaufort/Delta Self Government Negotiations office set up
      Nov   Chamber of Commerce agrees to merge with Western Arctic Tourism Association
      Nov 18   Cessna 170 plane crashes from its post next to Western Arctic Tourism Centre

1997 Feb 21   50th Anniversary of Branch 220 Royal Canadian Legion founded in Aklavik
      Jun 1   Inuvik Chamber of Commerce dissolved
      Jul   Midnight Sun Driving Range opened at Intown Airstrip
      Aug   Boot Lake Apartments vacated for foundation and building repairs
      Sep   Opening of new Midnight Sun Recreation Complex
      Oct   Northwestel changes Inuvik phone prefix numbers from "979" to "777"

1998 Jan   Bank of Montreal branch closes
      Jan   Grollier Hall arena to become community greenhouse
      Mar 1   First Air takes over route to Inuvik from NWT Air
      Jun 22   Inuvik TV moves into geodesic dome studio/offices
      Aug 19   Piles collapse under Mitchener house

1999 Jul 3   Sod turning ceremony for new Community Garden Society greenhouse
      Aug   Mackenzie Delta Hotel Group amalgamates Mackenzie, Eskimo and Finto hotels
      Sep 10   Inuvik Gas limited starts gas flow from Ikhil field to Inuvik customers
      Oct   Indian Affairs Minister Robert Nault visits Inuvik
      Oct 2   NWT Senator Nick Sibbeston visits Inuvik
      Dec   Floyd Roland and Roger Allen elected to NWT Legislative Assembly

2000 Jan 9   New Anglican Church of Ascension opens in former warehouse
      Mar   42nd anniversary of Muskrat Jamboree
      Mar   Inuvik self-government meeting at Recreation Complex
      Apr   Spirit 2000 Conference hosted by Western Arctic Business Development Services

	Apr	Inuvik Council takes over utilidor responsibilities from NWT Power Corporation
	May	Approval to construct young female offenders facility on Wolverine Road
	Jul 25-30	30th Anniversary of Northern Games
	Aug 9	Governor General Adrienne Clarkson visits Inuvik
	Aug 22	Approval for construction of new $37 million hospital facility
	Oct 16	Peter Clarkson elected Mayor
	Dec	Armed forces fighter jet exercise at Inuvik Forward Operating Location
2001	Jan 6	14th Annual Sunrise Festival held at the Intown Airport with $10,000 fireworks display
	Feb 1	Annual General Meeting of reorganized Inuvik Chamber of Commerce
	Mar	Group of Russian officials visit Inuvik to understand aboriginal rights
	May	12th Annual Firefighter's Ball, Scott Young firefighter of the year
	Jun 21-23	First Annual Inuvik Petroleum Show with 300 delegates and 70 exhibitors
	Jul 13-22	13th Annual Great Northern Arts Festival with over 100 artisists
	Aug 25	3rd Annual Knights of Columbus Fil Petrin Memorial Taber Feast
	Sep	9th Annual Demolition Derby
	Oct	Lion's Club Delta Daze
	Oct	25th Anniversary of Ingamo Friendship Centre
	Dec	Youth Justice Committee formed
2002	May 2	Arctic Tern Young Offender Facility opens
	May 3	Kunnek Reindeer Development holds public meeting on reindeer
	June	Inuvik Petroleum Show
	Jun 10	Beaufort Delta Education Council develops Inuvialuit and Gwich'in curriculum
	Jun 21	First Annual Aboriginal Day at Jim Koe Park
	Aug	Inuvik's Razzamajazz group formed
	Sep 20	IDC celebrates 25 years in business
	Oct 15	Aboriginal Pipeline Group threatens to pull out of Mackenzie Gas Project
	Nov	Inuvik ratepayers support Inuvik Family Centre project
2003	Jan	NWT Premier Stephen Kakfwi starts off the year with a major speech in Inuvik
	Feb	Aboriginal Pipeline Group secures $71 million in funding for project definition
	Mar	Inuvik Council passes first reading for a bylaw to restrict smoking in public places
	Apr 16	Beaufort Delta Self Government meeting in Inuvik recreation complex
	May	New Inuvik general hospital opens after 2.5 years construction
	Jul	2,000 hectare forest fire theatens Inuvik airport and Shell Lake properties
	Jul	Fred Carmichael re-elected to head the Gwich'in Tribal Council
	Jul	15th Annual Great Northern Arts Festival with 100 artists from across the North
	Aug	Gwich'in Land Use Plan signed after 20 years in the making
	Jun	Inuvik Gas increases residential rates by 45%
	Sep	Richard Nerysoo elected to head the Inuvik Native Band and Nihtat Gwich'in Council
	Nov	Floyd Roland acclaimed in Boot Lake riding and Roger Allen wins in Twin Lake riding
	Dec	Hiram Oscar missing while monitoring the reindeer herd north of Invik
2004	Mar	Northern Property Real Estate Inestment Trust purchases 200 rental units for $15 million
	May	Hearne High School foyer roof collapses due to accumulated snow
	Jul	Western Canada Provincial and Territorial Premiers meeting in Inuvik
	Jul	Prime Minister Paul Martin visits Inuvik
	Jul	First Annual End of the Road Music Festival
	Oct	Twin Lake MLA Roger Allen resigns
	Oct	Peter Clarkson re-elected Mayor
	Oct	New $12 million Aurora Campus of Aurora College opens on Loucheux Road

	Nov 24	Inuvik Council changes name of Loucheux Road to Gwich'in Road
	Dec	Robert McLeod wins Twin Lakes riding byelection
	Dec	Inuvik hosts 100 community leaders from around the Northwest Territories
2005	Jan 26	NEB Mackenzie Gas Pipeline Project hearings begin in Inuvik
	Apr	Inuvik Family Centre opens with large indoor pool, fitness centre and squash courts
	Jun 15	Western Energy Alliance meeting in Inuvik
	Jun15-16	Inuvik Petroleum Show
	Jul	17th Annual Great Northern Arts Festival
	Jul 27	Angry mob runs eight suspected drug dealers out of town
	Aug 26-28	End of the Road Music Festival
	Nov 29	Petition urging RCMP to act on Inuvik crack problems
2006	Jan 25	National Energy Board's Joint Review Panel first hearing
	Feb	Billy Day honoured with National Aboriginal Achievement Foundation award
	Feb	Perry Building closed by NWT Public Works
	Mar	Fred Carmichael honoured with 2006 Aboriginal Business Person of the Year Award
	Mar 15	East 3 Movie: Exploring A Frozen Frontier, filmed in Inuvik, premieres in New York
	Jun	6th Annual Inuvik Petroleum Show with 800 delegates
	Jun	Aklavik flood victims put up in Inuvik with some at the Forward Operating Base
	Jul	Beaufort Delta residential school reunion coordinated by John Banksland
	Aug	Gwich'in Biennial Gathering held in Inuvik
	Oct 17	Derek Lindsay elected as new Inuvik Mayor
2007	Jan 10	Distributor Street renamed Veteran Way
	Apr	50th Muskrat Jamboree
	May	Bertha Allen receives Order Of Canada award for her efforts to assist northern women
	May	Frosty's Bar closes after owner purchases Mad Trapper Lounge
	Jun 13-14	Inuvik Petroleum Show
	Jul	North Star Construction stops operation
	Aug	Demolition Derby at Navy Road gravel pit
	Sep	Roman Mahnic new Hearne High principal
	Oct	Robert McLeod wins NWT election for Twin Lake riding
	Oct	Floyd Roland selected as NWT Premier
	Oct 21-26	Oil & Gas Land Management Symposium in Inuvik
	Nov 29	Mackenzie Valley Pipeline hearings wind up in Inuvik
	Nov	North of Normal Theatre Group formed with plans to perform "East 3" in July 2008
2008	Jan	Nellie Cournoyea awarded Governor Generals Northern Medal
	Jan	Imperial Oil brings in transport loads of gasoline due to shortage caused by early freeze-up
	Feb 1	Aurora College residence opens
	Mar 18-21	51st Muskrat Jamboree
	Apr 1	Inuvik Muslims to build permanent mosque
	Apr 5	40th Annual Top of the World ski meet
	Apr 13-17	Gov. Gen. Michaelle Jean visits Inuvik, presents Northern Medal to Nellie Cournoyea
	May 3	19th Annual Fireman's Ball
	Jun 18-21	Boom Bust Economics Conference on impacts for rural and remote communities
	Jun 11-12	8th Inuvik Petroleum Show
	Jul 11-20	Great Northern Arts Festival 20th annual program
	Jul 18	Inuvik's 50th Anniversary Celebrations

Chapter Seven

Consolidation, 1993-2008

By the early 1990s, most community institutions in Inuvik were relatively stable. Citizens continued to make significant improvements to educational and recreational facilities and programs. Aboriginal land claims organizations took on a much greater role in the regional economy, buying existing businesses and investing in new ventures.

Around the turn of the millenium, rising oil and gas prices again brought major petroleum interests to Inuvik to renew plans for a Mackenzie Valley pipeline. This time aboriginal groups negotiated an ownership stake in any such pipeline, but after several more years of preparations, it still remains unclear if construction on this resource megaproject will actually begin any time soon.

Northern Government

Elected politicians from the Inuvik region continued to play a major role in territorial government, with two local politicians serving as premiers of the NWT – Nellie Cournoyea from 1991 – 1995 and Floyd Roland 2007 –.

Inuvik also gained more representation in the Legislative Assembly. In November 1999, there were elections for the first time of two members for Inuvik, in the ridings of Boot Lake and Twin Lakes. Floyd Roland was elected for Boot Lake and Roger Allen for Twin Lakes.

Aboriginal Self-Government

The 1992 Bourque Commission proposed a federal form of government organization of the western Northwest Territories with two levels of government. A district and a central government would coexist, each with its own constitutionally protected sphere of authority, lawmaking capabilities and structures of government (Commission for Constitutional Government, Ottawa 1992).

The Beaufort/Delta Self-Government Negotiations Office opened in October 1966 to pursue a self-government agreement on behalf of the Gwich'in Tribal Council and the Inuvialuit Regional Corporation in accordance with their land claim agreements. Local staff were hired to consult with local residents. This is the only case in Canada where a native self-government is being negotiated jointly by two Native groups, and within a public government context. Democratic and other rights of all Canadian citizens are to be balanced with the inherent indigenous rights. A review and amendment process will allow the Inuvialuit and Gwich'in to ensure that they retain control over how their inherent right is being implemented. The negotiations are based on legal and policy frameworks in the land claims provisions, the 1998 GNWT Self-Government Vision, and 1995 Federal Self-Government Policy.

On March 31, 2000 a Self-Government Political Accord was signed between the Inuvialuit, Gwich'in, Northwest Territories and Federal government. The aim was to have a final self government agreement in place by 2002.

A meeting of the Beaufort Delta Self-Government program was held at the Midnight Sun Recreation Complex in April 2003 with NWT Premier Stephen Kakfwi, DIAND Minister Robert Nault, Western Arctic Liberal MP Ethel Blondin-Andrew, Gwich'in Tribal Council President Fred Carmichael and Inuvialuit Regional Corporation CEO Nellie Cournoyea. There was an agreement-in-principle signing ceremony.

Parks and Tourism

Western Arctic Visitors Centre opened in 1995 to support tourism throughout the Western Arctic. The Centre, operated by GNWT, welcomes visitors to Inuvik and provides information on all Western Arctic communities. There are interesting geographic, wildlife and cultural displays.

Gwich'in Territorial Park

Gwich'in Territorial Park is approximately 20 km south of Inuvik on the east and south shores of Campbell Lake. Campbell Lake is readily visited off the Dempster Highway or along the East Branch. It was named by James Anderson (1812-1867) after Robert Campbell (1808-1894), Chief Trader for the HBC and in the Mackenzie District 1854-1862 (source DCB XII). The French explorer Count Eduard de Sainville, who was in the Mackenzie Delta area from 1889 to 1894, published a map in his book showing Campbell Lake as Camsell Lake (*Journey To The Mouth of the Mackenzie River* 1898). This name probably referred to Julian S. Camsell, who was a Hudson Bay Company factor at the time de Sainville travelled north on the Mackenzie River in 1889.

The area is recognized internationally under the International Biological Program. The land and waters of this area contain many significant natural, cultural and recreational features in this extension of the Mackenzie Delta. A park had been proposed for this area by the Inuvik Council and the Western Arctic Visitors Association (WAVA) in the 1970s.

Following passage of the Gwich'in Comprehensive Land Claim Agreement Act in 1992, the Gwich'in Tribal Council and the GNWT negotiated a Memorandum of Agreement concerning a territorial park. A master plan was completed in 1995 by a Gwich'in company as part of the Memorandum of Agreement.

INUVIK YOUTH BEHIND THE CAMERA

In 2005 a 19-minute video was produced by Dr. Janet Ip titled "We Don't Live In Igloos: Inuvik Youth Speak Out". A group of Inuvik teens were given cameras so they could capture what mattered to them. They were then interviewed about the photos they had taken, in particular as the pictures related to their health concerns. (Moving Images Distribution Vancouver)

The area has now been reserved for park purposes. The park is classified as an Outdoor Recreation Park and encompasses an area of approximately 8800 hectares. Two existing wayside parks and one existing campground have been incorporated within this park. Any proposed developments will not be permitted to affect sites associated with the past and present uses of the land. There will be a new focus on tourism but the traditional use will continue and is considered an asset to park development.

Town Parks

Jimmy Adams Peace Park, including the walking trail around Boot Lake, was proposed by Mary Beckett and Sue Rose as part of Peace Parks Across Canada program. The Inuvik Council passed a supporting motion for the park on August 25, 1993.

In November 2001 the Inuvik Council considered plans to establish a new gateway entrance to Inuvik and redevelop Jim Koe Park into an amphitheatre and marketplace.

Notable visitors

In July 1992, 200 Inuit representatives from Chukota, Alaska, Northern Canada, Greenland, plus hundreds of others, gathered in Inuvik for the Inuit Circumpolar Conference, to discuss issues of mutual concern and to socialize. Entertainment included the Delta Drummers and Dancers, Gwich'in Dancers, Kashtin Band, Susan Aglukark, Snowbirds and Greenland Theatre. The ICC General Assembly is scheduled every four years, and this was the sixth such conference.

Governor General Adrienne Clarkson and party visited Inuvik on August 9, 2000. She was presented with a northern painting at the Inuvik Centennial Library.

Governor General Michaelle Jean visited Inuvik from April 13 to 17, 2008 and participated in the National Inuvik Education Summit. While in Inuvik she presented the Governor General's Northern Medal to Nellie Cournoyea.

Major construction projects

Starting in the mid-1990s, many of the buildings housing Inuvik's original public institutions were either replaced or substantially renovated, and additional public services were added in entirely new facilities.

Midnight Sun Recreation Complex

In 1993 the Inuvik Town Council and recreation groups planned a replacement for the Dave Jones Community Centre that would include a standard size hockey arena, a four-sheet curling rink/lounge and a 350-seat community hall and conference centre with central utility core and kitchen/catering facilities. The rough estimate for this complex was $5 million, of which private funding would provide $500,000, the Town of Inuvik $1 million and the GNWT the remaining $3.5 million.

In February 1997 the new complex costs were estimated at $6.3 million or $1.5 million more than the Town Council had approved. In March 1999 the total complex costs were nearing $8 million. Tetlit Zheh Construction, a Gwich'in Development Corp. company, which had been awarded the project without open tendering, said that the increases were due to design changes and delays in construction.

The Midnight Sun Recreation Complex officially opened in September 1997 over budget and long after the targeted completion date ... just like Inuvik's first Recreation Centre (see Chapter Four).

Inuvik Centennial Library

In May 1996 the Inuvik Centennial Library moved to its new location in the renovated NWT Liquor Warehouse. On June 20, 1996 the official opening of the new facility took place with citizens forming a line to pass the Centennial Symbol from the old to the new building, where it again hangs above the entrance. Ellen Binder's grandson cut the ribbon. Cynthia Hill cut the cake. The Dick Hill Northern Collection, consisting of over 10,000 items, was accepted as a major donation. Computers were linked to a library in Christchurch, New Zealand. A special children's centre donated by the Legion Ladies and the Lions Club was inaugurated.

Inuvik Youth Centre

The Inuvik Youth Centre Society was formed in 1996 after a survey of the needs of youth between 13 and 19 who were at risk from drugs and alcohol. The Inuvik Council donated the use of the original Centennial Library building and many volunteers worked to provide building renovations and suitable furniture where youth could "hang out" in a drug-free environment. A coordinator was hired and supervision was provided by the Aurora College's Recreation Leaders Program.

Inuvik Community Greenhouse

In 1999 the old Grollier Hall ice arena was converted into a community greenhouse by the Community Garden Society. There are 75 raised garden plots and 4000 square feet of commercial area for vegetables. It is the largest greenhouse north of the Arctic Circle and serves as a focus point for community development.

CHAMBER OF COMMERCE PRESIDENTS 1993-2003	
1993	Allen Stenzell
1994	Sue Rose
1995	Harry Joujan
1996	Rolund Peters
2000	dormant
2001	Derek Lindsay
2002	Paul Watters
2003	Paul Watters

Anglican Church

The New Anglican Church of the Ascension was opened January 9, 2000 by Bishop Larry Robertson. It replaced the original temporary church hall which held only 100 people. The church had operated for 40 years in a small building that originally was supposed to be the church hall. The new project began when the Church bought an old warehouse for $1.00, spent $30,000 moving it to site, and attached it to the original church hall in an "L" configuration. The total project budget was $200,000. Chris Robertson of Hamilton, Ontario, who had bicycled to Inuvik in 1997, raised $30,000 towards the new building.

Young Offenders Facility

In May 2000 the NWT Government announced a $5 million Young Offenders Facility for Inuvik. It was to be the first stand-alone facility in Canada for girls. Nearly half of the girls sentenced to serve time in Yellowknife were from Inuvik.

Inuvik Regional Hospital

On August 22, 2000 the NWT Government announced the construction of the new 9,000-square-metre Inuvik Regional Hospital costing $37 million. This facility was planned to have 10 doctors and 35 nurses, 25 acute care beds, outpatient and emergency services, a transient centre and telehealth capability. The new hospital opened in April, 2003.

Inuvik Family Centre

This new facility is attached to the Midnight Sun Recreation Centre and was opened in April 2005 at a cost of $8.5 million. The centre has a large 25-metre, four-lane, combined lap pool and leisure pool plus a water slide and swirl pool. Also, there are two squash courts and a 24-hour fitness centre. The pool construction is unique with the "in-ground" pool built above ground with refrigerated piling below to maintain the permafrost. Another northern adaptation is the stainless steel pool lining.

Sir Alexander Mackenzie School

In June 2007 it was announced that the SAMS school would be demolished in 2013 after the construction of a new school for 1060 students, at a cost of $16 million, to be completed by 2011.

DISTRIBUTOR STREET TO VETERAN WAY

On the request of Fred Church, the Inuvik Council passed a motion to rename a portion of Distributor Street to Veteran Way in honour of those who fought for Canada (Council minutes 10 January 2007). The name change applied to the section between Mackenzie Road and Franklin Street and Distributor Street was extended along River Road to Duck Lake Road. Many residents support recognition of the town's military members but objected to changing a historically significant street name and suggested that another street be designated for veterans respect.

A changing business community

Chamber of Commerce

The Inuvik Chamber of Commerce has had an on-again, off-again existence in the last two decades. The Chamber remained active until 1994, but the Inuvik Independent Business Committee was organized in 1995 to provide basic coordination and representation for Inuvik businesses.

In 1996 the Chamber published an Inuvik Business Directory with assistance from NWT Economic Development. There were 50 members listed at the time. Shortly after taking this government funding the Chamber collapsed.

In November 1996, the Chamber and Western Arctic Tourism Association members merged to form the new Beaufort Delta Board of Tourism and Trade. This organization folded in 1999.

In 2001 the Inuvik Chamber of Commerce was reinstated with President Derek Lindsay, Vice President Kevin Braun, Secretary Tamie Littlechilds, Treasurer Paul Watters and directors Brian Desjardins, George Doolittle, Lyle Neiss, Tom Zubko, Gene Nikiforuk, Dennie Lennie, Lilian Brewster and Mary Backett. After operating for the next three years, the Chamber has again been dormant since 2004.

New Landlords and Hotels

Mackenzie Delta Hotel Group, an Inuvialuit holding company, amalgamated the Mackenzie Hotel, Eskimo Inn and Finto Motel in August 1999. In January 2004 the 32-unit Mackenzie Hotel built in 1960 was torn down to make make way for the New Mackenzie. The Finto Lounge shut down in October 2006 with the hotel closely shortly afterwards.

In 2003 three new hotels were commissioned increasing the number of rooms available by 50%. In 2004 Capital Suites opened with 82 units, in 2005 the Noval Inn opened with 42 units and in 2006 the new Mackenzie Hotel opened with 97 units. The new Mackenzie hotel is a three-story facility and sits on steel piles drilled 10 metres into the permafrost at a cost of $13 million. In addition the Arctic Chalet became upscale with 12 units. In 2008 there were a total of 300 hotel rooms in Inuvik.

In April 2005 a multi-million-dollar real estate deal involved many of Inuvik's key commercial sites. Northern Property Real Estate Investment Trust (Northern REIT) partnered with the Gwich'in Tribal Council and the Nihtat Gwich'in Council to purchase eight buildings including the Semmler Building, Jim Koe Building and Mack Travel building.

Canadian Reindeer Project

In 1996, Lloyd Binder of Inuvik began discussions that culminated in the purchase of the reindeer herd to the north of Inuvik. The herd originally had been brought to the Mackenzie Delta by the Canadian Reindeer Project in 1935. In the following decades, the herd had been owned by several private individuals and companies, but the Inuvialuit land claim agreement had resulted in controversies about grazing rights and fees that might be payable for the herd. Binder formed a company called Kunnek Resource Development Corp., owned by family members as well as the Inuvialuit Community Development Organization.

Although the reindeer herd had been operated in the same area for half a century and has caused no known environmental damage, Kunnek's application for a land use permit through the Inuvialuit Game Council took two years and involved extensive public hearings. Binder estimated that the hearing process cost the company $50,000 to $75,000.

The petroleum industry returns

The Mackenzie Delta and Beaufort Sea petroleum exploration programs were sporadic in the 1990s after peaking at close to $1 billion in the mid-1980s. Exploration moneys spent were $35 million in 1990, $9 million in 1991, $19 million in 1992, $4 million in 1993 and nil in 1994. In 1992 Shell drilled two dry wells at Unipkat. By 1994 discovered resources were 240 million cubic metres of crude oil and 360 billion cubic metres of natural gas. It was estimated that the Beaufort Mackenzie Basin contains 13.5 tcf of discovered natural gas and 42.4 tcf of undiscovered natural gas.

A new type of exploration began in 1998, when the Japanese company Japex drilled an off-shore well at Mallik in the Beaufort Sea. They were investigating the potential of natural gas hydrates, which had been discovered near Richards Island in 1972. An evaluation of this considerable resource was carried out in co-operation with the Geological Survey of Canada. Each cubic foot of hydrate yields 650 cubic feet of methane gas when melted. Several showings of Mackenzie hydrates has been found earlier by researchers such as Dr J. R. Mackay.

Anderson Oil moved into the Mackenzie Delta in 1999, picking up several licences on Inuvialuit land. Anderson was bought out by Devon Energy in October 2001.

Inuvik Petroleum Show

The Inuvik Petroleum Show was organized by Inuvik Town Council to promote petroleum exploration activities in the Mackenzie Delta and Beaufort Sea region. The first annual show was held in 2000. It is well attended with around 250 oil patch exhibitors participating.

Ikhil Gas Project

In 1997, the Inuvialuit Petroleum Corporation, in a joint venture partnership with Alta Gas Services and Enbridge Inc., developed the Ikhil gas field, located 55 km northeast of Inuvik. The gas field was discovered in 1986 by Gulf Canada. It was sold to Shell Oil and then to the Inuvialuit Petroleum Corporation. A test well proved up 14 billion cubic feet of gas, enough to last Inuvik for at least 20 years.

A delineation well was drilled in 1998 at the Ikhil gas field northwest of Inuvik to outline additional reserves. In the 1999 winter a 50 km 6" pipeline was built to Inuvik and was completed in June 1999, as the first gas pipeline north of the Arctic Circle. It is mostly buried at one metre. The cooled gas is piped to a gate station at NWT Power Commission. The NWT Power Commission plant, businesses and homes were connected in the summer of 1999.

The $23 million project is one-third owned by each of the Inuvialuit Petroleum Corporation, Alta Gas Service and Enbridge Consumers Gas. The Ikhil natural gas supplied to Inuvik homes and businesses sold for an average of 25% less than fuel oil and 32% less than propane (Gleason Media 2001). This alternative fuel source will provide economic benefits to Inuvik businesses and residents for many years to come.

The NTPC power plant converted to natural gas fuel in the fall of 1999 with installation of two Wartsilla generators. Residual heat goes to the town's water treatment plant. Installed capacity is 10,920 megawatts with one 720 KW, two 2500 KW and one 300 kW diesel backups. In 2003 there were 62 customers connected to Inuvik Gas Ltd. In 2007 this number had increased to 700.

Pipeline megaproject proposals

The euphoria of planning the Mackenzie Valley Pipeline returned to Inuvik in 2000 with consideration for five main northern natural gas pipeline proposals: (1) Mackenzie Valley only; (2) Mackenzie Valley with an offshore link to Alaska; (3) Mackenzie Valley with an onshore link to Alaska; (4) Alaska Natural Gas Transportation System (ANGTS) to Fairbanks and Alaska Highway to Alberta; and (5) ANGTS to Fairbanks and Alaska Highway to Alberta with a Dempster Highway lateral to the Mackenzie Delta.

The Mackenzie Gas Project involves the construction of a 1200-kilometre, 30-inch pipeline to ship Mackenzie Delta gas south to connect with existing pipelines in Alberta, construction of a gathering system to a processing plant near Inuvik, and development of the natural gas fields to production. A memorandum of understanding has been signed between the Mackenzie Delta producers and the Aboriginal Pipeline Group for the right to own up to one third of the Mackenzie Valley pipeline.

The Aboriginal Pipeline Group (APG) was created in 2000 following meetings in Fort Liard and Fort Simpson. Thirty aboriginal leaders signed the agreement, with the goals of maximizing the aboriginal ownership and benefits of the gas pipeline project, and to support greater independence and self-reliance among residents. It has been pointed out that the Dene Nation turned down a 10% ownership of the Norman Wells oil pipeline which would now be worth $100 million. Nellie Cournoyea was the first APG chairman with Fred Carmichael taking over the chair in 2002.

In June 2003, Aboriginal Pipeline Group unveiled a deal to secure a one third interest in the Mackenzie Valley natural gas pipeline (*Globe and Mail*, 20 June 2003). APG chairman Fred Carmichael stated that the agreement would support "economic self-sufficiency for northern aboriginals". Carmichael said they have two main concerns, their environment and their economy. "Too often we spent so long talking or arguing about what to do, that opportunities passed us by. We are united in our desire to maximize the benefits of a pipeline. It may get confusing wearing two hats. But better two hats than none" (*Oil & Gas Review*, Summer 2002).

The Northern Route Gas Pipeline Project (NPGPR) proposes to construct a new natural gas pipeline from Prudhoe Bay along the Arctic coast to Edmonton via the Mackenzie River Valley. The Canadian segment would be 2400 km and the Alaskan segment is 310 km for a total of 2710 km. Much of the Alaskan section would be offshore. The project is structured as a partnership with ArctiGas Resource Corporation of Calgary and Arctic Resources Company of Houston. A consortium of stakeholders would build the pipeline and operate it for 25 years, after which ownership would be held by the Aboriginal communities of the Mackenzie Valley. It proposes to develop a north-south corridor along the Mackenzie Valley including a road from Yellowknife to Inuvik, a fibre-optic right-of-way connecting northern communities, gas power generation and heating to the communities.

Joint Review Panel

The National Energy Board's Joint Review Panel for the Mackenzie Valley gas project started on January 25, 2006 to consider the environmental and social aspects of the proposed 1200 km natural gas pipeline from the Mackenzie Delta to Alberta. The initial estimated project cost was $7.5 billion. Imperial Oil is the lead player with partners including Shell Canada, Conoco-Phillips, Mobil Corporation and the Aboriginal Pipeline Group (APG). The Panel's first hearing was in Inuvik on February 14, 2006. Its closing hearing was held nearly two years later at Inuvik on November 16, 2007. Its final report was not expected for another year or so.

Since the JRP hearings started the estimated project costs have nearly doubled to $12 billion.

Anne Crossman, Permafrost Media editor, commented the panel members and staff were of good spirit but that they had vague guidelines, no finishing commitment date, no financial constraints and answered to no one. Most people at community hearings thought the JRP was another Berger Inquiry and were allowed to speak of grievances that had nothing to do with the panel's responsibility or pipeline construction (Permafrost Media 25 January 2008).

There were excessive information requests from Federal and Territorial government departments, on subjects only slightly related to northern development. The questions were mostly "what if" questions which are difficult or impossible for a proponent to answer for a proposed project.

Peter Ross, Tsiigehtchic Chief, told the Mackenzie Valley Environmental Impact Review Board in Inuvik on March 31, 2004 that "Many Delta residents feel they are over-consulted on pipeline matters, saying they are tired of answering the same questions they were asked 25 years ago" (MVEIRB 2004). The similarities of the 1974-to-1979 Berger Commission to the 2005-2008 Joint Review Panel are startling.

Kristen Wenghofer

In the late 1990s the former Grollier Hall arena was converted to a community greenhouse which soon drew a waiting list of residents wanting a garden plot. Kristen Wenghofer, above, was greenhouse co-ordinator 2005 – 2007.

Inuvik's arctic location has always been a big attraction to adventurers. In 2007 the 6633 Ultra Marathon race was begun, for cyclists or skiers willing to spend a March break travelling from Eagle Plains to Tuktoyaktuk. Below, the first team to finish the race was Denise & John Whyte, shown pedaling their tandem bike on the ice road north of Inuvik.

Martin Like

CHAPTER EIGHT

Retrospect: 50 Years

One way to begin an interpretive review of Inuvik's progress is by discussing the four goals for the town as expressed in 1961 by Prime Minister John Diefenbaker.

Four Goals For Inuvik

When Prime Minister John Diefenbaker officially dedicated the new community of Inuvik in 1961, he endorsed four main goals for the community which are engraved on the town monument's plaque. In the following fifty years Inuvik has met and exceeded all of Diefenbaker's challenges.

> "This was the first community north of the Arctic Circle built to provide the [1] *normal facilities of a Canadian town.* It was designed not only as a [2] *base for development and administration* but as a [3] *centre to bring education, medical care* and [4] *new opportunity to the people of the Western Arctic.*"

1. "Normal facilities of a Canadian town"

As a planned new community constructed with Federal government funds, Inuvik started off with complete facilities, including roads, airport and utilities, which at the time were not generally available throughout the Northwest Territories and small Canadian communities. Despite its remote Arctic location, the need to provide complete services for the military and government personnel necessitated "normal facilities" for all residents. Hence, telephones, refrigerators, running water, toilets, sewers, radio, TV, autos, retail stores, fresh foods, etc. became readily accessible for both indigenous Northerners and newly arrived Southerners.

At first Inuvik utilities were priced around the same as in Ottawa. During the 1960s water and sewer connections cost only $10 a month, electricity cost only 5 cents per kwh, telephones cost $8.00 a month and gasoline was 40 cents a gallon (9 cents a litre). Some Delta residents who voluntarily came to Inuvik in the early years experienced an accommodation shortage, but this shortcoming was rectified as fast as possible. Some services such as TV broadcasting, jet aircraft transportation and high-speed internet were available in Inuvik long before they were available in many southern communities.

2. "Base for development and administration"

When Inuvik was conceived in 1950 there was very little development and administration taking place in the northwest corner of Canada. At the time the RCMP detachment at Aklavik provided most of the Western Arctic government services. Inuvik flourished as a government centre, bringing social services and government direction to over 500,000 square kilometres, approximately one eighth of the Canadian land mass. With the establishment of transportation and communication services at Inuvik the petroleum exploration, transportation and tourism industries evolved.

As the largest community in the Western Arctic, Inuvik is a natural base for government administration. Federal and Territorial government offices which serve the region and surrounding communities are located in Inuvik. Native organizations, business and industry offices are located in Inuvik. Inuvik retail shops and commercial businesses serve the Western Arctic and are strong players in the "assessment and development of resources".

3. "Centre for education and medical care"

The Federal Day School, later Sir Alexander Mackenzie School (SAMS), was the first composite education facility north of the Arctic Circle. It attracted students from a 1500 km radius who initially had the choice of going to SAMS or no school at all. In the early years there were small schools only in Aklavik and Tuktoyaktuk.

The Samuel Hearne Secondary School opened in 1969. Many students came and received a full primary and secondary education. Several students went on to university and became doctors and engineers. Now most of the teaching staff and administrators are local residents.

The Inuvik Regional Hospital was the first government medical facility in the Western Arctic region. A series of nursing stations in the surrounding settlements provided full medical coverage for all residents.

From the beginning the Inuvik Research Laboratory has been a centre for "scientific investigations of concern to the North and to Canada". As many as 350 researchers working on 72 projects were active at the Inuvik Research Laboratory.

4. "New opportunities for the people of the Western Arctic"

Inuvik education, medical and administrative services opened up new business and service opportunities for the people of the Western Arctic. From the construction period onwards, there were commercial and employment possibilities for all interested local residents. Education and training provisions enabled them to participate in the northern economy. The new opportunities included politics, administration, commerce, transportation, communications and teaching. Inuvik has facilitated the change from a Mackenzie Delta trapping economy to a world economy. Inuvik is where "Indians, Eskimos and Southerners are working together".

Ten Community Strengths

Inuvik was able to meet Diefenbaker's goals through the interplay of ten community strengths, initiated in his Inuvik speech and carried out as federal policy. These strengths remain a big part of the way Inuvik meets its challenges.

RETROSPECT: 50 YEARS

1. First modern Canadian community north of the Arctic Circle

Inuvik had a distinct advantage of being new and starting free from the heavy baggage of history and social biases. Nobody was forced to live in the community. It had all the facilities and ingredients for success as a new community starting fresh in a location where there was little previous activity.

Inuvik remains the first and only Canadian community north of the Arctic Circle with the full services of piped water and sewage, medical facilities, jet airport, highway connection, commercial services and resource development. It has evolved as a river town, a highway town and an aviation town.

2. Notable social progress in education, health, housing and employment

Inuvik provided opportunities for entrepreneurs resident in the North and coming from the South. As local residents participated in the abundant education and training programs, they were increasingly employed in positions which initially had to be filled by Southerners. The 1955 decision of the Federal government, the Roman Catholic church and the Anglican church to make Inuvik's new education facility non-residential was a brilliant decision. The student hostels, for students from other communities, were separate institutions, and within the school, all students were treated the same.

For quality of life measurement, Inuvik remains on a par with or above any other Canadian community of a comparable size. Community statistics on education, health, housing and employment all show a strong positive trend. Most of the perceived social problems, discrimination and alcohol abuse have been greatly reduced or eliminated.

3. Introduction of democratic self-government institutions

Prior to the establishment of Inuvik there was no elected local government. The NWT Government had an elected representative for the Mackenzie Delta since 1955 and the Federal Member of Parliament for the Western Arctic was first elected in 1952. At Inuvik an advisory council was initiated in 1967, a village government in 1969 and a town government in 1970.

Now Inuvik democracy is flourishing at the municipal, territorial and federal levels. The Inuvik Council is strong, effective and representative. Also, the Inuvialuit and Gwich'in residents have elected organizations looking after their special interests.

4. Recognition of indigenous cultures and rights

Inuvik developed with no ethnic biases and provided full opportunities for all races and cultures. Any perceived biases could be related to lack of education and experience. Native cultures have always been recognized in Inuvik, and from the beginning Inuvik's indigenous residents have had full Canadian rights and freedoms.

Native organizations in Inuvik are as sharp and aggressive as any national or international corporation, union, environmental or special interest group. They look out for themselves using modern administration and communication skills.

5. Application of community planning to improve life quality

Inuvik is a planned community – with many plans. All of the government stakeholders had plans for the evolution of Inuvik, but in reality there was little coordination between the government planners, and Inuvik evolved naturally by adapting to both internal and external pressures with grace. Inuvik's existence and evolution has been an exercise in flexible community planning.

Inuvik's organization from conception to the present has been directed to improve life quality for all Inuvik residents. The original town layout addressed social and cultural issues. Later planning action was used to extend utility services and to provide practical housing for young and old.

6. Technical success of building a community on permafrost

When Inuvik was first built there was very little practical experience with permafrost construction problems. National building code standards were enforced for all construction, and adequate air circulation was required under structures to keep the ground ice from melting. As a result there have been very few structural problems. The recent pile degradation problems are not due to permafrost and could happen anywhere in Canada where moisture comes into contact with wood. Inuvik is an overall technical success providing full community services in a difficult Arctic environment.

7. Practical application of frontier development theories

Experiences with developing countries and ethnic relations were applied for community organization and social relationships. Provision of education and training for both community leadership and for employment opportunities has been the key to Inuvik's success. Development theories were applied practically in Inuvik.

8. Research studies documented community activities

The Inuvik Research Laboratory supported "Scientific investigations of concern to the North and to Canada," and provided documentation of the community's evolution. A continuous stream of researchers investigating technical and social problems has led to their understanding and solution.

9. Extensive economic benefits

The Federal government initiated policies of "Assessment and development of resources" and to "Serve the people of the Mackenzie Delta, Arctic Coast and Western Islands". These schemes provided positive economic benefits with everybody thriving. The evolution of Inuvik's economic base seemed to be a natural plan. First build the community, provide employment and training and then encourage resource development with the conditions of local employment, social responsibility and environmental protection.

10. "Indians, Eskimos and Southerners working together"

Inuvik has been a "social melting pot" with all races coexisting. All cultures have worked together while maintaining their pride and spirit. The social services of housing and allowances available for those in need are provided regardless of ethnicity. There has been full support for settlement of northern native land claims.

National Northern Objectives

As Inuvik was created by the Federal Government, its evolution has been greatly influenced by federal aboriginal and northern development policies. Inuit were included with Indians under all programs. In June 1969 the Hon. Jean Chrétien as Minister of Indian Affairs and Northern Development issued a Statement of the Government of Canada on Indian Policy, 1969 which stated that:

- Canada has changed greatly since the first Indian Act was passed.
- Past policy of separation had become a burden.
- Previously Indians only had two choices: live in a reserve community or lose their Indian identity.
- Indian people have the right to full and equal participation in the cultural, social, economic and political life of Canada.
- Indians were persuaded that property taxes were an unnecessary element in their lives and hence did not develop services for themselves as in other communities.
- No Canadian should be excluded from participation in community life.
- No Canadian should expect to withdraw from community life and still enjoy the benefits that flow to those who participate.
- New policy offers a third choice, a full role in Canadian society and in the economy while retaining, strengthening and developing an Indian identity which preserves the good things of the past and helps Indian people to prosper and thrive.

These policies were to be implemented through adequate communication among all people of Indian descent and between them and the Canadian community as a whole with programs for:

1. *Legal Structure:* Legislative and constitutional bases of discrimination must be removed.
2. *Indian Cultural Heritage:* There must be positive recognition by everyone of the unique contribution of Indian culture to Canadian society.
3. *Programs and Services:* Services must come through the same channels and from the same government agencies for all Canadians.
4. *Enriched Services:* Those who are farthest behind must be helped most.
5. *Claims and Treaties:* Lawful obligations must be recognized.
6. *Indian Lands:* Control of Indian lands should be transferred to the Indian people.

This 1969 policy statement recognized the central and essential role of the Indian people in solving their own problems and provided a nondiscriminatory framework within which, in an atmosphere of freedom, the Indian people could, with other Canadians, work out their own destiny. In effect, these Federal policies were applied in Inuvik's evolution.

Later on March 28, 1972, Hon. Jean Chrétien recapitulated Federal northern policies in the paper "Government of Canada's Objectives on Northern Development in the 70's". The aim was to:

1. Provide for a higher standard of living, quality of life and equality of opportunity for northern residents which are compatible with their own preferences and aspirations.
2. Maintain and enhance the northern environment with due consideration to economic and social development.
3. Encourage viable economic development within regions of the Northern Territories so as to realize their potential contribution to the national economy and material well being of Canadians.
4. Realize the potential contribution of the Northern Territories to the social and cultural development of Canada.
5. Further the evolution of self-government in the Northwest Territories.
6. Maintain Canadian sovereignty and security in the North.
7. Develop fully the leisure and recreational opportunities in the Northern Territories.

As a dynamic northern community, Inuvik has benefitted greatly in the implementation of these Federal government northern development policies, and its community strengths have withstood the tests of time.

During the 1950s and 1960s when Inuvik was conceived and built, there was a prevalent frontier development theory which was presented at the time as being "modern". It was not expressed as a single thesis but had evolved from earlier Canadian social economists such as Harold Innes, who wrote a powerful book, titled *The Fur Trade In Canada*, which included early Mackenzie Valley commercial activities. Innes described the overall Canadian social evolution as "staple theory". With the founding of the United Nations and the World Bank a new emphasis was placed on assistance to "third world" and "developing countries" which included studies, education, planning and political evolution for many regions throughout the world. Many books were written on development theory and new institutes were set up to examine related issues. The new Federal government activities in the Lower Mackenzie Region and the Western Arctic were based subconsciously or directly on these new economic theories with the best of intentions.

The results for Inuvik and the Western Arctic can be considered quite successful when compared to other parts of Canada and the world.

Inuvik through southern eyes

Since Inuvik's conception in 1950 there has been extensive media coverage of the community in newspapers, magazines, books, radio and television. Much of the media coverage has been competent and understanding, providing interested Northerners and Southerners with the objective Inuvik situation. There was also considerable sensational media comment on Inuvik.

Writing in the *Globe and Mail* in 1959, Bruce West raised many of the questions that were being asked. Under the heading "A Noble Dream Or A Foolhardy Enterprise" he wrote:

> the cost of building the new town is running into astronomical figures ... it is estimated the project will cost $100 million before it is completed ... as the native population of Aklavik is about 1000, the cost will be $100,000 each which represents a lot of muskrats ... there is a question whether many of the native residents will want to move ... the project may be a laudable gesture on the part of the white man towards the natives or it may be a foolhardy enterprise that may go down as one of the Government's biggest failures (*Globe and Mail*, 23 May 1959).

In 1962, the same writer presented a more favourable slant. Under the heading "Far North's Place Of Man Good Place For Women Too", West wrote:

> Inuvik is an "astonishing community ... a sparkling town that looks like a pleasant place not only for man but for women and children too ... neat buildings finished in various bright and pleasant colours ... ubiquitous utilidor, an unlovely device but the brilliant answer to the problem of providing the normal comforts to the families who live in this stern land ... the Hudson's Bay Co. store has a self-service groceteria just like the stores 'up south' ... fine landing strip where even DC-8s of Pacific Western Airlines can arrive and depart ... (*Globe and Mail*, 3 July 10, 1962).

Sounding a very different note, Farley Mowat, writing in *Canada North*, used these phrases to describe Inuvik:

> a showplace costing many millions ... elegant homes ... linked by a multi-branched umbilicus known as a utilidor ... but called the 'tin lizard' by Indians and Eskimos ... which linked the fine homes for government people ... but arranged nothing for the Indians and Eskimos ... [who] had to live outside the 'utilidor palace' ... in West Inuvik, one of Canada's newest slums ... without sanitation or water ... (Mowat 1967).

John Honigman, in his 1970 book *Arctic Townsmen*, wrote:

> Over 150 years there has been a considerable degree of assimilation on the part of local people to the Eurocanadian culture but it has not acted as a melting pot ... other populations funneled into the Delta from the Central Arctic, the upper Mackenzie Valley, Yukon Territory and southern Canada. In the process, the Delta acquired a permanent

population. Before it had been a place where both Indians and Eskimos visited but neither group had settled because the area could not provide the diet they were accustomed to. That limitation disappeared once stores began to stock flour, lard and a variety of other foodstuffs .... Around 1906 numerous Alaskan Eskimo moved to the Delta where they introduced their recently learned brewing practice ... more Alaskans came in the late 1940s ... Schools were defended and helped to make English a language shared by all ethnic groups, allowing communication between themselves and the rest of Canada. The schools brought together Indian, Métis and Eskimo children who continued to live together afterwards ... [and] contributed to the social integration of native Inuvik" (Honigman 1970).

Steve Hume in 1973 wrote:

Canadians, and the news media that serve them, must shed romance for reality if together they are to assist in the development of Canada's North. The trouble with the North is tomorrow. Too much of it is happening too soon. The trouble with the media, on the other hand, is yesterday. The media and Canadians are plugged into the past in the frames of reference used to evaluate how and why things happen in the North. Viewing and presenting the North as a treasure chest of resources waiting to be developed and as the last untamed wilderness are 19th century visions. Few see the North for what it really is, an extremely complex society faced with incredible change. Abandon the common clichés and stereotypes (*Edmonton Journal*, 8 March 1973).

The differences in perspective were clearly evident in discussions about northern development and possible effects on the environment.

Len Cardinal, an Inuvik native contractor, said in 1977 that "too many northern natives have been spoiled by the government and should get off welfare because they feel the country owes them a living without having to work for it." He pointed out that there was little concern about the land until the pipeline proposals arrived and noted the mythology about the delicate Arctic ecology and environment, which "can generally look after itself in competition with people" (*Oilweek* 1 August 1977).

Dr. Max Dunbar, professor of zoology at McGill University, has pointed out that the Arctic's reputation for fragility is based on possible damage to the tundra, a serious hazard which is now well understood and easily avoidable. He said "the Arctic environment is not fragile, certainly when compared to other dynamic ecosystems such as the tropical rain forests" (*Canadian Research & Development*, March-April 1993).

Yet "the fragile Arctic environment" has remained a common theme in national media for more than 30 years. Perhaps the myth remains so strong because "Never in the history of the world were there so many experts on any variety of subjects that affect all walks of life as there are today in the North. A good portion of them don't live there, have little likelihood of ever doing so, and others never in the past, present or future will ever set foot in the country" (Stuart Hodgson, Commissioner of the Northwest Territories, quoted in the *Edmonton Journal*, 2 November 1973).

Since 2003, Permafrost Media's internet presentation of world and national news items that affect Inuvik and the North provides new opportunities for all northern stake holders to see what is being reported about them. Anne Crossman of New North Networks in Inuvik emails early every weekday morning a selection of socio-economic and political stories. With this current information, northern leaders can take immediate action to support, oppose or correct the national and international media impressions which influence present and future northern developments. This service provides an opportunity for understanding and progress that was not available before in the time of limited media access, when Northerners were generally not aware of what was being written about them.

A natural community

The oft-cited view that everything was planned for Inuvik is quite misleading. There were so many planners and plans that Inuvik, in effect, just evolved naturally. Delta people tend to handle problems with the thought "If there's a problem, don't worry. It will go away." This pacific attitude is applied to both individuals and material things. For Inuvik, there were so many outside saviours solving problems that the community leaders just relaxed and allowed natural community evolution to work. As a result, all Inuvik residents have benefitted.

As a "planned community" with flexible designs, all aspects of Inuvik living have blended into creative success. Problems have been addressed and solved on local terms. Now Inuvik is a cultural mosaic with the positive blending of Canadian and world societies. Native residents look out for themselves whether they choose to live traditionally on the land and small communities or to live in the larger Inuvik community. Inuvik's diverse culture demands mutual respect as an individual's freedom is dependent on every other person's freedom whether in agreement or culturally different. Inuvik has not had a racial caste system despite efforts from Southern media and activist groups to heighten ethnic differences.

Social, cultural and political aspects were added to economic considerations in the new frontier development theory. Brundtland's 1987 United Nations Commission on the Environment and Development introduced sustainable development for growth with a human face. Education was seen as the most significant activity to assist a people to become viable and independent (Brundtland 1987). This goal blended well with the traditional Eskimo theory of total education, "Illihavik", where teaching involves all life skills and is a family responsibility.

Adaptations to "modern living"

Cece McCauley, a veteran business leader, former chief of Inuvik Native Band and land claims negotiator, wrote recently in *News North* that "I'm like this old Indian who said once in Inuvik 'I don't like this government! I like Hudson Bay and the mission government!' At least we knew where we were going and what to expect. HBC taught us about debit and credit and the missions taught us to read and write and about religion. Simple as that – no promises and we didn't expect anything" (*News North*, February 11, 2008).

During the 1940s and 1950s most Delta residents and family groups were independent and modern, using the latest technologies such as schooners, quality rifles, radios, and adequate accommodation. Their lifestyle was supported by high fur prices. Their children attended school in Aklavik. Technology was brought in by the many Southern trappers who lived in the Delta. When East 3 and Inuvik opportunities evolved, many Delta residents moved in as contractors and employees. In effect, the Delta residents were ready for Inuvik and its community advantages. The evolution of Inuvik involved integration, not assimilation.

Prior to Inuvik's founding, most of the Mackenzie Delta population was based in bush camps and predominantly lived off the land. With the opportunities of education, health, employment and entertainment, local people naturally migrated to Inuvik following the same rural-to-urban trends happening elsewhere in Canada. NWT Commissioner Ben Sivertz compared the North's community evolution to parts of Quebec, where in one generation the population changed from predominantly rural and agricultural to urban and industrial (Sivertz 1959).

Inuvik residents have successfully lived the social programs coming from modern frontier development theory. That the development process was working well is shown by the rapid rate of change and participation of indigenous residents. Gwich'in Chief Jim Koe, speaking to a *Toronto Star* reporter in 1963, said that his ambition was "to have educated Indians wrest control of the North from the whites." His son, Fred, made use of the education and employment opportunities to become Director of Economic Development for the Inuvik region and later was elected as the Inuvik MLA.

Inuvik schools were often criticized for taking away aboriginal culture and not teaching the life skills of trapping and subsistence existence. This situation has been largely rectified with the hiring of native teachers and including outdoor programs in the curriculum. In the early years this was not possible as local teachers had not been trained and at the time there was little interest shown by Inuvik parents.

The Mackenzie Delta's Inuvialuit and Gwich'in residents settled their land claims with the Federal government with considerable funding and now have recognized group rights to land and resources. They chose a form of communitarianism where the interests of communities and groups take precedence over those of the individual. Some consider the rights settlements as "assimilation" while others consider it as "integration." Julius Grey writing in September 2007 said "'Assimilation' is odious when force is used to achieve it… But it's positive when citizens of varied origins in an open society live together. It is not a one-way street as each group can learn and improve their well being from the other" (*Globe and Mail* 13 September 2007).

Social relations

Inuvik institutions including schools, hostels, hospital, government administration and businesses have been severely criticized by individuals and groups with special agendas. Unfortunately, this condemnation is a worldwide phenomenon with roots in past injustices which generally are no longer relevant. For example, youth abuse at Inuvik hostels was not an issue until after they were closed, while a much greater problem of abuse within Inuvik families was ignored.

Many community leaders have been harassed while trying to help improve the quality of Inuvik life. There is a need for awareness of the impossible decisions facing government, welfare and church officials, confronted with children often suffering from abuse and neglect, of the sacrifice and heroism of many who cared for them, of their honourable humanitarian desire to provide education and opportunity. There have been difficult times for many Inuvik "providers" to keep their cool while being punished for helping.

Most residents support criminal charges for specific offending individuals but oppose the concept of bringing old grievances into the present by formal apologies or cash payments. They believe that present day politicians and taxpayers should not be held responsible for what happened in earlier times for which they were not directly responsible.

The "shameful legacy of residential schools" is a phrase often applied to Inuvik's Grollier Hall and Stringer Hall student residences, but there is little justification for such a statement. The Inuvik situation was different from that of southern Canada. Basically these hostels were well run and assisted many youth who had no other choice. Any student abuse in the hostels has to be considered in context with northern times, as apparently during the same period, there was considerable child abuse in homes of both locals and outsiders.

The rhetoric of group victimhood can strongly affect perceptions of Inuvik. A simplistic view of group dynamics insists that every aboriginal is oppressed, every white person is a racist and every institution is discriminatory. An examination of Inuvik's history and present day situation confirms that these persistent claims of victimhood have little validity for Inuvik. However these claims can turn into a terrible trap, nourishing white guilt and racism, and deflecting attention away from obvious local problems such as the school drop-out rates, Fetal Alcohol Syndrome, substance abuse and incest. Exploiting aboriginal feelings of victimhood has become big business for several northern natives and for others, mainly lawyers.

Environmental concern

Inuvik is the only Mackenzie Valley community that started off with the environmental ethic of protecting its natural vegetation. All of the other communities cut down the trees in and around the settlements for firewood. During Inuvik's initial construction any contractor who unnecessarily damaged the trees and vegetation was fired. Curt Merrill worked hard to protect the broad band of spruce trees along the north side of Mackenzie Road between Bompass Street and Tuma Drive, but unfortunately when the road drainage altered the soil conditions, these trees had all died by 1970.

The Town Council passed a Community Plan Bylaw for protecting trees and vegetation. The initial rule required Council approval to cut down any tree greater than 6 inches in diameter. However, in recent years the Delta environment has suffered from the large number of trees cut for fuel in winter along lakes, creeks and riverbanks, despite Forestry regulations requiring any cutting to be at least 50 feet back from the water edge. Airport Creek in particular has been badly trashed by snowmobilers hauling in firewood.

In the longer term, world environmental change appears to provide a significant risk for Inuvik residents who live on permafrost in a low-lying area. Should the world temperature rise, the permafrost melt and the ocean levels increase significantly there would certainly be problems. However, it would be much more productive to adapt to any changes when they happen rather than just attend meetings and travel to distant capitals. As environmental change is continuous, it is better to adapt to it than to fight it. Inuvik should predict the consequences and prepare to deal with them, find advantages, minimize disadvantages and deal with the effects. As global warming appears to be a religion and not science, research and open debates are essential. Data from the Inuvik Research Lab's neutron monitor, which has operated continuously since 1964, indicates that the current global warming panic relates to sunspot activity and that there could be the reality of global cooling in the future.

Inuvik Without Berger?

Although it is heretical to question the activities and recommendations of the 1974-to-1978 Berger Commission, there is a haunting question of "What would Inuvik and the North be like today if the Berger Inquiry hadn't happened?" Northern democracy was established and dynamic at the time with an elected native majority on the NWT Council and most community councils. Self-government by these councils could have developed better social, environmental and economic solutions than those provided by Berger's well-funded external group.

Berger held 275 days of hearings, heard from over 1600 people and created 50,000 pages of transcript. Berger stated that his inquiry cost over $5.3 million (Berger 1977). When the costs for CBC radio and television services plus government expenses and industry outlays are added, the overall estimated cost of the inquiry was at least $10 million.

During the Commission hearings and afterwards there were many criticisms voiced, including:

- Berger had a large staff of at least 75 people but not one of them was a native.
- Berger sent an organizing group into each community to "set the stage" for each hearing with no opportunity for criticism or alternate viewpoints.
- Large response funds were provided to special interest groups on an arbitrary basis.
- Berger said different things to different groups such as the Inuvik Inuvialuit and Chamber of Commerce.

- Berger lived in the $600-a-night Factors Suite at the Explorer Hotel in Yellowknife while championing the "poor Northerner".
- Berger had not been to the Northwest Territories before he started his pipeline inquiry.
- Berger virtually ignored that democracy was alive and well throughout the Northwest Territories at the municipal, territorial and federal levels with effective native control before the Commission started.
- The Berger Commission was a "native rip off" and the North would have been better off without the delays and "apartheid" development he fostered.

The prime risk with the Berger Commission was that the Mackenzie Valley gas pipeline would not be built, and that all of the community infrastructure of education, medical facilities, housing, and utilities built up in Inuvik and along the Mackenzie Valley would not be utilized. The large capital expense advanced by southern Canadians would be left on the books, without the income generated from petroleum production and transportation. Northerner employment and training experience and business infrastructure would be wasted.

Prime Minister Jean Chrétien, in his book *Straight From The Heart*, stated that "Berger's mandate was to tell us how to build the pipeline. Instead he told us not to build it … for ten years … it took a bargaining tool away from the Indians. The minute the pipeline was stopped, there was no more pressure to settle the native claims" (Chrétien 1985).

On the day that the Berger report was released some 300 senior students, graduates and school dropouts in Inuvik signed a petition expressing their concern for their future and urging the government to proceed with pipeline plans (United Church of Canada, 16 May 1977).

The impact of the Berger Inquiry confirmed Inuvik residents' fears. While Berger recommended a ten-year delay in constructing a pipeline, the actual result was worse – pipeline development was stopped for at least a generation. The effect on employment prospects for northerners was dramatic.

Allan Fotheringham, a columnist for the *Vancouver Sun*, suggested that allowing Berger "to make his own pronouncements on the social, environmental and economic aspects of the Mackenzie Valley pipeline was comparable to one person holding up the building of the CPR across Canada many years before" (*CBC News In Review*, December 2001).

As Tom Zukbo, a life-time local resident, businessman and one-time mayor, said in 2008, the actions of the far-away government in Ottawa "left the majority of capable young northerners with only one practical career prospect – to involve themselves in regulatory hearings and reviews as a board member or consultant. Then they could chase those per diem fees." The legacy, which remains clearly evident today, is that "The regulatory process expands, everyone makes money at the taxpayers' expense and nothing gets done" (*Nickle's Daily Oil Bulletin*, 11 February 2008).

The Miracle of Inuvik

The miracle of Inuvik is that, from its beginnings in the 1950s to the present, all social, economic, government, and industry groups have cooperated to develop a better community.

Inuvik does have a future as it is the administrative centre for a large part of the Canadian North, around 500,000 square kilometres and one eighth of Canada. The region's petroleum resource potential will continue to be developed and tourism will thrive with national and international visitors. Any problems will be met and solved by residents who are accustomed to working together for mutual benefit.

This miracle started in Aklavik where all the interest groups got together and moved in the same direction to Inuvik. As nobody was forced to come to Inuvik, or forced to stay, Inuvik's beginnings were natural. For those who griped about the Inuvik situation the standard rebuttal was "If you don't like it here, go back to where you came from!"

During its first 50 years Inuvik has been dynamic with many threads making up its strong fabric. It has experienced rural-urban trends as in the rest of Canada. Its aboriginal residents have lived off the land, and have been involved in industry and petroleum exploration. The town has had many visitors, and new residents from east, west and south, due to its proximity to Yukon, Alaska and Alberta. Residents have observed aboriginal religious practices, Christian religious practices, and many others. The town has been of national strategic importance, for military reasons and because of its resources. Due to its arctic delta location, Inuvik is at the confluence of very distinct ecozones, and as a result it has been a meeting place for very distinct aboriginal cultures. These are just a few of the factors that continue to make Inuvik such a vibrant social experience.

Concluding Reflections

No matter who comes to Inuvik, for whatever reason, they will find new and distinctive experiences. John and Irma Honigman wrote that "Outsiders can be just as much affected by northern culture as the other way around" (Honigman 1970). For the many people involved in the Inuvik story it has been a shared experience with mutual respect.

Although I was actively involved in Inuvik politics, I have tried to present Inuvik activities impartially. I have been very supportive of social responsibility for all groups and was vigorously involved in bringing self-government to Inuvik. As a matter of principle and from familiarity with ethnic evolution in other countries, I purposely stayed out of Inuvik's native politics. I believed that I could be most helpful in providing information and encouraging groups to make their own decisions, without imposing the prejudices of another southern "manipulator". This was a difficult position as many native leaders strongly criticized my alleged inaction and accused me of being racist and against them. The success of the Inuvialuit and Gwich'in groups in Inuvik in finalizing their land claims confirms the correctness of my standoff position.

I believe that Inuvik has been a highly successful community in many ways, due in large part to the initiative and co-operation of its diverse residents. Nevertheless, the town must grapple with many problems, some of them common to many towns and others quite specific to Inuvik's unique circumstances.

As a government researcher and as an Inuvik resident, I had several administrative frustrations such as finding the Federal government's early northern social research programs funded and controlled by nonresident Southerners. Also, I was disappointed that none of the many social research projects in Inuvik picked up on Inuvik's obvious FAS (Fetal Alcohol Syndrome) problems, or the epidemic of parental apathy, or the improper selection, treatment and maintenance of wood piles under buildings.

Researchers and advisors came in waves relating to Inuvik development, technical problems, social issues, resource utilization and native rights. There are many articulate individuals influencing Inuvik residents so that real problems are often missed, even though residents are asked to attend endless meetings and are consulted to the point of boredom about trivial details.

I sense that the Federal solution for native rights has tended to weaken Town Council responsibilities through the legal and financial strengths given to native organizations. Currently, self-government provisions enshrined in both the Inuvialuit and Gwich'in claim settlements have created a difficulty for many Inuvik residents, as the process appears to be in conflict with both municipal government and native government. Steps towards self-government were taken by the Inuvik Council by including an Inuvialuit and a Gwich'in representative at the Council table. Some argue that they will lose land and treaty rights with a self-government agreement. Also, there could be legal action from claim beneficiaries if the land claim and treaty rights aren't fully protected.

Optimists think that self-government can be worked out in the typical Inuvik spirit of cooperation. Democracy is alive and well in the North. But one result of the development of separate native organizations, stimulated by many factors including the effect of the Berger Inquiry, is that there are multiple levels of authority and local democracy has been poorly served.

The combination of Federal funding, excitement about possible petroleum development, and self-government negotiations has led to a collection of little feudal systems with their individual agendas, and little action toward resident betterment and community improvements. There are as many organizations in the North as the Federal government funds. If a government pays people to be different, they will be different.

Inuvik's mixture of Inuvialuit, Gwich'in and others provides a classic situation for understanding ethnic relations. The national issue of aboriginal group rights vs individual rights provides insight applicable to all Canada. Through the native claims settlements, Inuvialuit and Gwich'in groups are very successful. However, many question the communitarian aspects of claims and would prefer to promote individual rights, so that individuals would be treated as special citizens integrated into Canadian society and not members of a tribal collective. As Pierre Trudeau wrote in *Cite Libre*, "ethnically based governments are by nature intolerant, discriminatory and, when all is said and done, totalitarian" (*Cite Libre* 1960).

The "two hand" approach that I applied as Mayor applies to Inuvik's current issues. There are two sides involved in everything and I have respect for both sides whether I agree or not. For example, the Inuvik school hostels provided an education opportunity for students from distant settlements and camps at the time when there was no alternative. Student abuse cannot be tolerated. At the same time the hostels provided a home for orphans and children whose parents chose to abandon them.

Today, the old fashioned values of helping and sharing remain in Inuvik. Race relations between native groups and with "others" are good. The entry of women into the workforce is relatively new but highly successful in Inuvik. For most Inuvik residents there is mobility within the North and to the South. Hunting and trapping remains a viable pursuit for interested Inuvik residents, with greater success on weekends, holidays or during evenings after work. Most Inuvik residents are not excited by outside pressures or radical concepts. They apply "ayorama", an Inuit concept for situations beyond one's control where "it can't be helped".

Rapid social change has been the norm in Inuvik and everywhere around the world. Fortunately for Inuvik residents, there's always change and there's always choice.

Acknowledgments

It has taken many years to collect the information presented here and to shape it into a presentable format. Most of the information was collected before the availability of the internet and Google searches. The study started as a social responsibility and has evolved into an obsession. I felt a responsibility to write down the many Inuvik information bits before they were lost or forgotten. Most of the information and data included here came from personal files, diaries and recollections. Several sections are not complete due to my innocence and selective memory.

There are several books on Inuvik and area that provide comment on Inuvik's development including:

> *The Mysterious North*, Pierre Berton, 1956
> *Mackenzie Delta Area, NWT*, J. Ross Mackay, 1963
> *Arctic Townsmen*, John and Irma Honigman, 1970
> *On Blue Ice: The Inuvik Adventure*, Jane Stoneman-McNichol, 1983
> *The Aklavik Journal*, Bern Will Brown, 1996
> *The Changing North*, Jack Grainge, 1999
> *Arctic Journal II*, Bern Will Brown, 1999
> *Natural History of the Western Arctic*, Western Arctic Handbook Committee, 2002

Information on current Inuvik activities were available from copies of the *Drum* newspaper and CBC Inuvik daily news broadcasts. A Northern Information clipping service of newspaper and magazine comment on Inuvik developments was initiated in 1970. Also, verbatims of pertinent CBC Inuvik broadcasts started in 1971. These news items were distributed to interested Inuvik residents so they would be more aware of what reporters were saying about community activities.

Retrospect: 50 Years

Every effort has been made to insure the completeness and accuracy of information but lack of space, personal knowledge and data blanks have left many significant gaps with projects and individuals unintentionally left out. More community detail is presented on Inuvik's earlier years, although I have included a brief overview of recent developments to carry the story right up to Inuvik's 50th birthday.

As no one can write a book alone, I have benefitted from the opinions, encouragement and support of many people. Effort has been made to provide correct event dates and accurate name spelling. Comments and criticism on the contents in this Inuvik story are welcomed as they will stimulate discussion and better understanding amongst all involved. Hopefully, those who disagree or find fault with information in this study will contact me directly for correction or explanation.

In the sense that "the past is unpredictable", future generations will undoubtedly see Inuvik's history differently from the way it is presented here. So be it.

Dick Hill
43 Niagara Street
Collingwood, Ontario L9Y 3X1
phone 705-446-2947
email dickhill@rogers.com
April 2008

John Diefenbaker's Speech at Inuvik's Dedication Ceremonies, July 21, 1961

Today is an occasion – for you, for me, and for the Western Arctic. We are here – all of us – to join in dedicating a town for which there is no counterpart in Canada. How else can I speak of such an opening ceremony but as an act of dedication? A promise made to the future of the north and its people, and to Canada.

Everywhere I look today with the fresh eyes of a stranger to the western arctic, history comes rushing to meet me. First the colourful history of this region of the Mackenzie Delta and the Western Arctic coast – history that the fathers and grandfathers of many of you helped to make. History – some of it – that had time to find its way into books and the children are learning about in the schools to remind them to be proud of a northern heritage.

Explorers and Missionaries

Here at Inuvik – in the beautiful Sir Alexander Mackenzie School, in Grollier Hall and Stringer Hall – you have the best possible reminder of the lives of men who dared the north as it was in those days equipped with little more than courage. This is why our largest schools in the Northwest Territories, and the student residences associated with them, bear famous names – of explorers and missionaries – names known and honoured not only in the north but far beyond it.

First Prime Minister North of Arctic Circle

That is one kind of history. And there is history of another sort in the fact that I am here with you today – the first Canadian Prime Minister to travel north of the Arctic Circle. I could not help thinking as we flew north from Fort Simpson – and this vast unrolling landscape kept pushing the horizons always farther away – of another Prime Minister of Canada, the first. I thought of Sir John A. MacDonald and how he would have wished to be at this ceremony today.

It was just 75 years ago that Sir John made his famous journey to the west coast by the newly-completed trans-continental railway – an event full of the drama of nation-building. He sparked the imagination of Canadians with his vision of a greater Canada – one that would stretch from coast to coast. How he would have relished this moment – his coast to coast dream immeasurably enlarged by this north-south dimension which I doubt ever occurred to that quick mind or for that matter some our better brains of today. For too long we have forgotten the Arctic.

Only A Future For Inuvik

And there is a third kind of history. The history we are making today and that you will make here in the years to come. This is a town with no past to leave behind – only the future to look to. The future not of one race, or two, but of the people of all cultures who choose to make it their home.

The monument is more than a striking design added to the Western Arctic landscape. Its meaning goes deeper than that. The design symbolizes the friendship and mutual aid of the peoples and governments – the federal and territorial governments and the people of the wide community of the Mackenzie Delta. Its three bronze arches curve strongly upwards from a secure base. The foundation of a friendship that will withstand any weather. The arches meet at the apex in a shining dome that mirrors the trees. In winter the outline will be furred by snow. Snow as clean and free from city grime as the winter pelt of an Arctic fox.

Permafrost

I wish I could see Inuvik in winter – a town with fewer chimneys surely than any town in Canada and with no furnaces to stoke! I – who am no engineer – can only guess at the number and complexity of the construction problems that had to be solved to raise up such a town. I say "raise" because it is the word to describe Inuvik – a town built above the permafrost, resting on piles frozen solid as iron. How many thousand piles must have been cut, hauled, and driven in by steam jet to create the foundations! If Inuvik should ever follow Yellowknife's example and adopt an insignia surely a pile driver rampant should surmount the shield!

One does not have to be an engineer to realize that the construction of Inuvik must have called on the full resources of Canada's Arctic building research. For so far north, you are contending with some of the most difficult frost conditions in Canada. And we are not a country that had been engaged in large-scale Arctic construction in the past like some other northern countries. Canadians have never attempted to build a town comparable to this so far north.

Construction

Great reserves of resourcefulness and ingenuity had to be summoned to work out new and special types of construction. You will say – and I agree – that since 40% of our country lies north of the provinces it was time we took major Arctic construction seriously. Inuvik is the teacher, which will stimulate the thirst for more knowledge of the Arctic. I am glad that some many of the men whose work contributed to the building of Inuvik have found it possible to be here today. They must feel proud of their work. They do not need this monument although they must share in it. Their best monuments are all around them. All that the architects, the engineers and the many men who worked for them could do, they have done. Now the future of your community lies in the large part in your hands – to carry the spirit of cooperation that built Inuvik into the years ahead. And they will be important years – for Canada and for the north.

The interesting thing about Inuvik is that it is a modern town yet with the most unmistakable Arctic characteristics. And I do not mean only in the pile construction or the system of utilidors that act as such vital supply lines for essential community service. I do not minimize that fact that here – almost with sight of the northern seas – is a town with amenities that many others of comparable size in southern Canada could envy – school, churches, hospital, a power plant, radio station, hotel, stores, dwellings …. These are essentials. But what gives them purpose and meaning to the north is people.

Appendix A: Diefenbaker's 1961 Dedication Speech

Residents

Our northern territories today include many different types of residents – more than at any time in the past. And many of them are here today. There are those born in the north – second- and third-generation families from many different countries of the world. There are the Indians, the Eskimos and the Metis who have shared with them – and still do – life on the land in all sorts of economic weather. There are men and women from southern Canada and other countries who – years ago – came north, made it their adopted land and would not now live anywhere else. And there are the most recent immigrants of all – the men and women whose duties have taken them in the north in recent years, sometimes for long periods, sometimes only on field trips. They are the scientists and the engineers, the administrators, doctors, nurses, teachers, technical experts, welfare workers – a cross section of many of Canada's most respected professions who are here to work for the north and with Northerners.

Local Workers

This was not a town that Canadians from the south came north and constructed single-handed. Far from it. Built into the town – in places we cannot see – thousands of man hours of work put there by men from surrounding communities of all races. This urgent need for local labour was in fact utilized in the most practical way and made part of the government's program of vocational education. Young Eskimos, Loucheux Indians and Métis worked side by side. Some had taken a training course in the use of heavy equipment out of the north and came back to jobs waiting for them. But for the majority of young trainees this was the first job of its kind that they had ever worked on.

I do not need to remind you – with the facilities you have here for the industrial arts at the Sir Alexander Mackenzie School – how much importance the government attaches to vocational education. This is as true in the rest of Canada as it is in the north where, as you know, vocational training is built right into the curriculum wherever facilities can be provided. Life is hard now on the unskilled and the half-skilled, no matter where they live, north or south. In the Territories this type of trade skill is more than acquiring the ability to drive a bulldozer or build a house or run an engine. It is a particularly vital form of insurance in an economy where the game is subject to cycles and demand affected by the whims of the fur market.

Floods

I have learned with deep regret of the floods suffered this spring by the Aklavik area with the tragic loss of fur-bearing animals, and the hardship this brought to many trappers, many perhaps relatives and friends of yours. Happily, there seems to have been no loss of human life. But 61 families, I am told, had to be evacuated from their homes at Aklavik and many others must have suffered varying degrees of inundation and flood damage. Floods of this proportion – though they be exceptional – illustrate the threat that hangs over a community whose foundations are so much at the mercy of the river.

Education

When I see the Sir Alexander MacKenzie School and the residences I regret – and I know that Mrs. Diefenbaker does too – that we are here too late to see the children. When one flies here – even though we flew over a relatively small part of this immense Mackenzie Delta – it is not difficult to know why the problem of providing education for the children who live in far-off hunting camps has to be solved by air lift.

Racial Diversity

Our northern schools have a responsibility even wider than to their own people. Through them Canada has an opportunity that is unique to show the rest of the world that we mean what we say when express our views on race discrimination. Those of you who are familiar with the Bill of Rights I advocated for some many years and Parliament enacted into law for them will know how strongly I feel about discrimination. But here in Inuvik there is more than an invitation to show our deep distaste of according privileges to one race that are not available to another. It is a wholly positive opportunity to show the future of the north will be influenced by young people who have been taught in a way to honour their racial distinctiveness. This is a pride of race that has no taint of arrogance. It is a source of strength.

Research

As you know, the government is building a centre here for Arctic research – for research into resources, into a wide range of problems and possibilities common to an Arctic environment. Its facilities are not limited to government scientists but are to be available to industry and the universities too, research is yet another field where Canada takes her northern responsibilities seriously. It is teamed with what we have done with roads, communications, mining, agriculture, surveying and community development.

World Peace

Perhaps with stimulus from all these developments Canadians will become more conscious of their tri-oceanic inheritance. It took us a long time to progress from the Atlantic watersheds to the shores of the Pacific, but, we did it. Now, there looms the horizon of the Arctic and all it might hold in wealth, knowledge of climate and peace in the world.

Our northern territories look toward a future that few Canadians would have pictured for them even a few years ago. You, and your neighbours in Aklavik and other neighbouring communities, live on wide horizons.

Circumpolar Cooperation

You have a brand new monument in a brand new town. In its graceful upward curves it could be a symbol of the world. It is a symbol of racial unity yet at the same time its sphere is the contour of the world. What could be more appropriate than this new "world" emerging above the Arctic Circle out of the spirit of cooperation that built your town? It is this world – a new world for all the people of the Arctic regions – that we in Canada are working to build.

Inuvik Town Council Members By Term, 1970 – 2007

*served part term

Year	Mayor	Deputy Mayor	Councillors	Manager/SAO
1970-71	Dick Hill	Tom Butters* Barney MacNeil*	Gordon Campbell Frank Hansen Tom Yate Jim Robertson Gary Wagner Agnes Semmler Victor Allen* Alex Illasiak*	Dave Prowse
1972-73	Leonard Holman	Barney MacNeil	Gordon Campbell Doug Bailey Doug Dittrich Frank Hansen Fred Carmichael Les Gardiner* Brian Cousins John Roska Ismail Alunik* Julian Tsafaroff*	Al Algar
1974-75	Leonard Holman* Jim Robertson*	Frank Hansen	Barney MacNeil John Hill Bertha Allen Ellen Binder Jack Heath* Malcolm McConnell Earl Holley Alex Foreman Gwen Davis Susie Huskey John Roska Carrol Bennett	Al Algar

1976-77	Jim Robertson	Jack Heath	Gwen Davis Bertha Allen John Komaromi John Roska Ellen Binder Art Polen Susie Huskey Carrol Bennett Cynthia Hill Tom Zubko Terry Buckle	Don Cave
1978	Jim Robertson	Jack Heath	Cynthia Hill Tom Zubko John Komaromi Terry Buckle Susie Huskey John Burch	Don Cave
1979-80	Cynthia Hill	Alex Foreman Dan Holman*	John Hill Tom Zubko John Komaromi Terry Buckle Bill Farmer Susie Huskey Carrol Bennett Dave Northrop Pauline Duggan	Don Cave
1981-82	Cynthia Hill	Dan Holman Barry Clarkson*	Doug Billingsley Tom Zubko Susie Huskey Pauline Duggan Dave Northrop Gary Kaulbach John Komaromi Edward Lennie Gordon Campbell	Don Cave Dan Strelioff
1983-84	Jim Robertson	John Hill	Rita Pasiciel Tom Zubko Carrol Bennett Edward Lennie Gary Kaulbach Don Cave Gordon Campbell Steve Roche	Elaine Lavigne

1985-86	John Hill	Carrol Bennett	Tom Zubko	Elaine Lavigne
			Don Cave	
			Barry Clarkson	
			Gordon Campbell	
			John McEachern	
			Victoria Boudreau	
			Paul Komaromi	
			Dan Holman	
			Bruce Barr*	
1987-88	Gordon Campbell	Victoria Boudreau*	Roger Israel	Diane Cheyney
		Don Cave*	Paul Komaromi	
			Jeff Gardiner	
			Alan Davis	
			Dan Holman	
			Bruce Barr	
			Terry Fellows	
			Roger Allen	
1989-90	John Hill	Cynthia Hill	Paul Komaromi	Diane Cheyney
			Roger Israel	
			Loretta Balsom	
			Arlene Hansen	
			Larry Gordon	
			Dave Sullivan	
			Tom Zubko	
			Vince Sharp	
			Wayne Litster	
			Diana Tingmiak	
			Bob Desautels	
			Doug Billingsley	
			Vivian Hunter	
			Billy Aleekuk	
			Don Patterson	
1991-92	John Hill*	Cynthia Hill	Doug Billingsley	Diane Cheyney
	Cynthia Hill*	Vivian Hunter	Don Patterson	Terry Testart
	Don Patterson*		Bob Desautels	
			Vivian Hunter	
			Billy Aleekuk	
			Diana Tingmiak	
			Shirly Kisoun	
			Vince Sharpe	
			Gordon Campbell	
			Dick Hill	
			Edward Lavoie	

1993-94	Paul Komaromi Tom Zubko*	Tom Zubko	Allan Davis Dennie Lennie Bob Simpson Tom Wright Floyd Roland Gordon Campbell Edward Lavoie Don Cave	Michael Richards
1995-96	Tom Zubko	Dennie Lennie Floyd Roland Bob Simpson*	Don Cave Richard Barnes Harry Joujan Tom Wright Vivian Hunter Allan Davis Gordon Campbell* Dennie Lennie Julian Tomlinson Eddie Kolausok Gary Smith Richard Barnes	Ken Anderson
1997-99	George Roach	Eddie Kolausok* Peter Clarkson	David Connelly* Derek Lindsay Joey Amos* Vince Sharp Vivian Hunter Richard Barnes* Gary Smith** Donna Allen Dan Davis* Don Craik* Shirley Kisoun* Richard Binder Denny Rogers Clarence Wood	Don Howden
2000-03	Peter Clarkson	Arlene Hansen	Richard Binder Don Craik Denny Rogers Gary Smith Clarence Wood George Doolittle Vince Sharpe	Jerry Veltman

Appendix B: Inuvik Town Council Members By Term, 1970–2007

2004-6	Peter Clarkson	Arlene Hansen	Gayle Gruben	Jerry Veltman
			Terry Halifrax	Tom Lie
			Derek Lindsay	
			Denny Rogers	
			Karen King	
			Clarence Wood	
			Paul Komaromi	
			Marja VanNieuwenhuyzen	
			Tom Wright –Gwich'in	
			Shirley Kisoun – Inuvialuit	
			Rebecca Robertson – Youth	
2007–9	Derek Lindsay	Chris Laroque	Vince Brown	Tom Lie
			George Doolittle	Jerry Veltman
			Terry Halifax	Sara Brown
			Grace Loreen	
			Brian McDonald	
			Jim McDonald	
			Clarence Wood	
			Cam MacDonald – Youth	
			Terry Peterson – Gwich'in	
			Gayle Gruben – Inuvialuit	
			Bernie MacNeil – Métis	

Note: Inuvik Council is made up of a Mayor and eight Councillors. Vacant Council positions are filled by appointing a person who ran for Council and through by-elections. The Deputy Mayor is selected from the elected Councillors. Some Councillors in a by-election only serve one year. Councillors served two-year terms up to 1997 and then three-year terms.

APPENDIX C

Inuvik Community Leaders, 1958 – 2008

An arbitrary selection of Inuvik residents who made an extra effort to make Inuvik a better place. All elected Community Councilors are included. There are separate listings where a spouse is known by a different family name or was involved in special activities. When available, information is presented on birth and death, spouse, spouse dates and significant activities.

Jules Adam – 1907-1977, OMI, sometimes known as Joseph. Born on a farm in Belgium 23Nov07, ordained 1935, posted to Aklavik in 1936, arrived Inuvik 1958. Pastor Igloo Church 17 years 1958-1975. Gardener, artist, had extensive 50' × 100' vegetable garden garden behind church rectory with greenhouse and cold frames, proved that vegetables will grow in Inuvik with tender care. semi-retirement at Aklavik August 1975, died in Belgium 26Jul77.

Len Adrian – Fire Chief, IA&ND Works Foreman, moved to Yellowknife.

Rosie Albert – 1934- , *(Freddy 1932-1988)*, Inukialuktun teacher. Daughter of Alex Stefansson, went back to school in 1979 and earned a teaching degree, Berger Inquiry interpreter, retired in 1998.

Bill Aleekuk – *(Louise)*, Aircraft engineer, Town Council 1991, left in 1971 back in 1985, Air Safety Inspector in 1998.

Charlene Alexander – Photographer. Co-founder with Sue Rose of Great Northern Arts Festival in 1988. Moved to Whitehorse.

Bertha Allen – 1934- , *(Victor)*, from Old Crow, came to school in Aklavik, Town Council 1973, Order of Canada 2007.

Roger Allen – *(Vanessa)*, TEST Program, President COPE 1986-87, Mayor of Aklavik, Inuvik Council 1988, NWT MLA 6 Dec 99, NWT Cabinet Minister.

Owen Allen – Delta leader, trapper, spoke at Carrothers Commission hearings in August 1965.

Victor Allen – 1928- *(Bertha)*, Family from Kobuk River area in Alaska, on initial construction team, linguist, Mackenzie Institute instructor, oil industry, CFS driver, *Drum* reporter 1966, Town Council 1971, library, speech at Edmonton Northern Development Conference in November 1963 on "The Eskimo and Indian Today", northern book collector, COPE.

Ishmael Alunik – 1922-2006, *(Ruth 1926-)*, trapper, Town Council 1973, author *Call Me Ishmael* (1998) and *Across Time And Tundra* (2003).

Bob Baetz – *(Greta)*, Baetz Trucking, early entrepreneur, Deputy Mayor Advisory Council in 1967 & 1968, first Chamber of Commerce President in 1964, Lions Club, Territorial Liquor Vendor in 1965, moved to Yellowknife around 1969.

Doug Bailey – *(Bea)*, electrician, moved to NWT in 1959, Deputy Fire Chief, Alano Club, Inuvik & District Aviation Council, Town Council 1971, moved to Campbell River, BC.

Carol Bennett – Arrived in 1968 with CFS Inuvik husband. Polaris Theatre. Town Council 1975.

Doug Billingsley – 1944-1993, *(Vicki)*, to Inuvik in 1973 as NWT Economic Development officer. Norm's Building Supplies in 1978, Town Council 1990-91, Chair of Inuvik Education Committee 1980, President of the Inuvik and District Chamber of Commerce in 1979-80, 1984-86 & 1988, appointed to NWT Water Board in 1985. Peterborough Teacher's College in 1965, Waterloo Lutheran University in 1967, University of Edinborough in 1973 with PhD in Geography. Active in Inuvik Centennial Library, Great Northern Arts Festival & Inuvik Choral & Theatrical Society.

Vicki Billingsley – 1941-2004, *(Doug)*, Norm's Hardware, Inuvik Centennial Library Board, Inuvik Choral and Theatrical Society (ICATS), Great Northern Arts Festival.

Ellen Binder – 1930- , *(Otto)*, arrived in the Delta in 1931 at six months with parents Mikel and Anna Pulk, operated a reindeer herd. Librarian at SAMS school in 1965. Librarian at Inuvik Centennial Library in 1967. Town Council 1967-8.

Richard Binder – IRC wildlife management, Town Council 1998-2000.

Vicki Boudreau – *(Dave)*, Delta Electric, Inuvik Housing, Town Council 1985, Inuvik Library Board.

Bern Will Brown – OMI, set up first RC church in Inuvik, published the *Aklavik Journal* from 1955 to 1957, artist, photographer.

Dick Bulloch – *(Marka)*, Army Signals in Aklavik, member Inuvik Advisory Committee in 1965, DOT radio operator, TEST Program volunteer.

John Burch – Arrived 1969. Ran for Inuvik MLA in 1979, Town Council 1978, taxi driver.

Tom Butters – 1925- , *(Peggy)*, born in Vancouver, to Yukon in 1947, to Inuvik in 1961 as Rehab Manager, Regional Administrator in 1963, started *Inuvik Drum* in 1965, Chair of Inuvik Community Association in August 1963. Offered to buy Departmental House on Lot 10, B l 14 (Aug 1963). Western Arctic and Inuvik MLA 1970-91, many portfolios including Finance and Housing, retired to Gillies Bay, BC.

Gordon Campbell – *(Bertha)*, arrived 1963 from Hay River, DINA Public Works, North Star Construction, Town Council 1970-73, Mayor 1987-88, retired to Yellowknife in July 2007.

Dolly Carmichael – Gwich'in Tribal Council vice-president, Inuvik Native Band

Frank Carmichael – 1900-1964, *(Caroline Kay)*, arrived Aklavik in 1927, began working as a trapper. First elected member of the NWT Legislative Assembly representing Mackenzie West 1951-54 and the new Mackenzie Delta 1954-57, Inuvik Liquor store manager. Active in planning for Inuvik.

Fred Carmichael – 1935- , *(Minnie Lucas)* (1), *(Micki O'Kane)* (2) to Inuvik in 1960 from Aklavik. Pilot's licence in 1954, commercial pilot in 1958, started Reindeer Air Service in 1959, on Inuvik Town Council in 1972, in 1982 started Antler Aviation, Western Arctic Nature Tours in 1990, elected head Gwich'in Tribal Council in November 2000 beating out Richard Nerysoo, in 2002 appointed chair of the Aboriginal Pipeline Group. In February 2006 he was inducted into the Aboriginal Business Hall of Fame. He holds a lifetime honourary membership in the Northern Air Transport Association.

Lloyd Carruthers – Inuvik Liquor store, ICA chairman in 1964 & 1965.

George Castle – Member Inuvik Advisory Committee 1965.

Don Cave – 1937-2004, NCPC stores in 1963, Council Secretary Manager in 1980, TLR Leasing in 1983, Councilor 1983-1991, Arctic Tire in 1988, Justice of the Peace for 10 years, Fire Department from 1963-1983.

Peter Clarkson – *(Sue)*, to Inuvik in 1986, GNWT biologist, Gwich'in Renewable Resources Board, Council, Mayor -2006, GNWT Regional Director 2006.

Lloyd Cole – *(Dorothy)*, to East 3 in 1958. Inuvik Community Association 1965, Postmaster.

Eddie Cook – *(Mary)*, from Good Hope, appointed Indian Agent at East Three in 1957, at the time Eddie had been a government employee for 11 years.

Nellie Joy Cournoyea – 1940- , born in Aklavik to Maggie and Nils Hvatum, worked for CBC Inuvik as an announcer/operator and as manager. In 1969 co-founded the Committee for Original Peoples Entitlement (COPE) to act as a native rights organization. She was active in negotiating the Inuvialuit land claim settled in 1984. She was first elected for the Nunakput (Tuktoyaktuk) riding in 1979 and held numerous cabinet portfolios between 1983 and her selection as government leader in 1991. Government leader (premier) 1991-1995. She retired from politics after her one term as government leader and became president of the Inuvialuit Regional Corporation. Awarded Honourary Doctorate at University of Toronto on 5 June 1996. Honourary degree at Carlton University on Jun 12, 1996. Elected to IRC chair first in 1996. Chair of the Inuvik Region Health and Social Services Board. Founding chair of the Aboriginal Pipeline Group (APG) 2000-2001, 7th term as IRC Chair in 2008, awarded Governor General's Northern Award in January 2008.

Brian Cousins – CBC announcer. Member 1969 Village Council, moved to Saskatchewan.

Peggy Curtis – arrived 1962 from Victoria, SAMS Phys-Ed teacher, Inuvik Home & School Association, TEST Program, 15 years in community recreation, Social Services in 1961, left to Victoria 1997. Curtis Field named after her.

Alan Davis – Davis Construction, Town Council 1987, first councilor who was child of a previous councilor.

Gwen Davis – Town Council 1975.

Billy Day – 1931- , *(Maggie)*, Trapper. Cook for crew cutting road to E3 in December 1955, NWT Social Services for 14 years to 1975. President COPE from 1984 to 1987. Chief Inuvik Community Corporation. President COPE from 1984 to 1987, Inuvik Drummers and Dancers story teller, National Aboriginal Achievement Award in 2006.

Doug Dittrich – *(Jean)*, Anglican church 1967-73, Town Council 1971-72.

George Doolittle – *(Violet)*, NCPC, Arctic College, Town Council 2000-2004.

Pauline Duggan – IAND office services in 1968, Town Council 1981.

Bertha Allen

Dolly Carmichael

Doug Dittrich

Wally Firth

Roy Goose

James Firth – *(Verna)*, Northwestel 1972, Inuvik Native Band, Chief Nihtat Gwich'in Council in 1990, Aboriginal Pipeline Group.

Shirley & Sharon Firth – 1953- , TEST program, on Canadian National Ski Team for 17 years. Received the Order of Canada in 1984.

Stephen Firth – Trapper, member Inuvik Advisory Committee 1965.

Wally Firth – First announcer for CBC Inuvik on 26 Nov 60, pilot, from Fort McPherson, Western Arctic Federal MP 1972 -79 as first aboriginal member.

Alex Foreman – *(Nan)*, came North in 1948, Foreman's Super-A Store, moved from Fort McPherson, Town Council 1974.

Les Gardiner – Town Council 1972.

Roy Goose – 1950- , *(Annie Rose)*, CBC, *Tusaayaksat*, Inuvialuit Communications Society, moved to Cambridge Bay.

Wallace Goose – *(Agnes)*, Wallace Kunak Joseph Goose, 24Mar24 - 25Dec85, born along East Branch, married Agnes Nanogak Banksland, children Bill, Roy, Walter, Douglas, Rex and Wayne, brother Jack Goose in Aklavik, (Roy and Ann-Rose. Roy Jr., Donna, Dianna, Benjamin).

Alex Gordon – *(Hope 1918-2001)*. Inuvialuktun name Kakianan, 1910 -2000, Drum dancer, retired to Aklavik.

Larry Gordon – *(Dianne)*, Teacher Education Program, taught at SAMS 1973-1995, Beaufort Delta Education Board, Inuvialuit Projects.

Pauline Gordon – *(William)*, SAMS teacher, Director, Beaufort-Delta Divisional Board of Education, Asst Dep Minister NWT Education, Vice Principal SAMS, SAMS Teacher, TEP Program, born at Stanton.

Alex Greenland – 1920-1980, *(Elizabeth 1921-)*, Gwich'in elder, IAND Engineering in 1968.

Roger Gruben – *(Winnie)*, born Tuktoyaktuk, graduated Hearne High in 1973, CBC announcer 1973-1980, Western Arctic Coordinator for Beaufort Sea Environmental Assessment Review Panel 1980-1984, . Chairman Inuvialuit Regional Corporation in 1986 to 1991, moved to Tuk.

Willard Hagen – *(Silvia)*, Aklak Air cofounder, president Gwich'in Tribal Corporation, Beaudel Air.

Sid Hancock – Inuvik Region Director in 1967, appointed Reeve of Village Council, moved to Yellowknife.

Arlene Hansen – Maiden name Prince, came to Inuvik in 1978, married Moses Hansen in 1985, Esso Resources, Originals On Mackenzie, Education Council, Town Council.

Cece Hansen – 1946- , Reindeer Air pilot, B737 pilot for Dome Petroleum, B747 pilot for Ansett Air in Australia, back to Canadian North in 2002, living in Calgary.

Frank Hansen – *(Sandy)*, 1946- , school in Aklavik, High School in Inuvik, University of Alberta Civil Engineering in 1969, Town Council, NWT Asst Region Engineer in 1970, Hansen Petroleum Products, 1995 Aboriginal Achievement Award, Northwestel director, Inuvialuit Investment Corp director, Norterra chairman, Inuvialuit Development Corporation chairman, Inuvialuit Communications Society, CBC director, Kavik Group of Companies.

Glenna Hansen – 1956- , *(Robert 1959-1999)*, Storr Contracting, Inuvik Community Corporation, IRC, NWT Commissioner March 2001.

George Harry – 1921-1998, *(Martha)*. Drum dancers, on original Inuvik construction team, IAND Engineering in 1968, Martha's photo on Camnadian stamp in April 1999.

Jack Heath – 1932-2005, *(Bubbins)* (1), *(Bonnie)* (2), RCN in Aklavik, CFS Inuvik, Town Council 1974, Community Business Services, Jack Heath Insurance, Legion club manager (1983).

Cynthia Hill – 1931- , *(Dick)*, arrived Inuvik 1963, Inuvik Day Care, SAMS special beginners, NWT Adult Education, councillor and mayor. Farewell Open House in her honour 26 Jun 1991, moved to Calgary in 1991.

Dick Hill – 1930- , *(Cynthia)* (1) *(Brigitte Huebner)* (2), to Inuvik in 1963 to direct Inuvik Research Laboratory, Mackenzie Institute, Inuvik Centennial Library, TEST program, 1975 formed Arctech Resource Management Services (Arctech), president 1973, exec dir. Chamber 1975-1993, Council 1968-69, Mayor 1970-71, Council 1992, started Boreal Books in June 1965, moved to Collingwood, ON in 1995.

John Hill – 1973- , *(Skip)*, born in England, to Canada in 1959, CIBC Inuvik manager in 1971, 1973 GNWT Ec Development, 1977 Polar TV, Deputy Mayor and Mayor. 1989 Chairman of NWT Public Utilities Board and NWT Highway Transport Board. Moved to Hay River.

Earl Holley – CFS Inuvik, CBC News, Airport Fire Dept, Town Council 1974, moved to Wallaceburg, ON.

Dan Holman – *Inuvik Drum* Editor 1978-88, Town Council 1980, Deputy Mayor 1981.

Leonard 'Hank' Holman – *(Dorothy)*, Stringer Hall Administrator, Town Council 1972-74, moved to Peterborough, ON.

Bob Hunter – *(Alice)*, Inuvik Research Laboratory, Inuvik Dairy, NWT Game Officer, Town Council 1969.

Vivian Hunter – GNWT Social Services, COPE, Town Council 1990-92.

Susie Huskey – 1936-1995, daughter of Jimmy and Mary Huskey, interpreter, nurses aid, Town Council 1975.

Alex Illasiak – 1935- , DOT Radio, NWT Renewable Resources Officer, Beaufort Delta Education Council, Town Council 1971.

Roy Ipana – Town Public Works firstman, Muskrat Jamboree starting in 1984, Northern Games, Ingamo hockey rink, hockey coach.

Dave Jones – *(Mary)*, Aklavik Relocation Advisory Committee, Imperial Oil agent, moved from Aklavik, Inuvik Village Reeve in 1969, Lions Club president 1964, sportsman, chair community council, left Inuvik 1978 to Edmonton.

Bill Kikoak – 1924-1994, *(Rhoda)*, Billie Edward Coates Kikoak, Arctic Clean Services. Pentecostal church.

Gerry Kisoun – *(Rosa)*, Mackenzie Valley Pipeline Research, RCMP 1974-1996, Parks Canada, dog mushers association, Gwich'in Land and Water Board, Siuliq Tours.

Shirley Kisoun – 1956- , first child born at Inuvik, Town Council 1992, IRC, *Tusaayaksat*, Northern Games.

Fred Koe

Eddie Kolausok

John Komaromi

Knut Lang

Robert McLeod

Fred Koe – 1947- , born in Aklavik, Fort McPherson settlement manager, 1984 Mackenzie Delta/ Beaufort Sea coordinating office in Inuvik, 1987 NWT Ed Development & Tourism, Northern Affairs, NWT Economic Development, Inuvik MLA 1991-1995, avid curler.

Jim Koe – 1908-1980, *(Vivian)* 1911-1999, Chief of Aklavik. Anglican mission school in Hay River until 1922 when he went to Aklavik and started working for the RCMP. Later he worked for NT Traders and the Aklavik Navy Base. Married Vivian Bell of Fort McPherson. Became chief in Aklavik for 16 years. Commissioner on 1959 Nelson Commission to investigate the unfulfilled provisions of Indian Treaties 8 and 11. Anglican church, CBC Radio, CFS Inuvik, Gwich'in leader, translator, helped organize Ingamo Hall in 1970 in old Hudson Bay store. CHAK radio show "Yesterday Before". Inuvik Native band now called Ehditat Gwich'in Council. In 1978 presented with a Silver Jubilee medal to commemorate work with the Aklavik Rangers. Inuvik Council dedicated Mackezie Square park after him and a sign with his photo was erected in 1993.

Vivian Koe – 1911-1999, *(Jim)*, Vivian Aurora Koe, 19Oct11 -16Feb99, born Fort McPherson to Charlie and Dora Bell, Anglican school in Hay River, Married Jim Koe in 1929, six children, Janet, Marilyn, Allen, Gladys, Freddie and Janet.

Eddie Kolausok – *(Karen)*, Town Council 1995, WAVA manager, ICI entertainment, Arctic College, moved to Yellowknife, Kolausok Ublaaq Enterprises, writer, *Across Time And Tundra* (2003).

John Komaromi – *(Alphia)*, Inuvik Laundry, bought out business when sold by GNWT, Town Council 1975.

Paul Komaromi – Town Council 1986, Mayor 1993, Inuvik Laundry, New North Network. Resigned as Mayor by letter of 24Feb94.

Adolph Koziesek – Works foreman, carpenter, camp on Campbell Lake at Rengling River, moved to Powell River around 1960, also spelled Koziek or Koziak.

Knut Lang – 1895-1964, from Denmark, arrived Aklavik 1928. Supplied wood for stern-wheelers, independent trapper and fur trader in Aklavik and Peel Channel, involved in search for the Mad Trapper. In August 1957 elected to Mackenzie Delta riding and remained a MLA until his death in 1964. He was fully involved in the plans for Inuvik and made the motion to name the new community "Inuvik". A NTCL tug was named after him in the 1980s.

Dennie Lennie – 1956- 2004 , *(Barb)*, Arctic Esso Service, Town Council 1993, hockey, Inuvialuit Development Corp.

Edward Lennie – 1934- , *(Jean)*, working for CBC in 1970, northern games, Town Council 1984, Aboriginal Achievement Award.

Derek Lindsay – *(Clara)*, Accountant, 10 years on Inuvik Council, Mayor 2008, Legion manager.

Finlay 'Mac' MacInnes – *(Marie)*. RCMP, Mechanic at Reindeer Station, Inuvik Liquor Store, McInnes Branch Canadian Legion named after him.

Barney MacNeil – *(Clara)*, came from Montreal to Aklavik in 1948 with Royal Canadian Corps of Signals, Town Council 1970-71, MOT radio operator, moved from Aklavik, airport manager, Town Council, moved to Hay River.

Cece McCauley – 1922- , born at Fort Norman, to Aklavik in 1958, Mackenzie Hotel in 1960, Polaris Theatre in 1962, Inuvik Native Band founder in 1982 and first chief, Opened the Rec Hall on September 15, 1958 as Inuvik's first business with a bakery, restaurant pool hall and theatre. First Chief of Inuvik Native Band in 1981 and served till 1992. Cloud Nine Restaurant at Inuvik Airport, Chicken Chef, moved to Norman Wells in 1997. Weekly column in *News North*, Locally known as Miss Chief.

Jim Maher – SAMS principal 1964, Inuvik Community Association chair in 1966.

Margaret Nazon

Malcolm McConnell – Lawyer, Town Council 1974

Jim McDonald – *(Denise Kyrszewski)*, McDonald Bros Electric, Council 2007.

Robert McLeod – 1960- , carpenter, contractor, Inuvik Twin Lakes MLA in 2004.

Elijah Menarik – *(Grace)*, CBC Manager, from Northern Quebec, Village Council 1968.

Dan Norris

Curt Merrill – East 3 project manager, moved his family in 1956 with sons William (4) and Robert (6), environmentalist, transferred to Fort Smith

Margaret (Donovan) Nazon – *(Bob)*, sewing, clothing artist, from Tsiigehtchic, Gwich'in Tribal Council

Richard Nerysoo – NWT Council, NWT Premier, NTPC chairman Dec 02, president Gwich'in Tribal Council, Inuvik Native Band

Christine Norris – 1900-1992, *(Adolphus)*. Christine Norris (Biggs), born Fort McMurray area, East Branch in late 1920s, store and general contracting business in Aklavik, husband died in 1955. Son Fred, Dan (Margaret), George, daughters Agnes, Bernice, Clara (Barney) MacNeil, Elsie (Larry) Grsel, Jim Biggs of Caslan Alta.

Kenneth Peelooluk

Dan Norris – 1936- , *(Margaret)*, born at Big Rock in Mackenzie Delta. Returned to Aklavik after 2 years at an Edmonton trade school (Brown 1996, 15 Feb 56). DINA , transferred to GNWT in 1969, Asst Reg director to 1972, Sup't Personnel to 1982, Inuvik Region Director 1985, first aboriginal NWT Commissioner 1989-1994. Retired to Hay River.

George Roach

Fred Norris – *(Junis)*, East 3 Contractor, operated boat "Barbara Jean", Norris Taxi.

George Norris – *(Jackie)*, member Inuvik Advisory Committee 1965.

Miki O'Kane – *(Fred Carmichael)*, nurse, Arctic College.

Abe Okpik – 1927-1997. Abraham Allan Okpik, Auktalik, Abe, foreman on DEWline, Leduc Training School, Pres of Mackenzie Delta Trappers Association, south to serve Welfare Division. Appointed to NWT Council 1965-67, Disc jockey with Project Surname 1968-1970, Member of the Order of Canada. Moved to Iqaluit.

Jim Robertson

Vern Opel – Member Inuvik Advisory Committee 1965.

Kenneth Peelooluk – 1893-1980, *(Rosie)*, born Noatak area, Alaska, to Canada in 1921, drum dancer.

Stan Peffer – 1912-1999. Stanley Munroe Peffer, son of Harry J. Peffer 1898-1964. Born in USA, came down Liard and Mackenzie Rivers to Aklavik with father and brother. Was on New Town Advisory Committee in Aklavik in Jan57. Entrepreneur. Built Rec Hall, Mackenzie Hotel, Polaris Theatre and Bakery.

Sam Raddi – 1931-1990, *(Wilma)*. Blind from methyl alcohol in 1959, first eskimo in Western Arctic to join AA, Taxi dispatcher. COPE president.

Henry Rivet – Member Inuvik Advisory Committee 1965, from Aklavik.

George Roach – *(Nora Dixon)*, Hearne High teacher, businessman, Mayor 1997-99.

Jim Robertson – 1929- , born Edinborough, lived in Orkney, came North with HBC, EV manager 1962, HBC district manager in Winnipeg, return in 1969 with Mack Travel, Northwest Company, Tilden franchise. On Council, Mayor 1973-1978 and again 1981-1984, living on a lake 80 km northeast of Yellowknife. Pacific Airlines board, plus NCPC in 1959 as NWT Government rep, entrepreneur, northern success story, chair NWT Power Corporation in 1976.

Floyd Roland – 1961- , *(Shawna)*, NWT Public Works, Nuktigvik Tours, Inuvik Council 1992-95, Deputy Mayor 1994/95, NWT MLA 16 Oct 95 and 6 Dec 99, Premier 2007.

Sue Rose – Rose Arts graphics, co-founder with Charlene Alexander of Great Northern Arts Festival in 1988. Moved to Yelloknife.

Max Ruyant – 1920-1995, OMI in 1939, to North in 1945, Aklavik school and hospital administrator 1946-1959, Grollier Hall 1959-1987, business supporter, TEST supporter, Tuk church pastor 1987-1989, retired to Alberta.

Agnes Semmler – 1911-2002, *(Slim)*, to Inuvik 1956, Women's Institute president in 1964, Home and School Association, Catholic Women's League, Women's Institute, appointed Justice of the Peace in 1975, Selected as Woman of the Century for the North in 1967. First president of COPE. NWT Deputy Commissioner 1984-1987. Agnes Semmler was born near Old Crow, Yukon. Her mother was a Gwich'in and her father was a Swedish trapper. She spent much of her life among the Inuvialuit. "I've always called myself Canadian," she told an *Edmonton Journal* reporter in 1983. "I don't like this Dene, Indian or Metis or whatever crap. I'm Canadian."

Slim Semmler – 1900-1998. *(Agnes)*, born Lawrence Frederick Semmler in Newberg, Oregon. Homesteaded in northern Alberta. Arrived in Mackenzie Delta 1932. Trapped along Arctic Coast. In 1947 set up camp at Napoyak in the middle of the Delta. In 1957 set up a trading store in Inuvik. In 1960 built the Mackenzie Road store.

Vince Sharpe – Mackenzie Delta Construction, Town Council.

Bob Simpson – Arrived Fort McPherson 1970's, known as Gwich'in Bob, negotiator for Mackenzie Delta Tribal Council, Gwich'in Tribal Council, Beaufort-Delta Self Government Negotiations, Town Council 1993-94.

Charlie Smith – *(Madelaine)*, Eskimo name Anisaluk, from Alaska on Capt. Pedersen's ship Nigalik in July 1938, reindeer herder, CBC Eskimo language program in 1962, president Inuvik Cooperative Housing Association, Pentecostal Church, president, Innuit Cooperative Ltd. (July 1963), Eskimo stories from sweat house, IA&ND Development Office (1966), died 1967. Efforts were made to name new high school after him rather than after explorer Samuel Hearne who had no connection with the area.

Duane Smith – President Inuit Circumpolar Council (Canada).

Ken Snider – *(Aldene)*, Anglican church, first Church Captain in 1956, to Dawson, back in 1966, to Mayo where he retired in 1998, lives in Dawson, WAVA, IVC, became Anglican Archdeacon of the Yukon.

Bill Starling – Member Inuvik Advisory Committee 1965.

Helen Sullivan – *(Dave)*, FDR Sports, NWT Continuing and Special Education in 1987, Regional Superintendent Education, Culture and Employment, NWT Regional Administrator, Governor General's Golden Jubilee Award in June 2002, NWT Premier's Award in 2005.

Dave Sutherland – 1931-2004, *(Aiko)*, Rehab Centre Northern Crafts, TEST Program, GNWT Economic Development, left Inuvik in 1970. Spent three years in Churchill and then moved to Yellowknife until retirement in Victoria.

Wilf Taylor – Forest Management Officer, Mackenzie Forest Service, Indian Affairs and Northern Development 1968-70, commander for Inuvik forest fire in 1968, closed bar. Youth forestry training program with several future leaders. Wrote book, *Beating Around the Bush: A Life in the Northern Forest.*

Mona Thrasher – 1938- , unique artist with no formal training. Painted Stations of Cross in Igloo Church when when was 18. The success of these endeavours launched her career as an artist. Moved to Yellowknife.

Abel Tingmiak – Northern games, Inuvik Drummers and Dancers, Blanket toss.

Diana Tingmiak – *(Pat)*1953-1992, Town Council 1990.

Marja VanNieuwenhuyzen – Community Programs, Aurora College, Town Council, 2004.

Gary Wagner – Carpenter, Wagner Construction, Mackenzie Delta Construction & Building Supplies, Inuvik Council 1970, moved to BC.

Gwen Walmsley – *(Ken)*, member Inuvik Advisory Committee 1965.

Agnes Semmler

Charlie Smith

Dave Sutherland

Abel Tingmiak

Gary Wagner

Bruno Weidemann – 1897-1997, *(Maggie)*, emigrated from Germany, took over Livingston's Farm in Aklavik in 1938. Purchased first Bombardier in 1952. Established in Inuvik in 1959 with a service station and transportation services. By 1960, Bruno and son John had 5 Bombardiers providing freight and transportation services throughout the Mackenzie Delta. He held a taxi licence until he was 88 years old. Retired to Yellowknife.

Tom Wright – 1941- , *(Lilian)*, Golden Jubilee medal, Town Council 1993.

Mike Zubko – 1923-1991, *(Dawn)*. Came from Poland in 1929. Began his flying career in 1942 flying for Canadian Airways. Formed Aklavik Air Services with Stan Byer in 1945 using an Aronca Champion. This was the first commercial air service north of the Arctic Circle. President of the Inuvik and Western Arctic Development Association in 1961. Founding Director of the NWT Aviation Council in 1964. After retiring he sat on the Federal Civil Aviation Tribunal and was a member of the NWT Workers" Compensation Board. He died in Oct 1991. The Inuvik Airport was named after him on August 7, 1995. In 2003 he was inducted into the Canadian Aviation Hall of Fame in recognition that his charter service vastly improved the lives of Western Arctic people providing a vital link with isolated camps and communities.

Tom Zubko – *(Christine)*, Inuvik Utilities Committee, Town Council 1989-94, Mayor 1995-96, Pilot-manager with Aklavik Flying Services 1970-1985. Purchased Inuvik TV in 1990, changed to New North Networks in 1999.

Some Notable Residents, 1958 – 2008

Inuvik residents who have participated in community development who are not listed in the Community Leaders list. A special effort was made to include early Inuvik resisdents but many people are not listed through lack of information. Undoubtedly there are errors in some dates and name spelling which can be corrected in future editions.

If available a persons information is listed: Dates, *(spouse)*, arrival in Inuvik and activities. There are separate listings where spouse is known by a different family name or was involved in special activities.

Albert Adams – Adams Services, son of Jimmy and Lucy Adams, moved south 1990s

George Adams – Inuvik General Hospital

Jimmy Adams – *(Lucy 1931-)*, trapline in the Inuvik area before Inuvik was built. Classic story teller. Jimmy Adams Peace Park named in his memory

Len Adrian – IAND Public Works, Inuvik Fire Chief 1964

Hans Affolter – *(Georgina -2000)*, Inuvik Inn, moved to Whitehorse

Freddy Albert – 1932-1988 *(Rosie)*, Canadian army, may have been son of Albert Johnson (Mad Trapper), Inuvik construction team

Johnny Aleekuk – -1969, *(Ida 1914-1984)*, Reindeer herder, moved to Inuvik in 1967, school caretaker

Agnes Okpik Allen – 1963- , *(Murray Cutten)*, daughter of Elijah and Mable Allen

Almira Kayotuk Allen – 1956-1995

Anita Allen – 1951- , TEST program

Collin Allen – Rita, SAMS caretaker

Delma Allen – Northern Games Association in 1981

Dennis Allen – Musician, film producer

Donna Allen – Inuvik Baseball

Elijah Allen – *(Mabel)*, Kendall Island Whale Watching Tours, worked on airport construction in 1950s

Gloria Allen – IRC, sports, Ingamo Hall

Owen Allen – 1909- , trapper, Community leader

Titus Allen – 1947-1997, from Aklavik, Inuvialuit Game Council

Wayne Allen – SAMS custodian

Yvonne Allen – CBC

Regina Amagonaiok – 1951-2002, "Little Regina", star of Inuvik TV's Mackenzie Road Show, moved to Yellowknife

Albert Ammon – Carpenter, worked with Gary Wagner

Beverly Amos – Tusasyaksat, language translation

Collin Amos – SAMS caretaker

Jeff Amos – Timberline Painting, Inuvik Youth Centre coordinator, Muskrat Jamboree

Joey Amos – Muskrat Jamboree

Adolph 'Red' Anders – Initial construction team

Andy Anderson – Lions Club

Ray Anderson – Midarctic Transportation, MATCO

Lloyd Anderson – Teacher, Matco Transportation

Alestine Andre – Student, CBC, cultural researcher, from Arctic Red River

Paul Andrew – Grolllier Hall resident, TEST program, CBC Inuvik

William Apsimik – 1933- , *(Eva)*, reindeer herder

Alfred Aquilina – NWT social services 1975-81, wrote book *Mackenzie And Beyond*

John Arey Sr – 1932-1998, worked NCPC in 1960s, moved back to Aklavik in 1973

Renie Arey – IRC

Sydney Ayak – 1898- , at Rehab Centre, good bone carver

Marlene Bailey – Inuvik Research Lab, Fisheries and Oceans, daughter Agnes Raddi

Donna Ballas – Place of Man

John Banksland – *(Annie)*, 12 years in residential schools, scouts, public health inspector in 1964, IRC

Claire Barnabe – 1940- , NWT Inuvik Regional Director

Tom Barry – *(Pat)*, CWS biologist

Don Baryluk – *(Jane)*, HBC, Northern, arrived 1975

Jane Baryluk – Inuvik Hospital

Fred Beaulieu – Inuvik Research Lab, member 1964 Inuvik Advisory Committee

Steve Bessaw – IAND Engineering in 1968

Elaine Bell – SAMS principal

Albert Bernhardt – 1937- , IAND Engineering in 1968, Town heavy equipment

Ernie Bernhardt – Boy Scout in Aklavik, at Rehab Centre (1963)

Lucien Bernier – Ec Dev officer, craft shop

Hank Bertrand – IAND Engineer in in 1968

Ray Berube – Great Northern Airways, President Inuvik Chamber of Commerce 1970

Jack Betteridge – Shell Resources

Jim Biggs – D8 Cat operator on original site development (1962)

Lloyd Binder – 1952- , NWT Economic Development, Mackenzie Reindeer Ltd.

Otto Binder – 1921- *(Ellen)*, reindeer herder. RCMP special constable in Aklavik in 1956

Jim Birch – Hospital carpenter. Make shelves for Inuvik Centennial Library

Francis Blackduck – Pipeline studies in 1975, from Yellowknife

Ethel Blake – Executive Asst Gwich'in Tribal Council, researcher

Grace Blake – Mackenzie Gas Project

Herbert Blake Jr. – From Fort McPherson, electrician, NTPC, president Nihtat Gwichj'in Council

Jim Blewett – -2002, *(Marg)*, SAMS Vice Principal

George Blue – INA Oil&Gas in 1975

Bill Bock – SAMS principal (1963)

Eric Boettger – *(Louise)*, Engineer, draughtsman, building consultant, surveyor, in Inuvik 1987, Town Development Officer, Anuri and Associates, moved to Cambridge Bay as High North Enterprises.

Dave Boudreau – *(Vicki)*. CBC technician, Delta Electric, Davic, Lions Club

John Boudreau – *(Lianne)*, Inuvik TV, Deputy Fire Chief in 1996, New North Networks

Fred Beaulieu – Research Lab technician, Indamo Association

Wally Bourassa – IAND Property Management in 1968

Bill Bourque – NWT Power Corp transmission superintendent

Joe Bourque – First barber shop in E3

Stella Bourque – 1953-2007, IGH Human Resources

Frank Boyce – Doctor Inuvik General Hospital in 1970s

Ted Boyer – NWT asst regional director in 1975

Shane Brewster – *(Lilian Hvatum)*, teacher, sports coordinator

Bernard Brown – RC Priest OMI, arrived 1956, left 1957. replaced by Fr. Jules Adam

Mabel Brown – Anglican Church, NWT Health Services

Bob Brunette – CBC technician (1962)

Brian Bruser – NWT Judge

Louis Bryant – *(Carol)*, arrived 1975, CFS Inuvik, Norm's Hardware, Safety Sales & Equipment, Scouts

Norma Buchanan – *(Sven Johansson)*, Research Lab secretary

Greg Bulger – *(Josephine)*, Ram Air pilot, Jo Swimming instructor

Bert Bullock – *(Martina)*, Stanton Distributing

George Bunz – SAMS teacher

Jim Burch – Hospital carpenter

Norm Burgess – vocational education in 1963

Frank Burke – 1926-2007, to Inuvik in 1970, DPW

Bob Burnett – CBC Tech

Trevor Burroughs – Connelly Dawson Airways manager 1965

J.W. Burton – Northern Affairs sub district administrator in March 1956

Ian Butters – Development Impact Zone (DIZ) Society, NWT Economic Development

Dave Button – *(Myrna)*, teacher in 1970, University Calgary PhD Education candidate in May 2007

Stan Byer – *(Jean)*, RCMP, Aklavik Flying Service, PWA agent

Ernie Canning – Govt Clerk in 1964, Lions Club

Len Cardinal – 1930- 2003 , Contractor, river tug, arrived 1974 from Hay River, NWT Task Force on Northern Business Preferences

Maurice Cardinal – -2008, Aurora College

Rudy Cardinal Sr – Trapper from Arctic Red River

Rudy Cardinal Jr – Inuvik Native Band, Arctic College caretaker

Dan Carmichael – GNWT, Minor Hockey

Frank Carmichael – Arctic Wings and Rotors

Fred John Carmichael – 'Junior', 1960-2008

Dusty Caruthers – East 3 carpenter, vocational instructor

Agnes Carpenter – *(Fred Carpenter)*, nee Agnes Peffer, Inuvik General Hospital

Andy Carpenter – Chairman Inuvialuit Game Council in 1976

Frank Carpenter – 1930-2004 , *(Florence)*, RCMP

Les Lee Carpenter – Born in Fort McPherson, Hearne High, IRC President, Inuit Circumpolar Conference, CBC announcer

Margaret Carpenter – Northern Affairs secretary in early 1960's

Mary Carpenter – 1943- , *(Lyon)*, COPE, Rutger University graduate, teacher, DINA in Ottawa

Art Carrier – TH Mechanical Services

Martin Carroll – *(Ruth)*, active with Anglican church, NCPC, Community Justice Coordinator

Ruth Carroll – *(Martin)*, from Fort McPherson, CBC

Robert Charlie – *(Annie Jane)*, Northwestel Technician Gwich'in Renewable Resources

Olive Chesworth – Rehabilitation Centre superintendent in 1964

Red Cheyney – *(Diane)*, Arctic Plumbing, Legion President in 1994

Diane Cheyney – *(Red)*, Town Manager

William Chicksi – *(Rebecca)*, at Rehab Centre. Wood carver, died around 1966, used bark from giant Balsom Poplar trees from Liard River and found along Mackenzie Delta shores

Fred Church – CFS Inuvik, Cadets, Legion

Viktor Ciboci – V&V Contracting, taxi

Bide A.J. Clark – NCPC (1962), in charge of water treatment and utilidor operations, built a boat from CANOL bridge pontoons to sail away from Inuvik when he retired in 1973

Tommy Clark – 1916- , born in Winnipeg, HBC, Aklavik Construction, NCPC, Rehab Centre

George Clarke – Arctic Wings and Rotors, Tuk Traders, Mad Trapper

Lavona Clarke – Chair Inuvik Library Board 2007

Peter Clarke – Finning Tractor, President Chamber of Commerce 1976

Barry Clarkson – Samuel Hearne High School Principal, Town Council 1980

Joe Coady – NWT Education Superintendent in 1975

Rudy Cockney – 1948- , Canada Manpower, Northern Affairs Regional Director

Topsy Cockney – *(Terry Fellows)* , Inuvialuit Communications Society

Winnie Cockney – 1922- 2006, Inuvialuit elder

Peter Coolican – *(Fran)*, IRC finance

John Comeau – CIBC Manager (1961-1965), auditor for Inuvik Community Association

Roger Connelly – GNWT Inuvik Regional Administrator, Inuvik Regional Corporation COO

Al Cottrell – Indian Agent in Aklavik and Inuvik (1962), was Agent in Fort Norman

Ewan Cotterill – Regional Administrator 1968, left government and joined Dome Petroleum

Irish Coulter – Hired by Aklavik Constructors as chief oiler (AJ Feb57)

John Cournoyea – GNWT tourism officer

Russ Cournoyea – -2003, *(Nellie)*(1), *(Carolyn)*(2), CFS Inuvik, Inuvik Community Association, Postmaster in 1975

Ray Cox – *(Elvina)*, Contractor (1962), Inuvik Sales & Services, pilot

Liz Crawford – Teacher

Albert Cottrell – Supt Indian Affairs Branch 1964

Denis Croteau – 1932- , Bishop Mackenzie Diocese, north in 1960, Igloo Church priest in 1970s

Murray Cutten – *(Agnes Allen)*, NWT Economic Development

Ted Curtis – Tough Turtle Construction

Ian Dalziel – *(May)*, Husky Insurance, First Burns Society night coordinator, 1973-1981

Tony Darin – Inuvik Hospital worker

Harold Darkes – *(Mary)*, Education Superintendent in 1965

Ernie Davis – Gwen, GNWT Public Works in 1975

William Day – Northern Games,

Lena Dayman – ICS

Harry Debastien – (1962)

Braam DeClerk – Doctor

Ben DeKline – Village Council secretary-manager, 1969

Johnny Desrochier – Set up third store in Inuvik, working with Stan Peffer, diesel mechanic, boat captain

Emma Dick – *(Hebert)*, drum dancer

Hebert Dick – 1920- , original construction crew, Emma. DPW maintenance

Richard Dick – Reindeer Air Service, Gruben Transport tug captain

John Dillon – 1926-2007, *(Annie)*, IAND Property Management in 1968

Dan Dimitroff – Lilian, IGH doctor1970s

Rev Jeff Dixon – Rosalind, Anglican Church

Art Dodman – Cook at Rehab Centre, 1963

Don Doncster – Inuvik gun Club, shooter

Ray Douglas – PWA Otter pilot, Douglas & Loutit Trucking 1965

Ed Duggan – 1930-2006, Pauline, teacher, SAMS Principal in 1975, NWT Education, retired 1988 to Red Deer

Blair Dunbar – *(Linda)*, NWT Social Servcices, TEST, Inuvik Ski Club, moved to Yellowknife

Gordon Dyke – Teacher

Bruce Dyson – 1929- , *(Irene)*, Dyson Gun Shop, Inuvik Gun Club, taxi driver

Julia Edwards – 1914-1999, *(Alec Elanik)*

Edward Hoppy Elanik – Arctic Esso, addictions counselor

Albert Elias – 1942- , NWT Development Corp director

Lillian Elias – 1943- , NWT community government, moved to Yellowknife

Jim Elliot – CFS Inuvik, Town foreman in 1979

Marion Ellis – 1979-88, post office, Dome Petroleum, Pluim Construction

Bill Enge – *(Ann)*, NWT Public Works, formation of Ingamo Hall Association

Bill English – *(Mabel)*, NWT Economic Development

Mabel English – *(Bill)*, Gwich'in teacher, Gwich'in Elders Council

Ron English – Gwich'in artist

George Erasmus – Company of Young Canadians 1970-71

Gerhard Erler – restauranteur Raven's Nest, Pepermill, arrived 1989, departed 2007 to Calgary

Michael Fabijan – *(Lynda)*, arrived 1979, marine biologist, Fisheries and Oceans, Inuvialuit Joint Secretariat, Kavik-AXYS GNAF

Gerald Falk – Pastor Inuvik Christian Assembly 1965-1999

Olav Falsnes – *(Judy)*, pilot, B&B

Jack Familinow – 1963, Works painter, Arctic Painting & Development in 1973

Hugh Feagan – RCMP 1963

Alana Fehr – *(Marilyn)*, NWT Adult Education, Inuvik Research Lab, Inuvik Ski Club

Herb Figures – Arranged construction of HBC store in Inuvik

Frank Firth – *(Mary)*, first construction team. Operated government stores IAND Propery Management in 1968

Margaret Firth – GNWT secretary, IRL secretary

Verna Firth – *(James)*, Bank of Montreal, GNWT Economic Development

Jean Fleming – Welfare clerk in 1964

Vern Flexhaug – President, Inuvik & Western Arctic Development Association in 1962

Father Franche – OMI, Grollier Hall administrator in 1962 and Mackenzie Delta Mission supervisor

Carl Franzin – Inuvik Boat Shop1962, 1964

Gerd Fricke – NWT Economic Development in early 1990s

Terry Frith – Pentecostal Church 1963, moved to Edmonton

Frank Fulop – Inuvik Taxi

Sig Gaida – Peffer Enterprises comptroller, owner Eskimo Inn, accounting services, auditor, operated out of Edmonton

Roch Gagnon – *(Diane Nelson)*, Pilot with Aklak Air, Photo Script

Jeff Gardiner – *(Nancy)*, Inuvik Housing Association, Town Council, moved to Yellowknife in 1994

Carl Gardlund – *(Sarah-Ann)*. Operated first cafe above town wharf in 1958

Ken 'Busher' Gerry – 1963, CFS Inuvik, Gulf Resources

Pat Gerry – Ken, NWtel office

John Gilpin – PWA, Lions Club

Robert Girard – 1928-2003, Carpenter, arrived April 1959 to work on the Igloo Church

Shannon Goldsberry – Arctic College

Martin Goodliffe – Crafts, GNAF

Jack Goose – From Holman, employed by Akavik Constructors in 1957

Leanne Goose – aboriginal rock singer

Louie Goose – 1950- , *(Mae Cockney)*, from Aklavik, CBC, Trapper character, musician.

Wallace Goose – 1924-1985, *(Agnes)*, born near Inuvik

Alex Gordon – Rosalind, Asst Regional Administrator

Clayton Gordon – ICS, Inuvik Community Corporation, Inuvialuit Communications Society

Debbie Gordon – ICS, Eskimo dancer

Ernie Gordon – 1958-2000, Beluga Transportation, NWT Ferries, drowned while saving a young child

Jimmy Gordon – 1930- , *(Deva)*. Reindeer herder, boat captain, Beluga one freighting

Margaret Gordon – from Aklavik, 1976 Hearne High graduate, CBC Inuvik coordinator, Gwich'in Tribal Council regional coordinator

Olive Gordon – NWT Social Services

Stanley Gordon – 1931- , *(Christine)* 1933-1998, arrived in 1958

Tom Gordon – 1940- , started flying with Reindeer Air, first Inuit pilot, Gateway Aviation, Executive jets for Imperial Oil, Berkshire Avaiation

Wayne Gordon – Inuvialuit Development Corporation chair

Willie Gordon – CBC, fiddler

Roland Gosselin – arrived 1968, SAMS teacher, active in sports organizations, to Yellowknife in 1974

Pat Grandy – Inuvik hospital

Moe Grant – Mac's News, Midnight Express Tours, arrived 1975 from Hay River

John Greekas – *(Gloria)*, Mackenzie Hotel manager 1960s, in 1964, Lions Club

Nelson Green – 1948-1999, from Paulatuk

Peter Green – COPE, from Paulatuk

Barry Greenland – Subchief Nitat Gwich'in Council, Muskrat Jamboree

Peter Greenland – Inuvik Recreation

William Greenland – CBC, Inuvik Native Band, Northern Communications Society in Yellowknife

Ken Grey – PWA base mgr in mid '60s

Ron Grier – *(Donna)*, Post Office 1980-84

Bob Gulley – M. Burnhart, Bob's Welding

Clara Gully – Grollier Hall cook

Marlene Gustafson – Office services for petroleum industry in 1970s.

Peter Guther – Arctech Services, Inuvik TV

Ralph Guthrie – Mackenzie Valley Pipeline Research, showed Royal Family facilities in 1971

Val Haas – NWT Social Service

Mary Habgood – MD, Inuvik General Hospital superintendent in Nov1966

Cliff Hagen – Cat Skinner on original Inuvik construction crew

Larry Hagen – Reindeer Air, moved to Yellowknife

Ken Hamilton – *(Annie)*, cook

Elizabeth Hansen – Grollier Hall cook.

Hans Hansen – *(Kathleen)*, operated boat "Kings Highway" carrying freight between Aklavik and Inuvik

Dennis Hansen – *(Pat)*, 1942-1996, Reindeer Air, Hansen Petroleum

Clara Harrison – Canadian Nation Telecommunications manager 1965

Knute Hansen – IRC, tourism, manager Western Arctic Regional Visitor Centre in 1998

Moses 'Moe' Hansen – *(Arlene)*. Inuvik Community Corporation, Lakes & Rivers Consulting

Robert Hansen – 1959-1999, Glenna, Storr and Sons Contracting

Roy Hansen – Liz Crawford

Dave Hanson – *(Dale)*, Inuvik Funeral Service

Dale Hanson – *(Dave)*, Inuvik Regional Health Board

Art Hanvold – Expediting service in 1973

Lionel Harder – *(Judy)*, Wrangling River Supply

Grant Harding – New North Networks

Daisy Harrison – 1921-1996, Parka maker

Harry Harrison – 1930- , *(Cathryn)*, operated schooner "Golden Hind", trapper, early Inuvik contractor

Jim Harrison – Harrison Enterprises, Pingo Drilling, Roberts Rat Hole Drilling

Leonard Harry – Inuvialuit Communications Society

Vern Hawley – CWS muskrat biologist 1961

James Heath – Lorri, Born 4 Aug 57 in Aklavik, Navy commander

Cezar Heine – *(Joan-Cole)*, arrived 1975, Inuvik General Hospital, Lutheran Church, d 1990

Grant Hemming – *(Brenda)*, Hemming Communications

Jane Henson – planner, Mackenzie Delta Tribal Council, late 1980s

Keith Hickling – Sam, Game Officer, moved to Norman Wells

Bob Hewitt – Imperial Oil Enterprises manager 1965

Marnie Hilash – Great Northern Arts Festival

Bill Hill – Margo, Environment Canada, MOT

Greg Hill – Continuing & Special Education

Wally Hill – IAND economic development officer in 1965

Willy Ho – SAMS teacher in 1965, science club

Al Hockstein – Gulf Oil manager 1980s

John Hodgson – Draughtsman, 1980s

Ron Hodkinson – *(Jean)*, IAND Inuvik Regional Administrator, 1962-1963

Dorothy Holman – Grollier Hall

John Holman – 1946 CBC

Willy Hombert – Mackenzie Hotel manager

George Hudson – Inuvik Curling Club president 1965

Mike Hudson – *(Nina)*, Federal DPW Housing Manager

Rob Hunchak – MOT, ICATS Director for East Three and Wind Chill

Norris Hunt – *(Maureen)*, doctor Inuvik General Hospittal in 1970s, many of his photos now in collection of Inuvik Centennial Library

John Hunt – Fisheries officer

L.A.C.O. Hunt – Aklavik administrator at time of East three development

Alice Hunter – 1942- , *(Bob)*, northern clothing, *Alice Hunter's North Country Cookbook*, Eskimo Dancing

Bobby Hurst – Trapper, Arctic College custodian

Dennis Inglangasuk – Parks Canada

Roy Ipana – Inuvik Public Works, Muskrat Jamboree emcee

Sandra Ipana – Northern Games

Josie Irlbacher – Hospital

Fred Jacobsen – "Jake", delivered booze by boat from Aklavik before Inuvik Liquor store opened

Peggy Jay – IRC Communications, Inuvik Library Board

Bob Jenkins – 1963, teacher

Folmer Jensen – *(Elaine)*, Delta Water Ltd., water deliver and sewage pumpout services, bought out Inuvik KLK

Henning Jensen – Foreman for Aklavik Contractors on airport construction

Milkie Jensen – Gwich'in Tribal Council corporate secretary in 2002

James Jerome – 1949-1979, photographer

Sven Johansson – 1924- , *(Norma)*, spent 12 years working with Laplanders in northern Sweden managing reindeer herds, 1963-1968 as manager Canadian Reindeer Project, 1967 to 1972 chartered his boat "North Star" for work in Beaufort area, retired to Victoria

Albert Jones – *(Agnes)*, Albert Jones Construction, GNWT carpenter, Inuvik Christian Assembly

David Jorstead – Chartered Accountant

Simon Jozzy – Dental practioner

Zivojin Jovanovic – 'John'. Mechanic, garage operator, taxi driver. From Serbia

Herman Kaglik – Plummer

Donald Kagklik – 1928- , Story teller

Buster Kailik – *(Mary)*, 1914-1996, reindeer herder, Mary came from Cambridge Bay

Gus Karampelas – Peffer Enterprises, Rec Hall, baker, convenience store, bar tender

Rose Marie Karnes – Dome Petroleum, GNWT, ran for NWT Council

Ann Kasook – *(Charlie)*, Ingamo Hall

Roy Kasook – Zoo disc jockey

Stringer Kasook – 1915-1993, *(Ruby 1923-1995)*, a born mechanic

Ned Kayotuk – 1930- , *(Agnes 1932-1999)*, reindeer herder

Henry Keevik – SAMS custodian

Maureen Keevik – Worked for Cece McCauley at Rec Hall. Won a million dollar lottery in 1998 and didn't change, dart champion

Andrew Kendi – taxi driver, wood carver

Richard Kendi – 1938- , carpenter

Talal Khatib – Corner Store, Inuvik Theatre, Bowling Alley

Ed Kikoak – 1936- , on original constuction crew under Adolph Koziak, helped build Igloo Church

Freeman Kimiksana – 1917-1989, drum dancer

Tom Kimiksana – Drum Dancer

Cliff King – 1948-2003, *(Jodie)*, teacher in 1973, NWT Teachers Association, Arctic Winter Games Committee, Inuvik Minor Hockey Association

Wally King – CFS Inuvik, Northern Games, help on COPE formation

Rosemary Kirby – *(Tom)*, teacher, education consultant, Eskimo Dancing, Kalluk Consulting

Tom Kirby – *(Rosemary)*, teacher, Kirby Construction, Bahai, Northwest Lock & Safe, Justice of the Peace 2004

Greg Komaromi – CBC, moved to Whitehorse

John Kostelnik – Pat, game officer in 1960s

Roger Kunuk – Annie, Rehab Centre (1964)

Denise Kyrszewski – Jim McDonald, teacher, from Aklavik in 1960, Aurora College Board

Marla Kupfur – *(Bob Wilson)*, Lions, Inuvik Visitors Committee

Rosemarie Kuptana – 1954- , CBC Inuvik 1979, living in Ottawa

Marcel Lacerte – 1932- , arrived 1969, bar tender, Taxi driver

Ron Lalonde – *(Helene)*, teacher, retired in 1991 after 32 years of service

Bev Latham – CBC

Alfie Laroque – 1932- , *(Rosie)*, GNWT, Métis Association

Maurice Larocque – 1908-2001, Oblate brother. Carpenter. Designed and built Igloo Church in Inuvik

Bernice Lavoie – *(Joe)*, Grollier Hall administrator July 1991

Eddie Lavoi – Grollier Hall

Joe Lavoi – Grollier Hall, Arctic Foods

Rocky Lemieux – Rockey's Plumbing

Mario Lemieux – *(Joy)*, Rockey's Plumbing, car wash

Archie Lennie – 1963, Vice President of E3 Parent Teachers Association in 1957, IANF Engineering in 1968

Barb Lennie – *(Dennie)*, NWT Public Health

Beverly Lennie – School Liaison Officer

Johnny Lennie – in Aklavik and E3

Paul Leroux – Grollier Hall supervisor in 1970s

Freda Lester – 1960- , Whiteside

Ernie LeTeur – Crafts Officer 1964

Charlie Linklater – 1916- , *(Emily)*, worked at Stringer Hall. Came from Yukon with L.P. Holman to work in Aklavik

Robert Linklater – NCPC

Fred Linton – *(Agnes)*, Northwestel

Harry Lipscomb – 1939-2001, LGR Leasing, Town Works

Les Lokos – *(Lorraine)*, R. Angus, Finning Tractor

Lorraine Lokos – Inuvialuit Regional Corporation

Ken Look – CBC announcer, member1967 LID Advisory Council

Dez Loreen – *Drum* Editor 2000s, Grace's son

Grace Loreen – CBC

Steven Loreen – SAMS Custodian

Sweeny Loreen – 1934-1994, from Alaska

Al Luitit – welder in 1973

David Lowe – Town bylaw enforcement officer 1979-1984

Ed Lysk – Marion, RCMP Inspector 1960

Velma MacDonald – 1926- , *(Reg Daws)*, SAMS teacher 1959-1971, helped XC skiing, preparation of Charlie Smith's Eskimo stories, fonds in NWT Heritage Centre

Andy MacInnes – *(Margaret Gully)*, game officer, Sitidgi Lake Fishing Lodge

Marie MacInnes – *(Mac)*, Rehab Centre in 1968

Dave MacNaughton – *(Elaine)*, CBC tech

Bernie MacNeil – *(Debbie)*, "Dido", Arctic Digital, Inuvik Metis Assoc.

Mary Malloch – Secretary to Regional Administrator in 1964, Research Lab secretary

Peggy Madore – *(Don)*, Bank of Montreal, Joint Secretariat 1994-2006

Roman Mahnic – Hearne High principal in 2007.

Larry Mann – CO HMCS Inuvik 1964 –

Fanny Maring – 1937-1992, NWT Social Services

Paul Marks – *(Trudy)*, butcher, NWT Economic Development

Uli Mast – Butcher in 80's, photographer, Dempster video

Howard McDiarmid – GNWT Local Government in 1973 & 1975

Margot McDiarmid – CBC News

Jim McDonald Sr – *(Alestine)*, 1924-1995, E3 watchman in 1955, NWT Carpenter

Ken McDonald – McDonald Bros Electric

Velma McDonald – SAMS Teacher, skiing, drum dancing

Wanda McDonald – Gwich'in Business Development Corp.

Marg McGee – Inuvik Guides and Scouts, NWT Housing Corp in 1975

Gordon McInnes – Inuvik Community Assocation

Jack McKenna – DPW Manager in 1964

Donald Buster McLeod – 1929- , trapper

George Buck McLeod – 1924-1999, Legion president in 1995, Grollier Hall, Inuvik Tourism

Ruby McLeod – East Three Reelers, started in 1986

Vern McLeod – *(Sandy)*, Inuvik Sewing and Crafts

Veronica McLeod – Muskrat Jamboree starting 1999

Wanda McLeod – CBC Announcer, started in 1982

Brenda McNabb – Inuvik Justice Committee

Dave McNaughton – *(Jean)*, CBC Technician, Inuvik Health Board

Wally McPherson – Oil industry, Gwich'in Tribal Council, to Aklavik

Moe McRae – CFS Inuvik, Inuvik Research Laboratory

Max Melnyk – *(Agnes)*, CFS Inuvik, 25th Anniversary coordinator

D.P. Mush Mersereau – NWT Regional Engineer 1965, Regional Director 1972

Mick Michalko – Mackenzie Hotel bar manager 1964

Dusty Miller – *(Connie)*, in Aklavik in 1956 with an apprentice carpenter crew, trades teacher

Keith Miller – Postmaster 1981-1985

Ron Milligan – NWT Economic Development, former HBC employee

Bob Milner – Reindeer Air

Bev Mitchell – CBC

Catherine Mitchell – 1918- , from Aklavik

Jim Mitchener – *(Lilias)*, Grollier Hall, Customs and Immigration

Lilias Mitchener – *(Jim)*, Northern Images

Bert Mockford – 1939-2004, *(Kaye)*, Sams Teacher

Cliff Moore – *(Lucy)*, on first construction team, member Inuvik Advisory Committee 1965

Billy Moore – Town of Inuvik handyman

Ernie Moore – 1941-2001, first Grade 12 SAMS graduate

John Moore – Inuvik Taxi

Derek Morfit – musician

Maureen Morfit – Métis Association

Andy Morton – Anglican church 1964

Bob Mumford – to Inuvik in 1989, musician, Strings Across The Sky, Arctic College

Rod Murphy – *(Marilyn)*, teacher, artist

David Musselwhite – *(Sylvia)*, SAMS teacher 1976, NCPC, GNWT, pilot

Bill Nasogaluak – Carver

Eli Nasogaluak – *(Sheila)*, carver

Elsie Netro – secretary at Inuvik Research Lab, from Old Crow

Ed Newcombe – NCPC Manager in 1975

Eli Norbert – fiddle player, from Arctic Red River, oil patch

Lawrence Norbert – from Tsiighetchic, school in Inuvik, NWT Dept of Justice, Gwich'in Tribal Council communications advisor

Nap Norbert – 1917- , from Arctic Red River

Gordon Norberg – NWT Housing Corporation

Keith Nordstrom – Pilot

Adolphus Norris – Independent trader on East Channel

Fred Norris – *(Unice)*, East 3 contractor, trucking

Jackie Norris – *(George)*, secretary of Home & School Association in 1963, Member Advisory Committee

Margaret Norris – *(Daan)*, Ingamo Hall

Fred North – *(Vivian)*, third teacher at East 3 arriving in September 1957, later became SAMS principal

Vi North – *(Fred)*, Postmistress

Terry Norwegian – 1935- , northern sewing

Albert Oliver – 1921- , reindeer herder

Vern Opel – Lions Club

Ian Orbel – 1948-1996, *(Liz)*, Deputy Fire Chief in 1990, Fire Chief in 1993

John Ostrick – *(Ethel)*, Inuvik Research Lab

Ed Overbo – Education

Carol Palmer – *(Lyn)*, Bank of Montreal Manager in 1983

Wilbert Papik – IRC accountant, left in 199? to Victoria

Harry Peffer – 1947-2000, *(Susan)*

Jake Peffer – from Aklavik, Inuvik's first contractor

Wilbert Peffer – Peffer's Painting

Guy Pemberton – Dowland Contracting

Bertha Peter – CBC Gwich'in

Bjorger Pettersen – *(Anita)*, TEST program instructor, Inuvik Ski Club

Fil Petrin – 1926-2000, Inuvik Construction, Knights of Columbus Fil Petrin Memorial Corn Roast

Pam Petrin – CBC announcer

Clara Phillips – cook at Rehab Centre 1963, Grollier Hall, Inuvik Hospital

Frank Pielak – RCN in Aklavik, CFS Inuvik, GNWT Tourism

Jim Pitt – Inuvik Housing Association, NWT Local Government

Art Pollon – *(Del)*, Shell base manager, Town Council 1976

Lee Post – *(Lorna)*, Aklavik administrator in 1954, organized first Spring Carnival Queen Contest in 1957

Dave Prowse – Town Secretary-Manager, 1970

Mikel Pulk – 1904-1994, *(Anna)*, reindeer herder, Commissioner's Award in 1974

Nels Pulk – *(Ruth)*, reindeer herder

Joe Pyne – NCPC Manager

Johnny Raymond – 1912-1988, Story teller

Dave Reid – Samuel Hearne principal

Louise Reindeer – moved to Tulita (Fort Norman), Tulita Mayor in 2008

Eugene Rheaume – Welfare Officer (1959), later MP

Robert Rhodes – CBC Manager in 1975

Doug Robertson – Inuvik Crisis Line

Gord Robertson – *(Val)*, Robertson's B&B, Inuvik Ski Club, NWT Transportation

Larry Robertson – Anglican church, ICATS

Dorothy Robinson – early northern teacher, in Inuvik 1963, died in England May 1998

Denise Robson – *(T.K.)*, Mack Travel

T.K. (Karen) Robson – 1931-2004, *(Denise)*, SAMS teacher in 1963, Curling Club, Legion, went outside to Squamish in 1989

Big Jim Rogers – 1903-1988, trapper

Hank Rogers – Town heavy equipment operator, Northern Games

James Niulus Rogers – fiddler

Lawrence Rogers – ICS

David Roland – 1922- , *(Olga Tumma -2003)*, reindeer herder, SAMS caretaker

John Rooks – IGH Supt in 1965

John Roska – *(Jean)*, heavy equipment maintenance, Town Council 1972, Polar TV

Mary Ann Ross – from Tsiigehtchic, Gwich'in Tribal Council vice president in 2003

Tom Ross – *(Tina)*, PWA Manager 1963

Tommy Ross – *(Lois)*, first construction team, NWT Centennial Canoe race, from Aklavik

Les Roth – *(Irene)*, Treeline Aviation Services

Charlie Ruben – *(Lois Harwood)*, fisheries management

Stan Ruben – ICS

Tom Rusnak – NCPC (1962), Lion's Club President

Bill Rutherfod – Veggie man, from Okanagan, started trucking fruits and vegetables to Inuvik in 1985, featured in book *By Truck To The North* (Turnbull 1999) and CBC television documentary On The Road

Bob Ruzicka – dentist, singer

Pauline Schmidt – Boreal Bookstore

Herbert Schwarz – Doctor at Inuvik Hospital. Collected native legends and artifacts. Wrote book *Elik* in 1970

Eric Thrasher Schweig – 1967- , Inuvik-born actor, first film was *The Shaman's Secret*

Jim Scott, – *(Dorcas Allen)*, boat builder, Scott Construction

John Scullion – *(Colly)*, Regional Administrator

Dave Seabrook – *(Barbara Klengenburg)*, jumped ship at Tuk, only Southerner to arrive from the North

John Sealy – GNWT Social Development in 1975

Peter Selamio – Inuvik heavy equipment operator

Ella Shanahorn – First East 3 teacher in September 1956 in Distributor St 512 schoolhouse

Mike Shand – Asst Regional Administrator in 1964

Roland Shingatok – Inuit Housing Association

Doug Shinnon – PWA agent and business man, Shine-On Super A groceries, real estate, Suna Likka

Sarah Simon – Order of Canada October 18, 1991

Willie Simon – *(Joyce)*, trapper, entrepreneur, unauthorised house at Boot Lake and East Branch in 1991

Ron Simpson – GNWT safety inspector

Ed Smith – Ed Smith Construction, operated in 1970s, factory-built homes

Ken Smith – RCMP Western Arctic Subdivision in 1963

Jack Smith – Federal Public Works in 1975

Rosalind Smith – Phys Ed teacher, TEST

Tommy Smith – 1952- , Northern Games,

Norm Snow – *(Roseann)*, Dept Fisheries, Exec Director Inuvialuit Joint Secretariat in 1986

Karen Snowshoe – raised in Vancouver, member Tetlit-Gwich'in Band, Gwich'in Tribal Council Community Regional Manager

Norman Snowshoe – from Fort McPherson, Gwich'in Tribal Council resource manager

Fred Sorenson – 1926-2001, *(Irene)*, 1927-1998, arrived 1965 operated sawmill projects

Charlie Soupay – Rehab Centre, qualified in watch repair, hospital concession

Arnold Stadler – HBC manager 1965

Kuno Stahlberg – *(Minnie)*, carpenter, locksmith

Perry Stamatelakis – 1934-2001, *(Katia)*, ran Perry's Cafe in MacKenzie Hotel in 1970, Perry Building in 1988

Alex Stefansson – 1910- , *(Mabel)*, 1914-1993, on Aklavik Relocation Advisory Committee

Frank Stefansson – 1941- , Boy Scout in Aklavik, Carpenter

Georgina Stefansson – *(Bruce Tocher)*, granddaughter of Vilhjalmur Stefansson and Fanny Pannigabluk, daughter of Alex Stefansson 1910-

Willie Stefansson – ICS, NTCL

Don Stewart – 1963, Social Services, Sup't Welfare

Lin Stewart – *(Pauline)*, L.E.S. Arctic, President Inuvik Chamber of Commerce 1974

Ivor Stewart – Regional Director 1975

David Buck Storr – 1933-1996, contractor

Bill Stott – Manager, Northern Canada Power Commission Inuvik Plant 1962-1970

Norm Street – Norm's Building Supplies, 1974-78

Ray Suchodolski – *(Jean)*, MOT, Taxi driver, broomball

Dave Sullivan – *(Helen)*, RDR Sports, Town Council 1989

Steve Szabo – 1927-2000, born in Budapest, to Inuvik in 1965, worked at NCPC until 1985, retired to Alberta

Danny Sydney – 1925- , *(Ruby)*, reindeer herder, SAMS caretaker

Darielle Talerico – biologist, Delta tourism

Andy Tardiff – *(Doreen)*, Boy Scout in Aklavik, Herschel Island park warden

Doreen Tardiff – Andy, Dentist, graduated U of Manitoba in 1995

Mary Tapinen – 1930 - , arrived 1963, cook

Glen Taylor – *Drum* Editor in 1990s

Grace Tatti – Inuvik Hospital

Joe Teddy – 1926- , *(Mary)*, SAMS caretaker

Ron Thody – teacher, Hearne High principal in 1975

George Thompson – Asst Regional Administrator in 1968, Regional Administrator

Alice Thrasher – 1910- , Alaskan Inuvialuit married to Bill Thrasher, son of a Portuguese whaler. Mona was their first child

Willie Thrasher – musician, moved to Vancouver

Marci Tingmiak – IRC Deputy Enrolment Registrar

Ray Tingmiak – Town public works

Sarah Tingmiak – 1922- , Eskimo Dancer

Charles Tiza – Musician, from Old Crow

Jerome Tocher – *(Georgina Stefansson)*

Rudy Tornow – carpenter in 1964, later Mayor of Aklavik

Fred Trimble – GNAF, carver, moved to Vancouver Island

Lyle Trimble – *(Mary)*, Ram Air, RCMP, NWT Council, carver, painter, living in Nanaimo (2000)

Julian Tsaroff – *(Jeanne)*, Dentist, Town Council 1973

Ron Tuckley – Magician, NWT Public Works

Amos Tuma – 1889-1975, Delta person, early Inuvik resident, Tuma Drive named after him

Brian Turner – *(Maiie Ann)*, boat captain, carpenter

Mike VanBridger – *(Bobbie)*, 1956-2007

Bill Vehus – *(Charlotte 1896-)*, on Aklavik Relocation Advisory Committee, East 3 contracts

Jack Veitch – Industrial Division 1962

Jerry Veltman – Town Inuvik CAO 2000

Vickers, Ted – Lions Club 1963

Charlie Villeneuve – Minor hockey

Doug Villeneuse – Musician

Don Violet – Pentecostal missionary, pilot, owned Delta barge Tiliruk

Uli Wager – Doctor Inuvik General Hospital in 1970s

Don Waleski – GNWT Regional Engineer in 1966

Jack Wainewright – 1929-1999, *(Erica (Weiderman))* (1), *(Lena)* (2), pilot 1962, taxi driver, cigar smoker

Ken Walmsley – *(Gwen)*, PWA

Agnes Walsh – IHG nurse

Lee Wark – *(Audrey)*, 1962, teacher, hotel in Puerto Vallarta, Mexico

Al Warner – *(Iris)*, GNA mechanic, moved from Whitehorse

Bill Warren – *(Bea)*, teacher, big on basketball games

Peter Westaway – *(Balbir)*, Ingamo Hall coordinator in 1980s

Al Weaton – HBC

Agnes White – Inuvialuit translator, daughter Marlene Raddi Bailey

Dick White – plumber, Arctic Plumbing, from Aklavik

John Wiedermann – PRJ Mechanical in 1985

Paul Wiedemann – Arctic Dove, Esso agent

Walter Willkomm – 1931-2003, *(Hildegard)*, to Canada from Poland at 14, to Inuvik in 1969, Mackenzie Hotel, Walter The Roofer, W.W. Roofing

Heidi Willkomm – Artist, northern T-shirts with brother Arno

Ken Williams – DOT Airport Manager 1964

Ron Williams – Regional game officer in Aklavik and Inuvik, pilot, good citizen e.g. fighting Inuvik fire 1968

Tom Williams – Gwich'in Tribal Council chief operating office in 2001

Fred Wills – Dept Agriculture field technician in 1964 and 1965

Al Wilson – *(Mary)*, cook at Grollier Hall, AAA, Metis Association

Jim Wilson – carpenter, Inuvik Vice President NWT Federation of Labour in 1976

Bev Woslyng – NCPC utilidor management. Crashed plane in 1969 and survived 18 days until rescue

Ruth Wright – artist, Great Northern Arts Festival

Tom Wright – Lilian, Town Council 1994, Nitat Renewable Resource Council

Audrey Loreen-Wulf – 1942- , CBC, artist, Inuvaluit Communications

Harold Wulf – *(Audria Loreen)*, Co-owner of Finto Inn

Bill Yorga – CFS Inuvik, Inuvik Community Assocation

Don Yamkowy – *(Kerry)*, Northwestel Manager 1975, Chamber of Commerce

Tom Yate – *(Agnes)*, GNWT DPW

George Yelich – Kennaston Contractors/ Klondike Contractors, ran for Mayor in 1971

Mike Yip – SAMS teacher in 1971-1975, photographer, book *Inuvik*, 1971

Barry Zellen – *Tusaayaksat* editor 1990s

Influential Officials

Inuvik Secretary Managers
Ben DeKline	1969-1870
Dave Prowse	1970-1971
Al Algar	1972-1975

Inuvik Fire Chiefs
Mr McDerby	1960-1962
Len Adrian	1962-1970
Don Cave	1970-1975

Federal/NWT Administrators
Curt Merrill	1954-1955
Tom Taylor	1955-1956
Bob Langdon (Nor Affairs)	1955-1956
Ron Hodgkinson	1962-1963
Tom Butters	1963-1964
Ewan Cotterill	1965-1966
Sid Hancock (Nov 66)	1966-1967
George Thompson	1967-1969
Mush Mersereau	1969-1972
Ivor Stewart	1972-1975

Education Superintendents
Harold Darkes	-1967
Joe Coady	1968-

Indian Affairs Branch
Eddie Cook	1955-1956
Al Cottrell	1957-1966
Danny Norris	1967-

Sir Alexander Mackenzie School Principals
Bill Shaw	1959-1962
Bill Bock	1962-1965
Jim Maher	1965-1971
Fred North	1971-1975
Ed Duggan	1975-1977

Post Masters
Lloyd Cole	1958
Lloyd Carrothers	1960
George Castle	in 1964
Russ Cournoyea	in 1975

RCMP Detachment
Insp Ed Lysuk	in 1961
Insp Stewart	in 1962
Insp Ken Smith	in 1964
Insp Carl Smith	in 1971
Insp John Sebastian	in 1975

CFS Inuvik Commanding Officers
A.P. Johnson, Lt	1952
J.A. McDonald, Lt	1954
W.C. Wilinson, Lt	1956
J.M. Kempton, Lt	1962
D.W. Smith, Lt-Cmd	1962-64
Larry P. Mann, Lt-Cmd	1964-66
R.C. Eastman, Lt-Cmd	1966-68
W. Yorga, Lt-Cmd/Maj	1968-70
Jack "Tug" Wilson, Maj	1970-72
N.W. Van Loan, Major	1972-74
Harry J. Atchener, Major	1974-75

Hospital Superintendents
Dr. Dale at time of transfer from Aklavik, 1959
Dr. John Rooks,1964-1965
Dr. Mary Hapgood, 1971

CBC Radio Managers
Berkeley Macmillan	1962-1963
Elijah Menarik	1965-1969
Nellie Cournoyea	1970-1974
Robert Rhodes	1975-

Governors General

Lord Byng of Vimy	1921-1926
Viscount Willingdon	1926-1931
Lord Tweedsmuir (John Buchan)	1935-1940
Earl of Athlone	1940-1946
Viscount Alexander	1946-1952
Vincent Massey	1952-1959
Georges-P Vanier	1959-1967
Roland Michener	1967-1974
Jules Leger	1974-1979

Prime Ministers

Louis St. Laurent	Lib.	1948 -1957
John Diefenbaker	Cons.	1957-1963
Lester Pearson	Lib.	1963 -1968
Pierre Trudeau	Lib.	1968 -1979

Federal MPs Elected Constituency

Aubrey Simmons, 1947, Yukon-Mackenzie River

Merv Hardie, 1952, Mackenzie River

Isabel 'Tibbie' Hardie, 1962, Mackenzie River
Gene Rheaume, 1963, Northwest Territories
Bud Orange, 1965, Northwest Territories
Wally Firth, 1972, Northwest Territories

Northern Affairs Ministers

Robert Winters	Liberal	1950 to 1953
Jean LeSage	Liberal	1953 to 1957
Douglas Harkness	Conservative	1957
Paul Comptois	Conservative	1959
Alvin Hamilton	Conservative	1957 to 1960
Walter Dinsdale	Conservative	1960 to 1963
Arthur Laing	Liberal	1963 to 1968
Jean Chretien	Liberal	1968 to 1974
Judd Buchanan	Liberal	1974 to 1976
Warren Almand	Liberal	1976 to 1977

Northern Affairs Deputy Ministers

R. Gordon Robertson	1959
Ernest A. Cote, ADM	1964
Basil Robinson	1970

ACND Chairmen

Hugh Keenlyside	1948
General Hugh Young	1953
Gordon Robertson	1953-
Ernest Cote	1961-

NWT Commissioners

Hugh A. Young	1950-1953
R.G. Robertson	1953-1963
B.G. Sivertz	1963-1967
Stewart Hodgson	1967-1979

NWT MLAs Elected Constituency

Frank Carmichael, 1951-1957, Mackenzie West
Knut Lang, 1957-1964, Mackenzie Delta
Lyle Trimble, 1964-1970, Mackenzie Delta
Tom Butters, 1971-1975, Western Arctic
Tom Butters, 1975-1991, Inuvik

Inuvik Street Names

Inuvik street names provide a glimpse of the area's history. Kingmingya (cranberry) and Kugmallit (local tribe) are Inuit names. Bonnet Plume (prominent Gwich'in family) and Loucheux (early French name for Gwich'in people) are Indian names. Franklin, Dolphin, Reliance and Union are streets named after the Arctic Explorer and three of his ships. Adam and Ruyant streets are named after Father Joseph Adam of the Igloo Church and Father Max Ruyant who operated the Grollier Hall student residence for 25 years.

Adam Road	After Father Jules Adam, OMI.
Bompas Street	After Anglican Bishop William C. Bompas, the first Bishop of the Mackenzie River diocese in 1884.
Berger Street	After Hon. Thomas Berger who headed a commission into Mackenzie Valley pipeline developments.
Bonnet Plume Road	After prominent Delta family.
Boot Lake Road	After the lake shaped like a boot.
Breynat Street	After Roman Catholic Bishop Gabriel Breynat OMI, the first head of the Vicariate of the Mackenzie in 1901.
Camsell Place	After Juliam Camsell, Chief Factor of the Hudon's Bay Company Mackenzie River operations in the 1890s.
Carmichael Drive	Named after Frank Carmichael who was the first NWT Councillor representing Inuvik.
Carn Road	After Carn Construction Company owned by Milan Carnogusky who operated from the corner lot on Airport Road
Centennial Street	Named to commerate the 100th birthday of the Northwest Territories in 1971.
Council Crescent	Where the NWT Council and staff was accommodated in 10 new "512s" for their Inuvik session in August 1956.
Distributor Street	After the Hudson's Bay Company paddle wheel steamboat which was the largest ship on the Mackenzie River in 1918.
Dolphin Street	After Sir John Franklin's ship "Dolphin" used in his second voyage to the Polar Sea in 1825-27.
Firth Street	After the legendary John Firth who was the Hudson's Bay Company employee/manager in Fort McPherson from 1871 to 1920.

Franklin Road	After Sir John Franklin who in 1825 descended the Mackenzie River.
Gwich'in Road	After the Gwich'in residents, originally Loucheux Road
Inuit Road	After the local Inuvialuit residents.
Kingalok Place	Inuit word for King Eider Duck.
Kingmingya Road	From the Inuvialuktun word meaning "cranberry".
Kugmallit Road	After the Inuvialuit tribe traditionally living in Eskimo Lakes area.
Mackenzie Road	After Sir Alexander Mackenzie who in 1789 camped at the site where Inuvik now exists.
Marine Bypass Road	Built during the petroleum and pipeline construction era to connect the marine shipping yards north of the community with the Dempster Highway and Inuvik airport.
Millen Street	After RCMP Constable Spike Millen of the Arctic Red River detachment who in January 1932 led an attempt to capure "Albert Johnson, the Mad Trapper of Rad River". Constable Millen was killed in the gunfight with Albert Johnson.
Nanuk Place	After the Inuvialuit for Polar Bear.
Natala Drive	From the Gwich'in word "natialia" meaning "the place where serveral rivers come together" referring to Point Separation and the beginning of the Mackenzie Delta.
Navy Road	Named as the street leading from Inuvik to the HMCS Inuvik operations base to the north of Inuvik which operated from 1961 to 1986.
Oopik Street	after the Inuvialuit Snowy Owl.
Reliance Street	After Sir John Franklin's ship "Reliance" used during his second expedition to the Polar Sea in 1825-27.
Ruyant Crescent	After Roman Catholic priest Father Max Ruyant who operated the Grollier Hall students residence in Inuvik.
Tuma Drive	After Amos Tuma, a well known Inuk who lived in the Mackenzie Delta and Inuvik from 1889 to 1975.
Tununuk Drive	After Tununuk island off the south tip of Richards Island. Tununuk translated means the 'Place where you can see in all directions".
Union Street	After Sir John Franklin's ship "Union" used during his second expedition to the Polar Sea in 1825-27.
Veteran Way	Distributor Street from Mackenzie Road to Franklin Street renamed in 2007 in honour of those who fought for Canada. At the same time Distributor Street was extended along River Road to Duck Lake Road.
Wolverine Road	After a common Mackenzie Delta mammal.

Appendix G

Inuvik Humour

Humour is essential for complete living in an Arctic community. Hence, there are many Inuvik jokes and witticisms which are repeated with many variations. Johnny Raymond, an Inuvik old timer, always had a funny story to tell about his many experiences. Joe Adams was another classic story teller who often financed his drinking habit by telling tales about northern life. Here are a few of Inuvik's humorous anecdotes.

1. **"Inuvik's population is ..."**: Inuvik residents are mixed bunch. As many of the Southerners in Inuvik boast mixed parentage from England, Ireland, France etc. so also do the local indigenous people who claim ancestry from explorers, whalers, Bay Boys, RCMP, administrators, etc. Many Eskimos have married Indians and vice versa. The Métis population has always been sizable. As the initial Northern Affairs census records showed "Indians, Eskimos and Others", it is a standard comment to refer to the Inuvik population as being 50% Eskimo, 50% Indian and 50% Other.

2. **"Smartie town"** : In the early years, most of Inuvik residences were painted bright colours to compensate for the long periods of supposedly dreary winter weather. A fourplex row house would have each unit painted a dramatic pink, blue, green or yellow. Hence many jokes developed about Inuvik's appearance as a 'smartie town' or an 'easter egg town'. Pat Barry wrote "To old-timers in the Mackenzie Delta, Inuvik is Toy Town. And so it seems to have been planned: a toy town for toy people." (Barry 1965).

3. **"Typical Inuvik family"**: Visiting journalists spending time in Inuvik's restaurants and bars would invariably meet up with one or more groups of socioeconomic researchers doing their summer thing. Often these researchers would be seen going along on family expeditions. Hence, the standing joke developed that the "typical Inuvik family is made up of a husband, wife, two kids and a sociologist."

4. **"Let the Inuvik administrators control only themselves"**: Many times at Inuvik Community Association meetings when there was a heated debate on the supposed lack of Federal interest, a frustrated resident would call out "If we don't get more respect, we'll all leave and let the Inuvik administrators control only themselves."

5. **"Visitor sting"**: Northerners have a highly developed tradition of providing mischievious answers to inquiring researchers and journalists who generally bother people with many social questions which could be considered as none of the researcher's business. The ultimate sting is to provide a plausible, but way-out, story to see if the misleading information is published in a report or newspaper.

6. **"Researchers coming to Inuvik are like the birds"**: They arrive in the Spring and depart in the Fall. Abe Okpik in 1970 said that he had heard three people say the word "Inuit" that

morning. After the perfect pause, he said "The anthropologists must be early this year." (*Globe & Mail* Morning Smile, 20 Sep 97)

7. **"Major Accident"**: Back when Inuvik was under construction and there was no road connection, there were no cars on the streets, only big trucks and bulldozers. When people settled in to normal living they brought in cars by barge to be more 'normal'. However, there is a story about the first and second cars to arrive. One car ran into the other and Inuvik was back to having no private cars again.

8. **"Lawyer Problems"**: For several years Inuvik residents seemed to have few legal problems. Then Inuvik's first lawyer arrived to set up shop in 1971. He didn't have much business. But when the second lawyer set up in 1972 both legal offices were very busy with 'everybody' suing each other.

9. **"Welcome Sign"**: For a Spring curling bonspiel a large canvas welcome sign was made up and was strung across Mackenzie Road. On the saturday night of the bonspiel the sign disappeared but was found next morning strung between the two posts at the Inuvik cemetery entrance where those traveling on Airport Road could read the WELCOME.

10. **"Brown Jokes"** from the *Aklavik Journal* 1956-1957 (Brown 1996).

When an Arctic Red woman came to the "age" blank while filling out a government application form, she wrote "Atomic".

On the first day of school the teacher explained that if anyone had to go to the toilet, they should hold up two fingers. One puzzled little girl plaintively asked "How's that going to help?"

Mangileluk's Requisition: Old timers around Aklavik tell of Eskimo trader Mangileluk at Perry River Post who, unable to read, copied his orders from old boxes and one year ordered one case of "This Side Up" and three cases of "Handle With Care".

Donald Greenland claims he can't bear to see his wife get up in the cold and start the fire these frosty mornings … so he turns his face to the wall".

Old timers tell of the early Scotch trader up the Mackenzie who used to take off his reading glasses to save them from wear when he wasn't looking at anything.

Mrs X, an Aklavik housewife, looked high and low for her husband Charlie last Thursday night. Finally found him at a friend's drinking overproof rum. She grabbed the bottle and took a short nip, spat it out and said "How can you drink that poison, that tastes perfectly awful". And Charlie replied "You see, and you thought I was having a good time."

A carpenter at E3 putting on roofing slipped and fell into a trash can below. While he was sitting there trying to figure out how he could get out, two newly arrived Eskimos walked by and one said "White man very wasteful. That carpenter good yet for ten years".

Inuvik Acronyms

AB . . . . Arctic Bibliography

ACND . . . . Advisory Committee on Northern Development

AECL . . . . Atomic Energy of Canada Ltd.

AJ . . . . Aklavik Journal

BAY . . . . Hudson's Bay Company

CANEX . . . . Canadian Forces Exchange System

CBC . . . . Canadian Broadcasting Corporation

CFS . . . . Canadian Forces Station

CIBC . . . . . Canadian Imperial Bank of Commmerce

COPE . Committee for Original Peoples Entitlement

CPA . . . . Canadian Pacific Airlines

CWS . . . . Canadian Wildlife Service

DBR . . . . Division of Building Research (NRC)

DEW . . . . Distant Early Warning line

DIAND . . . . Department Indian and Northern Development

DOT . . . . Department of Transport (federal)

DPW . . . . Department of Public Works (federal)

EM&R . . . . . . Energy, Mines and Resources (federal)

E3 . . . . East Three Inuvik Construction Site

E4 . . . . Inuvik Airport Construction Site

EV . . . . Inuvik Airport Call Sign

EVTV . . . . Inuvik Television Company

FAS . . . . Fetal Alcohol Syndrome

FENCO . . . . Foundation Engineering Company

GNWT . . Government of the Northwest Territories

HBC . . . . Hudson's Bay Company

HMCS . . . . Her Majesty's Canadian Ship

ICA . . . . Inuvik Community Association

IGH . . . . Inuvik General Hospital

INAC . . . . Indian and Northern Affairs Canada

IAND . . . Indian Affairs and Northern Development (federal)

IRL . . . . Inuvik Research Laboratory

IVC . . . . Inuvik Visitors Committee

MADGAG . . . . Mackenzie Delta Government Administration Group

NA&NR . . . . Northern Affairs & National Resources (federal)

NAPO . . . . National Anti-Poverty Organization

NCPC . . . . Nothern Canada Power Commission

NCRC Northern Coordination and Research Centre

NFB . . . . National Film Board

NOGAP . . . . Northern Oil and Gas Action Program

NTCL . . . . . Northern Transportation Company Ltd.

NRC . . . . National Research Council

NRS . . . . Naval Radio Station

NTCL . . . . . Northern Transportation Company Ltd.

NTPC . . . Northwest Territories Power Corporation

NWT . . . . Northwest Territories

PCSP . . . . Polar Continental Shelf Project

PWA . . . . Pacific Western Airlines

RCASC . . . . Royal Canadian Army Signal Corps

RCMP . . . . Royal Canadian Mounted Police

RCS . . . . Royal Canqdian Signals

SAC . . . . Strategic Air Command (US)

SAMS . . . . Sir Alexander Mackenzie School

UCN . . . . University of Canada North

WAVA . . . . Western Arctic Visitors Association

"512" . . . . 512 sq ft house measuring 16ft × 32ft

APPENDIX I

References & Bibliography

Aasen, Clarence T., (1967), **Comprehensive Settlement Planning in the Mackenzie River Delta, NWT,** Waterloo, University of Waterloo, 91 p. A proposed planning theory and methodology.

Aasen, Clarence T. and S. Walter Wright, (1966), **Functional Evaluation of the Inuvik, NWT, Settlement Plan,** Ottawa, Indian and Northern Affairs, 19 p, Northern Coordination and Research Centre.

Alberta Business Journal, (1967), **Main Street In The Arctic,** Edmonton, Alberta Business Journal Sep-Oct 1967.

Alberta Business Journal, (1971), **Adolescent Growing Pains for Inuvik,** Edmonton, Alberta Business Journal, p 82-84, July-August issue 1971.

Allen, Victor, (1966), **Trapping Industry,** Inuvik, 3. Brief presented to the Economic Council of Canada.

Alunik, Ishmael, (1998), **Call Me Ishmael,** Inuvik, Kolausok Ublaaq Entrprises, 99 p, ISBN 096845710X.

Alunik, Ishmael, Eddie D. Kolausok and David Morrison, (2003), **Across Time and Tundra: The Inuvialuit of the Western Arctic,** Vancouver, Raincoast, 230 p, ISBN 1551926458.

Aquilina, Alfred P., (1981), **Mackenzie, Yesterday and Beyond,** North Vancouver, Hancock House Publishers, 204 p, ISBN 0888390831.

Arctic Circular, (1958), **Inuvik,** Ottawa, Arctic Circle, 2 p. Notes official proclamation, July 18, 1958, of Inuvik as name of the town built to replace Aklavik as a centre for the Mackenzie Delta district.

Arctic Circular, (1968), **Inuvik Research Laboratory,** Ottawa, Arctic Circle, 3 p. Brief report on the projects and activities of the laboratory at Inuvik, which provides logistical and technical aid, equipment, field camps and laboratory space free of charge to scientific investigators.

Arctic Institute of North America, (1970), **Man In The North Conference on Community Development,** Montreal, Arctic Institute of North America, 42 p, vertical, Inuvik, 18-21 Nov 1970. Under auspices of Mackenzie Institue.

Argue, Marilyn, (1967), **Woman of the Century Seeks Better Housing for Eskimos,** London, London Free Press. Agnes Semmler in Ottawa asking government support for housing and education in Inuvik.

Associated Engineering Services Ltd., (1973), **Water and Sewage System Analysis, Town of Inuvik, NWT,** Edmonton, Associated Engineering Services, 52 p. Prepared for Northern Canada Power Commission, Ottawa.

Atkins, Alison, (1983), **Inuvik: Coping With Beaufort Sea Hydrocarbon Development,** Inuvik, Town of Inuvik, 40 p, ISBN Vert File. A report for the Town of Inuvik in preparation for the 1983 Environmental Assessment and Review Process Hearings.

Atkinson, Ken, (1987), **Life On A Deep Freeze,** London, The Geographical Magazine, September 1987, p 444-449.

Baird, Irene, (1960), **Inuvik – Place of Man,** Winnipeg, Beaver Magazine, Autumn 1960, 13 p. Describes Inuvik, planned to replace Aklavik. Solutions to problems caused by permafrost are outlined.

Baird, Irene, (1969), **Canada's Far North,** New York, UNESCO, 7 p, outsize, UNESCO Courier 1969.

Barmann, George J., (1970), **9 to 5 Life Comes To Canada's North,** Cleaveland, The Plain Dealer, 1 p. Comments by Graham Rowley on naming of Inuvik and Dick Hill on northern development.

Barry, Pat S., (1966), **Utopia In The Arctic,** Edge 5, Fall 1966, 11 p. Details the problems of Inuvik, including the utilidor system and inequalities of the treatment and condition of permanent and transient residents. Original report published in Inuvik 15 May 1965.

Beaufort Industry Group, (1985), **Proceedings Big '85 Beaufort Development Conference, Inuvik, May 29-Jun 1, 1985,** Inuvik, Beaufort Industry Group, 58 p. Text of major addresses presented at the conference.

Berger, Hon Thomas R., (1977), **Northern Frontier, Northern Homeland: The Report of the Mackenzie Valley Pipeline Inquiry, Vol One and Vol Two,** Ottawa, Government of Canada, 1-213 p, 2-268 p, Vol two on Terms and Conditions.

Berton, Pierre, (1956), **Mysterious North: Encounters with the Canadian Frontier 1947-1954,** Toronto, 391 p. First published February 20, 1956.

Billingsley, Martha, (1985), **Inuvik Visitor Consultant Programme,** Inuvik, Western Arctic Visitors Association, 18 p. In 1984 Visitor Consultants were employed by the Western Arctic Visitors Association (WAVA) for a visitor hospitality program.

Bissett, Don, (1967), **Lower Mackenzie Region: An Area Economic Survey,** Ottawa, Indian Affairs and Northern Development, 520 p. An assessment of the economic situation and resource base of the Mackenzie Delta and the area immediately surrounding it and the diversity of physical and human landscapes. The present status of the economy is unsatisfactory in terms of productivity, the input of monies for development and the outflow of products. Marketing systems are unsatisfactory or ill-defined. A program of integrated resource use and the establishment of marketing systems appear to be absolute requirements. Continuing advances in education and the replacements of non-residents with residents in positions of increasing responsibility will partly solve the problem of increasing population. For the interim period continuous efforts should be made to encourage the out-migration of younger age groups.

Black, W.A., (1959), **Suggested Program of Economic Rehabilitation in the Mackenzie Delta Area,** Ottawa, Geographical Branch, Dept Mines and Technical Surveys, ISBN Vert File.

Boek, Walter E. and Jean M. Boek, (1960), **Report on Field Work in Aklavik and Inuvik, NWT,** Ottawa, Northern Coordination and Research Centre. Unpublished manuscript, March 1960. Report of an investigation to determine basic causes for resistance to the move to Inuvik on the part of Aklavik residents. Includes information on the economic and social situation in the Mackenzie Delta.

Bouchard, Lorne H., (1963), **Mackenzie: Misissippi of the Arctic,** Toronto, Weekend Magazine, Vol 13, No 1, 1963. Paintings and story of a trip down the Mackenzie River. Includes a painting of an Eskimo boy at Inuvik and the Mackenzie Delta at Tununuk. Bouchard (1913-1978) was a Montreal artist who made several trips to the Arctic.

Bowles, K., (1974), **Characteristics of Mackenzie Delta Natives and Their Relationship to Employment Policies,** Ottawa, Indian and Northern Affairrs, 38 p. Extracted from Natives and Outsiders, Derek G. Smith, 1974.

Boyd, William L. and Josephine W. Boyd, (1965), **Water Supply and Sewage Disposal Developments in the Far North,** Journal American Water Works Assoc, July 1965, 10 p. Reviews recent developments in water supply and sewage disposal in the north, including Inuvik.

Boyd, William L. and Josephine W. Boyd, (1967), **Microbiological studies of aquatic habitats of the area of Inuvik, NWT,** Montreal, Arctic, March 1967, 13 p. Report on chemical and microbiological studies fn lakes, ponds and the Mackenzie River near Inuvik.

Boyer, J. Patrick, (1980), **Town of Inuvik Interim Submission on COPE Agreement In Principle (Spring 1982),** Toronto, Fraser & Beatty, 47 p.

Brown, Bern Will, (1996), **Aklavik Journal: A Reprint of the Community Newspaper of Aklavik, North West Territories, 1955-57,** Colville Lake, Bern Will Brown, 125 p, ISBN 1550564730.

Brown, Bern Will, (1999), **Arctic Journal II: Time for a Change,** Ottawa, Novalis, 350 p, ISBN 2895070393.

Brown, Roger, G.H. Johnston and J.A. Pihlainen, (1954), **Site Investigations of East Three, 1954,** Ottawa, National Research Council, Division of Building Research, Report No 57, Prepared for the Department of Northern Affairs and National Resources.

Brown, R.J.E., (1957), **Observation on Break-up in the Mackenzie River and its Delta, 1954,** Ottawa, National Research Council, 8 p, ISBN Vert File, Journal of Glaciology, Oct, 1957.

Brown, R.J.E., (1957), **Permafrost Investigations in the Mackenzie Delta,** Canadian Geographer, 1956, 5 p.

Brown, R.J.E., (1970), **Permafrost in Canada, its Influence on Northern Development,** Toronto, University of Toronto, 234 p. Part of Canadian Building Series.

Brown, R.J.E., G.H. Johnston and J.A. Pihlainen, (1955), **Compendium of Field Notes from Aklavik Townsite Studies, 1954,** Ottawa, National Research Council, 211 p. Division of Building Research, Report No 64. Field notes from an intensive study of all possible townsites for the new town of Aklavik in the Mackenzie Delta. Photographs and maps.

Brown, W.G., G.H. Johnston and R.J.E. Brown, (1964), **Comparison of observed and calculated ground temperatures with permafrost distribution under a northern lake,** Canadian Geotechnical Journal, July 1964, 7 p. From a few ground temperature measurements around a small shallow lake near Inuvik, it was possible to estimate the thermal regime under and about the lake.

Brundtland, Gro Harlem, (1987), **Our Common Future: World Commission on the Environment and Development,** New York, United Nations.

Buker, Peter Edward, (1984), **Socio-Economic Impact of CFS Inuvik on its Host Region,** Ottawa, Department of National Defence, Operational Research and Analysis Establishment, 69 p, ORAE Project 96738, January 1984.

Burns, B.M., (1973), **Climate of the Mackenzie Valley-Beaufort Sea,** Toronto, Environment Canada, 279 p, Atmospheric Environment Climatological Studies Number 24.

Butters, Tom, (1974), **Inuvik Is Getting Restless,** Edmonton, Business Life, July/August 1974, p 31-35.

Byer, Doug, (1997), **Northern Service (Stan Byer's Arctic Experiences),** Calgary, Detselig, 151 p, ISBN 1550591495.

Canada, (1956), **Hydro Electric Potential for the Mackenzie Delta Area,** Ottawa, Canada Mines and Resources.

Canadian Architect, (1956), **The Old and the New Aklavik,** Toronto, Canadian Architect, November 1956, p 23-28.

Canadian Weekly Bulletin, (1953), **To Move Aklavik,** Ottawa, Canadian Weekly Bulletin Canada, 2 p. Plan for relocation of Aklavik, the largest community in the Canadian Arctic, is announced to have been approved in principal by the Canadian Governent. The town is to be rebuilt in a location safe from erosion of the Mackenzie River and from sinking through the melting permafrost, with conditions permitting proper sanitation and water supply. The new site will be chosen by experts during 1954; after roadways, water and sewage system, etc., are installed, transfer of buildings will begin in the winter of 1955-56. The move is estimated to require four years' time. (Canadian Weekly Bulletin, 11Dec1953 "Plan To Move Aklavik" AB33993).

Carrothers, A.W.R., Jean Beetz and John M. Parker, (1966), **Report of the Advisory Commission on the Development of Government in the NWT,** Ottawa, Indian and Northern Affairs, 1965 hearings, Vols 1 & 2., in Inuvik 22 & 23 August 1965.

Castonguay, Rachelle and David Sherestone, (1985), **Bibliography of Research Publication: Inuvik Scientific Resource Centre 1964-1984,** Ottawa, Indian and Northern Affairs Canada, 87 p, 658 entries to May 1985.

CBC North, (2002), **Berger Commission 25 Years Later,** Yellowknife, CBC North, 9May02, Review of the Berger Commission after 25 years. Prior to a CARC conference in Yellowknife, June 17-18, 2002.

Chretien, Jean, (1970), **Northern Development Issues in the Seventies,** Edmonton, National Northern Development Conference, p 131-133. Proceedings Fifth National Northern Development Conference, November 4-6, 1970, Edmonton.

Clairmont, Donald, (1963), **Deviance Among Indians and Eskimos in Aklavik, NWT,** Ottawa, Northern Affairs and National Resources, Northern Coordination and Research Centre, Publication NCRC-63-9.

Clairmont, Donald H., (1962), **Notes on Drinking Behaviour of the Eskimos and Indians in the Aklavik Area,** Ottawa, Northern Coordination and Research Centre, 13 p, NCRC-62-4.

Clifton, Rodney A., (1968), **Differences in the Adaptation of Three Groups of Indigenous Children Residing in a Northern Hostel,** Edmonton, University of Alberta, Dept of Education, ISBN Vert File. Children in Inuvik's Anglican and Catholic hostels.

Coates, Kenneth and Judith Powell, (1989), **Modern North: People, Politics and the Rejection of Colonialism,** Toronto, James Lorimer, 168 p.

Collins, Mary, Ernie Pallister and R.J. Orange, (1974), **Beaufort Sea Environmental Program Public Interface Project,** Calgary, Arctic Petroleum Operators Association, 37 p. Interim report to APOA steering committee, APOA Project 72. Purpose is to update the understanding of the concerns and perceptions of the various publics and to provide a design for future communication activities which will be directed to developing a climate of mutual understanding between all those with an interest in the long term status of the Beaufort Sea.

Committee, Western Arctic Handbook, (2002), **Canada's Western Arctic, Including the Dempster Highway: The Definitive Guide to Canada's Western Arctic,** Inuvik, Western Arctic Handbook Committee, 352 p, ISBN 09687100X.

Conaty, Gerald T. and Lloyd Binder, (2003), **Reindeer Herders of the Mackenzie Delta,** Toronto, Key Porter, 80 p, ISBN 1552632296.

Cooke, A.D., (1975), **Communities of the Western Arctic,** Edmonton, Boreal Institute, c75 p. Prepared for the 1975 Arctic Summer School.

Cooke, A.D., (1976), **Communities of the Western Arctic,** Edmonton, University of Alberta, c75 p. Prepared for the 1976 Arctic Summer School.

Cooper Jr, P.F., (1967), **Mackenzie Delta Technology,** Ottawa, Indian Affairs, 69 p, Mackenzie Delta Research Project.

Cooper Jr, P.F., (1968), **Comparison of hovercraft trials in northern Canada,** Ottawa, Indian Affairs and Northern Development, 14 p. Technical Notes -2. Summary of problems of operating hovercraft in northern Canada based on trials at Churchill and in the Mackenzie Delta.

Cooper Jr, P.F., (1968), **Engineering notes on two utilidors: a report on the Frobisher Bay utilidor system and the proposed new Inuvik utilidor.,** Ottawa, Indian Affairs and Northern Development, 38 p, Northern Sciences Research Group, Technical Notes -1.

Cowan, Edward, (1970), **Dark Season Brings Sluggishness To Arctic Town,** New York, New York Times, 13 Dec 1970.

Crawford, D.B. and G.H. Johnston, (1971), **Construction on Permafrost,** Canadian Geotechnical Journal 1971, Ottawa, 8 p.

Cwynar, Lee, (1999), **James C. Ritchie: The 1999 W. A. Johnston Medalist,** Montreal, Geographie Physique et Quaternaire 1999.

Detlor, Tom, (1989), **Inuvik History,** Inuvik, Town of Inuvik, 7 p, ISBN Vert File. Presentation to Aurora Campus of Arctic College, July 1989.

Devine, Marina, (1993), **The New Western Territory: Balkanization or Federation?,** Ottawa, CARC, Northern Perspective, Vol 21, No 1, Spring 1993, 8 pages.

Dickens, H.B., (1959), **Water Supply and Sewage Disposal in Permafrost Areas of Northern Canada,** Ottawa, National Research Council, Division of Building Research, 12 p, NRC 5169, DBR TEch Report 80, Polar Record, May 1959, p 421-433.

Dickens, H.B., (1961), **Work of the Division of Building Research in Northern Canada,** Ottawa, Arctic Circular, Dec 1961, 7 p. Describes work of the Permafrost Section since 1950. Construction and performances of facilities in continuous permafrost were observed at Inuvik.

Dickens, H.B. and R.E. Platts, (1960), **Housing In Northern Canada, Some Recent Developments,** Ottawa, National Research Council, Division of Building Research, 8 p, NRC 5902, DBR Tech Paper; 107, Polar Record, Sept 1960, p 223-230.

Dickie, F., (1964), **Inuvik, Canada's triumph over permafrost,** Canadian Municipal Utilities, 3 p.

Diefenbaker, Rt Hon John, (1961), **Opening Ceremonies at Inuvik, Northwest Territories, July 21, 1961,** Ottawa, Government of Canada, 7 p.

Dixon, Rosalind G., (1989), **On Top Of The World: The Four Seasons of Inuvik,** Inuvik, Rosalind G. Dixon, video. Locally created video, 27 min.

Dobson, A., (1962), **High Pressure Hot Water District Heating Scheme at Inuvik in Canada's Arctic,** Montreal, Montreal Engineering Company Ltd., 19 p. Prepared for Journal of the Institution of Heating and Ventilating Engineers.

Dodman, Stan, (1973), **College North Report,** Yellowknife, University of Canada North. Published in October 1973.

Downing, D.F., (1968), **Arctic Research: The Arctic Town of Inuvik and Its Research Laboratory,** London, Science Abroad November 1968, 5 p.

Drewery, E.M., (1963), **Seven Small Pots of Paint,** Ottawa, North, 1963, 3 p. Description of murals in Anglican Hostel at Inuvik painted by Erwin C. Flaig.

Drummond, Robie Newton, (1991), **Arctic Circle Songs: Fifty Delta Hushpuppies,** Calgary, Penumbra Press, 74 p, ISBN 0921254288. Drummond was a doctor at the Inuvik hospital in the 1980s.

Eades, J.W., (1971), **Locals and Outsiders in Aklavik, NWT: An Anthropological Analysis of a Multi-Ethnic Community,** St John, Memorial Univiversity, Mackenzie Delta Research Project, field work in 1969 and 1970. Much on reactions to building of Inuvik. In IAND library.

Edinborough, Arnold, (1995), **History of the Canadian Imperial Bank of Commerce, Vol IV 1931-1973,** Toronto, Canadian Imperial Bank of Commerce. Comments on opening a branch at Inuvik p 143-145.

Elkan, Walter, (1973), **Development Economics: An Introduction to,** London, Penguin Books, 150 p, ISBN 0140807470.

Ellis, D.V., (1962), **Observation on the distribution and ecology of some arctic fish,** Montreal, Arctic Institute of North America, 3 p, Arctic, September 1962. Reports on work during 1953-1955 in the Mackenzie Delta and Coppermine River. Twenty-seven species are listed with notes on their distribution and ecology.

Ellis, J.B., (1967), **Component System Construct for Settlement Planning,** Ekistics, Dec 1967, 5 p. Outlines a method for deriving a suitable physical plan without preconceived notions of "best solutions". The study area used in setting up the methodology was the Mackenzie Delta area.

Ellis, Roy, (2002), **The Estimated Impact of Mining Developments On the Demand for Housing In Inuvik,** Yellowknife, Ellis Consulting Services, 8 p., Study prepared for NWT Government and CMHC mainly initiated to understand the effects of the loss of 130 GNWT positions in Inuvik due to the downturn of petroleum activities and transfers to the Nunavut government.

Environment Canada, (1984), **Inuvik Principal Station Data,** Ottawa, Atmospheric Environment Service, 78 p. A summary of hourly weather observations, climate normals and extremes.

Ervin, A.M., (1968), **New Northern Townsmen In Inuvik,** Ottawa, Indian Affairs and Northern Development, 25 p, Mackenzie Delta Research Project 5. Northern Science Research Group. Assesses the degree of success enjoyed by native people in adapting to the new urban environment of Inuvik. A new social grouping, Northerner not based on ethnicity, has emerged in response to a feeling of being dominated by southerners. Analyzes various factors which hinder adaption of Northerners to the Inuvik environment.

Ervin, Alexander M., (1969), **Conflicting Styles of Life In A Northern Town,** Montreal, Arctic, 14(89), 15p.

Espie, Tom, (1980), **Inuvik Scientific Resource Centre: An Assessment,** Ottawa, Indian Affairs and Northern Development, Northern Social Research Division.

Appendix I: References & Bibliography

Eyvindon, Peter, (1994), **Missing Sun,** Winnipeg, Pemmican, ISBN 0921827296. Children's book on Inuvik.

Fairfield, Robert C., (1967), **New Towns in the North,** Journal of Canadian Studies, May 1967, 8 p. Discussion of new settlements in the North, including a detailed description of Inuvik.

Ferguson, J., (1971), **Eskimos In A Satellite Society,** Scarborough, Prentice Hall, 13 p, In Minority Canadians, Vol 1, J.L. Elliot editor. The situation in the Western Arctic in the mid-sixties, if allowed to continue unabated, would transform the Eskimo into an Arctic variety of the 'hill-billy'. Sporadic and minimal opportunities for wage labour have partially integrated the Eskimo into a cash economy. The traditional living-off-the-land life style is no longer feasible, but a modern alternative has not been satisfactorily developed.

Foundation of Canada Engineering Corp (FENCO) Ltd, (1955), **Town Plan and Utilities for Aklavik, Northwest Territories,** Montreal, Foundation of Canada Engineering Corp Ltd, 59 p, Submitted to tht Department of Public Works, Ottawa, on August 16, 1955. Report assembled by Norman D. Lea, assistant to the Vice President. Assistance of P.B. Parker and C.L. Merrill. Project steering committee of J.P. Carriere, F.J.G. Cunningham and R.F. Legget. Mechanical studies by A.H. Thompson. Electrical studies by E.J. Bartley. Soils work by B.I. Maduke. Report reviewed by R.E. Bolton of Durnford, Bolton and Chadwick and R.M. Hardy, Dean of Engineering, University of Alberta and Per Hall, Vice President, Foundation of Canada Engineering Corporation. It covers the development of the new town site for Aklavik at East 3 on the East Channel of the Mackenzie river. The report includes 13 drawings covering the town plan, roadways, utilidors, water treatment and soil conditions.

Foundation of Canada Engineering Corporation, (1955), **Site Investigations for Aklavik, NWT,** Toronto, Foundation of Canada Engineering Corporation, Report to Department of Public Works of Canada.

French, Alice, (1977), **My Name is Masak,** Winnipeg, Peguis, 110 p. "The story of her childhood in the NWT in the years prior to the Second World War ... and many changes in Eskimo life..." PB. Autobiography. With photographs. French's maiden name is Smith. Daughter of Charlie Smith, an Alaskan Eskimo who lived in the Mackenzie Delta.

French, Alice, (1992), **Restless Nomad,** Winnipeg, Pemmican, 183 p.

Fried, J., (1963), **Settlement Types and Community Organization in Northern Canada,** Montreal, Arctic, June 1963, 7 p. Inuvik is among the settlements cited.

Gallon, Gary, (1974), **Trip North: Observations of an Environmentalist,** Vancouver, Canadian Scientific Pollution and Environmental Control Society, ISBN Vert File, Section on Inuvik.

Garner, Sir S., (1961), **Impressions of the North,** Ottawa, North Magazine, May-Aug 1961, 3p. The British High Commissioner in Canada reports on a tour of the Mackenzie District in July 1960, visiting Inuvik and Tuktoyaktuk. Development prospects are considered.

Glassford, R.G., (1971), **Application of a Theory of Games to the Transitional Eskimo Culture,** New York, Arno Press, 340 p, ISBN 0405079206, PhD Thesis, University of Illinois.

Glassford, R.G., H.A. Scott, T.D. Orlick, E.T. Bennington and D.L. Adams, (1973), **Territorial Experimental Ski Training Program: Research Results,** Edmonton, University of Alberta, 88 p.

Gleason, Richard, (2001), **Gas Proves Popular: More Than Half of Inuvik Converted to Gas,** Yellowknife, Northern News Services, 5 Mar 2001.

Glover (ed), Michael, (1974), **Building In Northern Communities,** Montreal, Arctic Institute of North America, Report of a conference-workshop held in Inuvik, NWT, 10-15 February 1974.

Goodin (ed), C. Ross and Lynda M. Howard (ed), (1984), **Beaufort Sea, Mackenzie Delta, Mackenzie Valley and Northern Yukon: A Bibliographical Review,** Calgary, Arctic Institute of North America, 310 p, Arctic Science and Technology Information System. Prepared for the Office of Northern Research and Science Advisor, DIAND.

Graburn, Nicholls, (1964), **Permafrost preservation value proved in Inuvik, NWT, experience,** Ottawa, Public Works in Canada, Sept 1964, 2 p. Construcion experience at Inuvik has shown that piles driven through the active layer of soil into permanently frozen ground sucessfully resist uplifting and settling of structures built in permafrost areas.

Graham, Amanda, (1994), **The University That Wasn't: The University of Canada North 1970-1985,** Thunder Bay, Lakehead University. Thesis with the Department of History.

Graham, Amanda, (1994), **Not A Perfect Solution But A Good Illustration: The Life and Times of the University of Canada North, 1970-1985,** Whitehorse, Yukon College, 14 p. The Northern Review #12/13: 117-132.

Grainge, Jack, (1999), **Changing North: Recollections of an Early Environmentalist,** Edmonton, Canadian Circumpolar Institute, 251 p, ISBN 1896445152.

Grainge, J.W., (1958), **Water and Sewer Facilities in Permafrost Regions,** Municipal Untilities Magazine, October 1958, 5 p. The various sources of water in permafrost areas and their exploitation are discussed; the construction of water and sewer systems is described; experience at Fort Smith, Inuvik, Hay River, Tuktoyaktuk, etc is cited. Also sewage-discharge methods used at DEW Line stations are described. AB 51326.

Hall, K.L., (1971), **Performance of Experimental Pipeline at Inuvik, NWT In Relation to the Active Layer,** Vancouver, Trans Mountain Pipeline Co.

Hall, K.L., (1971), **Pipe Lines in the Arctic Environment: Challenge and Opportunity,** Toronto, American Society of Mechanical Engineers, 11 p. Paper with slides presented by Ken Hall, Operations Manager, Trans Mountain Oil Pipe Line Company. Includes Inuvik oil test line.

Hamilton, John David, (1994), **Arctic Revolution: Social Change in the Northwest Territories 1935-1994,** Comment on Inuvik's development p 75-79.

Hancock, Lyn, (1993), **Northwest Territories,** Toronto, Harper Collins.

Hankins, Gerald M., (2003), **Sunrise Over Pangnirtung,** Calgary, Arctic Institute of North America, ISBN 091034977. Includes first posting to Aklavik and Inuvik comments.

Hargrave, M.R., (1965), **Changing Settlement Patters Amongst The Mackenzie Eskimos of the Canadian North Western Arctic,** Edmonton, Boreal Instiute, U of Alberta, 6 p, vertical, The Albertan Geographer, No 2, 1965-66, Dept of Geography, U of Alberta.

Harrington, Lyn, (1973), **Polar Regions: Earth's Frontiers,** New York, Thomas Nelson, Comment on Inuvik p 130-131.

Harris, R.E., (1966), **Inuvik Experimental Plots,** Beaverlodge, Canada Agriculture, 16 p.

Harris, R.E., (1966), **General Outline of Horticulture in the Canadian Sub-Arctic and Arctic Regions,** College Park, Maryland, Proceedings of the XVII International Horticultural Congress, 9 p. Briefly outlines the history of horticulture in the North and the present-day activities of agriculture research stations, including one at Inuvik.

Harris, R.E., (1969), **Gardening at Inuvik,** Canada Agriculture, Winter 1969, 3 p. Discussion of various techniques which have been used to improve yields of common vegetables grown in the Mackenzie Delta.

Harris, Robert E., (1970), **Gardening On Permafrost,** Ottawa, Canada Agriculture, 16 p, Publication 1408.

Harrison, Alfred H., (1908), **In Search of a Polar Continent, 1905-1907,** London, Edward Arnold, 292 p. Journeys along the Mackenzie River to the Delta and Beaufort Sea. Account of the author's exploration and mapping of the Mackenzie Delta, his sledge trips in the region from Herschel Island east to Cape Bathurst, a boat trip to southern Banks Island. Includes descriptions of Eskimos, travel conditions and plight of the Beaufort Sea whalers. The author started out from Edmonton and provides descriptions of life at the time, esp of the Fort McMurray region. HB. With illustrations and a map.

Hart, Eliza J., (2001), **Reindeer Days Remembered,** Inuvik, Inuvialuit Cultural Resource Centre, 112 p.

Harvey, Hugh, (1958), **North of the Prairies,** Shell Aviation News, November 1958, 5 p. Reviews scheduled and non-scheduled aviation in the Northwest Territories, in particular such of Shell Oil Company geological field parties operating with small aircraft and helicopters out of East Three (Inuvik); the construction of this new settlement is also described in some detail. AB58560.

Harvey, H., (1959), **North of the Prairies,** World Petroleum, March 1959, 5 p. Engineering aspects of airport and town construction at Inuvik. Also information on Shell Oil Company exploration in the Canadian North.

Heginbottom, J.A., (1973), **Some Effects of Surface Disturbances on the Permafrost Active Layer at Inuvik, NWT,** Ottawa, Task Force on Northern Oil Development, Environmental-Social Committee, Northern Pipelines, Report 73-16.

Heinke, Gary W., (1972), **Evaluation of the Sewage Lagoon at Inuvik, NWT,** Toronto, University of Toronto, Dept of Civil Engineering.

Heinke, Gary W., (1974), **Report on Municipal Services in the Northwest Territories,** Ottawa, Indian Affairs and Northern Development, Northern Science Research Group Publication 73-1.

Helm, June, (2000), **People of Denendeh,** Iowa City, University of Iowa, 387 p, Ethnohistory of the Indians of Canada's Northwest Territories. Much information on Mackenzie Delta residents.

Hill, Cynthia, (1971), **Inuvik Region Community Survey,** Inuvik, NWT Education, Continuing and Special Education, ISBN vert file, June 1971.

Hill, Cynthia C., (1967), **Special Beginners 1966/67, Sir Alexander Mackenzie School,** Inuvik, Education Division, GNWT, 18 p.

Hill, Dick, (1965), **Sociopolitical Development in the Inuvik Region,** Inuvik, Northern Affairs and National Resources.

Hill, Dick, (1966), **Proposals for Mackenzie Reindeer Operations,** Inuvik, Northern Affairs and National Resources.

Hill, Dick, (1966), **Inuvik's Arctic Research Program,** Anchorage, 17th Alaska Science Conference, 31 August 1966.

Hill, Dick, (1966), **Abattoir Improvement Program – Mackenzie Reindeer Operations,** Inuvik, Northern Affairs and National Resources.

Hill, Dick, (1967), **Mackenzie Reindeer Operations,** Ottawa, Northern Coordination and Research Centre, DIAND, August 1967, Publication 67-1.

Hill, Dick, (1967), **The Canadian Reindeer Project,** Cambridge, Polar Record, Scott Polar Research Institute, Vol 14, No 8.

Hill, Dick, (1967), **Observations on Beluga Whales Trapped by Ice in the Eskimo Lakes,** Inuvik, Inuvik Research Laboratory.

Hill, Dick, (1967), **Research in the Western Arctic,** Inuvik, Inuvik Research Laboratory.

Hill, Dick, (1968), **Mackenzie Delta Recent History,** Inuvik, Mackenzie Institute, 13 p. From draft of Mackenzie Delta In Focus published by the Mackenzie Institute as a series of 10 public lectures by local experts.

Hill, Dick, (1968), **Research Facilities in the Canadian North,** Whitehorse, National Northern Research Conference, 26 August 1968.

Hill, Dick, (1970), **Community Development and Local Government in the North,** Montreal, Arctic Institute of North America, ISBN vert file, Man In The North Conference, Inuvik, 17 November 1970.

Hill, Dick, (1970), **Opportunities for the Petroleum Industry in Northern Research,** Calgary, Arctic Petroleum Operators Association, 25 October 1970.

Hill, Dick, (1971), **Concepts of a University of Canada North,** Inuvik, University of Canada North, ISBN vert file. Presented at University of Canada North Conference, Inuvik, 19 November 1971.

Hill, Dick, (1972), **NORTH – Northern Orientation, Research and Training Hostel,** Inuvik, Mackenzie Institute, March 1972.

Hill, Dick, (1972), **Dempster Highway – Benefits to the Arctic,** Whitehorse, Yukon Resources Conference, April 1972.

Hill, Dick, (1973), **Organization of Research in the Yukon and Northwest Territories,** Inuvik, Inuvik Research Laboratory, 20 December 1973.

Hill, Dick, (1974), **Development In the Mackenzie Delta Area,** Inuvik, Arctech Services, 3 p. Notes for a presentation to the 4th Arctic Summer School, Inuvik, June 29, 1974.

Hill, Dick, (1974), **Current Social Situation in the Mackenzie and Western Arctic,** Edmonton, University of Alberta Extension Seminar, January 1974.

Hill, Dick, (1975), **Polar Perspectives,** Inuvik, Arctech Services, 3 p. Notes for a "P" review of Inuvik and the Inuvik region.

Hill, Dick, (1976), **Parallel Progress,** Yellowknife, Northern News Services Ltd., Northern News Report, August 19, 1976.

Hill, Dick, (1977), **Inuvik Business Profiles,** Inuvik, Inuvik Chamber of Commerce, ISBN vert file, December 1977.

Hill, Dick, (1978), **Lower Mackenzie Tourism Opportunities,** Yellowknife, NWT Government, Travel Arctic, March 1978.

Hill, Dick, (1978), **Inuvik – A Canadian Development In Modern Arctic Living,** Inuvik, Arctech Services, 1 p. Originally published by the Inuvik Research Laboratory in May 1970.

Hill, Dick, (1981), **Sanitation in an Extreme Environment,** New York, American Society of Civil Engineers, ISBN vert file, American Society of Civil Engineers, International Convention, New York, 11 May 1981.

Hill, Dick, (1985), **Arctic College Training Programs for the Inuvik Region,** Yellowknife, NWT Government, 90 p, ISBN vert file, 31 August 1985.

Hill, Dick, (1988), **Town of Inuvik Waterfront Study,** Inuvik, Town of Inuvik, ISBN vert file, Northern Oil and Gas Action Plan.

Hill, Dick, (1989), **Inuvik Advantages for Petroleum Projects,** Inuvik, Arctech Services, ISBN vert file, National Energy Board, Gas Exports Hearing, Inuvik, 20 April 1989.

Hill, Jessie, (1987), **Inuvik, Northwest Territories: The Influence of southern perception on the development of a town in Canada's North,** Cambridge, Scott Polar Research Institute, Cambridge University, 86 p. Thesis for degree of Master of Philosophy in Polar Studies.

Hill, Jessie, (1989), **Community Base for Northern Development,** Vancouver, University of British Columbia, School of Community and Regional Planning, 77 p, Master of Arts Thesis, September 1989.

Hill, Jessie, (1990), **Uneven Development and Regional Planning: The Case of Canada and the Northwest Territories,** Vancouver, University of British Columbia, 23 p. Directed readings in Geography, Public Policy and Regional Development.

Hill, R.M., (1965), **Inuvik, NWT,** Inuvik, Inuvik Research Laboratory, 5 p, ISBN Vert File, Prepared for Northern Affairs and National Resources, Inuvik Regional Office, as Inuvik Post Report.

Hill, R.M., (1968), **Review of Inuvik Forest Fire, August 8-18, 1968,** Inuvik, Inuvik Research Laboratory, 10 p.

Hill, R.M., (1968), **Observations on white whales trapped by ice in the Eskimo Lakes during the winter of 1966-7,** Ottawa, The Arctic Circular, 9 p, Arctic Circular, May 1968.

Hill, Richard M., (1969), **Physical Geography of the Mackenzie Delta Area,** Inuvik, Inuvik Research Laboratory, ISBN vert file,.Presented to Mackenzie Delta Seminar, 30 October 1969.

Hill, Richard M., (1972), **Inuvik and the Role of the Inuvik Resarch Laboratory,** Inuvik, Inuvik Research Laboratory, IA&NR, 6 p. Paper in Mackenzie Delta Area Monograph, Denis E. Kerfoot (ed), 1972.

Hill, Richard M., (1975), **Review of the Science Council of Canada Discussion Paper on Northern Development,** Inuvik, Private, 8 p.

Hill, R.M. (Dick), (1972), **Employment Opportunities Related to the Mackenzie Corridor Petroleum Developments,** Inuvik, Resource Management Services, 32 p.

Hobart, Charles W., (1968), **Report On Canadian Arctic Eskimos: Some Consequences of Residential Schooling,** Washington, Educational Resources Information Center, in Journal of American Indian Education 1968. Comments on bed-wetting problems at Stringer Hall.

Hodgins, B.W., J. Benidickson, R.P. Bowles and G.A. Rawlyk, (1977), **Canadian North: Source of Wealth or Vanishing Heritage?,** Scarborough, Prentice-Hall, 257 p.

Holmen, K. and G.W. Scotter, (1971), **Mosses of the Reindeer Preserve, NWT, Canada,** Linbergia 1, p 34-56.

Holmes, Doug, (1984), **Buoyant Oil Industry Boosts Northern Hub,** Winnipeg, Trade and Commerce Magazine, October 1984, 10 p.

Holmes, Douglas, (1989), **Northerners: Profiles of People in the Northwest Territories,** Toronto, James Lorimer, 190 p, ISBN 15550282158. Includes Doug Billingsley, Sharon Firth and Cece McCauley.

Honderich, John, (1987), **Arctic Imperative: Is Canada Losing the North?,** Toronto, University of Toronto Press, 258 p, HB. With photographs and maps.

Honigman, John J., (1973), **Integration of Canadian Eskimo, Indians and Other Persons of Native Ancestry In Modern Economic and Public Life: Evidence from Inuvik,** Oxford, Pergamon Press, 9 p. In Berg, G. (ed), Circumpolar Problems: Habitat, Economy and Social Relationships in the Arctic, p 61-72.

Honigman, John J. and Irma Honigman, (1970), **Arctic Townsmen: Ethnic Backgrounds and Modernization,** Ottawa, Canadian Research Centre for Anthropology, St. Paul University, 303 p. Scholarly anthropological studies of northern communities, especially Inuvik, NWT 1967. With photographs. John Honigman was an anthropology professor at the University of North Carolina at Chapel Hill.

Houseman, Jan and Alan Fehr, (1996), **Listening for Cosmic Rays,** Inuvik, Aurora Research Institute, 14 p. One of three units in Canada, the cosmic ray monitor at the Inuvik Research Centre has been in operation since 1964.

Hunt, Barbara (editor), (1983), **Rebels, Rascals and Royalty: The Colourful North of Laco Hunt,** Yellowknife, Outcrop, 219 p, The life of Leonard Arthur Charles Orgar (L.A.C.O.) Hunt, 1909-1978. HB. Biography. With photographs.

Hunter, Alice, (1986), **Alice Hunter's North Country Cookbook,** Yellowknife, Outcrop, 85 p. Alice Hunter was born in Aklavik and grew up with wild foods. She picked up recipies throughout the North. They ecompass every season and region.

Huskey, Susie, (1994), **Aklavik Moves to East 3,** Inuvik, Tusaayaksat, September 23, 1994, p 16.

Inuvik Council, (1969), **Inuvik Utilidor Extension Program 1970-1971,** Inuvik, Village of Inuvik, 8 p.

Irvin, A. M., (1968), **New Northern Townsmen In Inuvik,** Ottawa, Northern Affairs, 25 p, Northern Science Research Group.

Jacobsen, George, (1968), **Canada's Northern Communities,** Ottawa, North, 1968, p34-37, 4 p.

Jacot, Michael, (1954), **Aklavik, Where Muskrat Is King,** Toronto, Imperial Oil Review, 5 p. Contains popular description of this town on the Mackenzie River, its inhabitants, permafrost problem, recreation, schools, trapping, whaling and history, also its proposed move to another site (Imperial Oil Review, Dec 1954, AB 35425).

Jacot, Michael, (1956), **Aklavik,** Toronto, Canadian Nature, Mar-Apr 1956, 5 p, AB 45760. A reprint of AB354525, Aklavik, Where Muskrat Is King.

Jenness, Diamond, (1957), **Dawn in Arctic Alaska,** Minneapolis, University of Minnesota Press, 222 p. Jenness recounts his experiences, versions of events and criticism of the ill-fated Canadian Arctic Expedition led by V. Stefansson. With illustrations by Giacomo Raimondi.

Jenness, D., (1964), **Eskimo Administration II, Canada,** Montreal, AINA, 186 p.

Johnston, G.H., (1981), **Design and Performance of Inuvik, NWT Airstrip,** Ottawa, National Research Council, Division of Building Research, DBR Paper 1069. Published in Proceedings of 4th Canadian Permafrost Conference, 2-6 March 1981, Edmonton.

Johnston, G.H., (1981), **Permafrost Design, Engineering and Construction,** Toronto, J. Wiley, 540 p, ISBN 047179918.

Johnston, G.H., (1982), **Design and Performance of the Inuvik, NWT Airstrip,** Ottawa, National Research Council, Division of Building Research.

Johnston, G.H., (1983), **Performance of an insulated roadway on permafrost, Inuvik, NWT,** Ottawa, National Research Council, Division of Building Research.

Johnston, G.H. and Roger Brown, (1955), **West Channel Areas: Summary of Soil and Permafrost Data with a Preliminary Site Appraisal,** Ottawa, National Research Council, Division of Building Research.

Jones, Mary Jane, (1969), **Mackenzie Delta Bibliography,** Ottawa, Indian Affairs & Northern Development, 119 p, Northern Science Research Group Publication No 6.

Kelland, Jenn, (2006), **Humble Olympian Prefers Quiet Life (Shirley Firth Larsson),** Edmonton, Windspeaker March 2006.

Kerfoot(ed), Denis E., (1972), **Mackenzie Delta Area Monograph,** St. Catherines, Brock University, 174 p, Contains a paper "Inuvik and the Role of the Inuvik Research Laboratory" by Dick Hill.

Kettle, John, (1956), **Old and New Aklavik,** Canadian Architect, Nov 1956, p 23-28, 5 p. Maps and describes the new town site, to accommodate an 80-bed hospital, two 250-student hostels, a 25-room school building, a rehabilitation centre for Eskimos, several federal buildings and nearly 200 dwelling units. The site is divided into two main zones, one to have electricity, central heating, sewer and water services, the other to be provided with electricity only. Utilities are laid in "utilidors" several feet above ground. Steam jets are used to melt holes (2 ft diametre and 16-25 ft deep) for the foundation piles. The soil is mainly granular, with gravel deposits in the form of terraces and ridges. The project is scheduled for completion by 1960-61. AB59149.

Kolausok, Eddie D., (1999), **Aurora Shining,** Yellowknife, Kolausok Ublaaq Enterprises, 105 p, ISBN 0968457118.

Komaromi, Greg J., (1983), **Inuvik 25 Years Later,** Ottawa, North Magazine, 1983, Inuvik celebrations July 11-18, 1983.

Koring, Paul, (1979), **Light In Darkness: Inuvik's Economy Gets A Boost From Dome and the Dempster,** Toronto, The Financial Post, Special Report, 1 Dec 1979.

Langford et al, J.A., (1966), **Inuvik NWT Town Planning Study January 1966,** Ottawa, Northern Affairs and National Resources, c60 p. Prepared by the Dept of Public Works, Building Construction Branch. The survey was carried out in August 1965. The DPW Town Planner was scheduled to visit Inuvik in February 1966 to review the study recommendations.

Legget, Robert Ferguson and R.J.E. Brown, (1956), **Rapid Disintegration of Alluvial-fan Material near Aklavik, NWT,** New York, Geographical Society of America, Bulletin Dec 1956, 2 p. Test drilling in permafrost on the western edge of the Mackenzie Delta disclosed some 40 ft of organic silt, no sand or gravel. Intense frost action causes rapid mechanical weathering of material from adjacent mountains. AB46296.

Legget, R.F. and H.B. Dickson, (1959), **Building In Northern Canada,** Ottawa, Nartional Research Council, Division of Building Research, 48 p, NRC 5108, DBR Tech Paper 62.

Leitch, A.F and G.W. Heinke, (1970), **Comparison of Utilidors in Inuvik, NWT,** Toronto, University of Toronto, Department of Civil Engineering, ISBN Vert File, Masters thesis.

LeVert, Suzanne, (1992), **Northwest Territories,** New York, Chelsea House, 64 p. Let's Discover Canada series.

Lockwood, C.M., (1975), **Perspective on COPE,** Edmonton, University of Alberta, 6 p. A panel discussion with Agnes Semmler, Addy Tobac, Rosalea Tiyza, Nellie Cournoyea. Chaired by Charles Hobart.

Lotz (ed), Jim, (1963), **Government Research and Surveys in the Canadian North 1956-61,** Ottawa, Northern Affairs & National Resources, 28 p. Northern Coordination and Research Centre Publication 63-1, January 1963.

Lotz, Jim, (1963), **Inuvik Research Station,** Ottawa, IAND, 3 p, ISBN Vert File, in IAND Intercom.

Lotz, Jim, (1970), **Northern Realities: The Future of Northern Development In Canada,** Toronto, New Press.

Lotz, J.R., (1962), **Inuvik, NWT: A Study of Community Planning Problems in a New Northern Town,** Ottawa, Northern Coordination & Research Centre, IA&ND, 45 p, outsize, Review of Inuvik situation. Northern Affairs Library Box 711.42(2)C, unpublished.

Lubart, Joseph M., (1971), **Psychodynamic Problems of Adaptation: Mackenzie Delta Eskimos, A Preliminary Study,** Ottawa, Indian Affairs, 49 p.

MacKay, J. Ross, (1963), **Mackenzie Delta Area, N.W.T.,** Ottawa, Canada. Department of Mines and Technical Surveys, 202 p. "This memoir presents the results of surveys carried out over eight years, five summers of which the author spent in the field. The field work was supplemented by airphoto interpretation and the most modern methods of statistical analysis were applied to most of the data obtained." Geographical Branch Memoir 8, Cat. No. M66-8.

Mackay, J. Ross, (1969), **The Mackenzie Delta,** Ottawa, Canadian Geographic Journal May 1969, p 146-155.

Mackay, J. Ross and Larry Dyke, (1990), **Geological Features of the Mackenzie Delta Region, N.W.T.,** Yellowknife, Science Insitute of the Northwest Territories, 16 p, ISBN Vert File, Scientific Report No 1. Guidebook to Geological Localities in the vicinity of Inuvik. Pingos of the Western Arctic Coast.

Mackenzie, Sir Alexander, (1801), **Voyages from Montreal through the Continent of North America to the Frozen and Pacific Oceans in 1789 and 1793, with a Preliminary Account of the Rise and State of the Fur Trade,** London, T. Caldwell & W. Davies, 412 p. With maps. Commonwealth library edition.

Mackenzie Valley Environmental Impact Review Board, (2004), **Reasons for Decision and Scoping Report for the Environmental Assessment of the Mackenzie Gas Project,** Yellowknife, MVIRB, May 21 2004, 34 p.

Mackenzie Valley Pipe Line Research Ltd., (1972), **Arctic Pipe Line Feasibility Study,** Vancouver, Mackenzie Valley Pipe Line Research Ltd., 109 p. Consortium of 16 companies formed in 1969 to sponsor research and related engineering and economic studies of the feasibility of a 1738-mile oil pipeline from Prudhoe Bay, Alaska to Edmonton, Alberta. A full-scale 48" diameter experimental pipeline loop was constructed on piles and in a berm off Navy Road in Inuvik to study the effects of permafrost behaviour.

Mackenzie Valley Pipe Line Research Ltd., (1970), **Research At Inuvik,** Vancouver, Mackenzie Valley Pipe Line Research Ltd., 33 p, ISBN Vertical file. Construction of the pipeline research facility at Inuvik operated by Canadian Bechtel.

Macpherson, N.J., (1975), **Northern Education,** Edmonton, University of Alberta, 17 p. In Arctic Summer School Notes.

Maillot, Jose, (1968), **Community Structure – Inuvik – Summer 1965,** Ottawa, IAND, Northern Science Research Group, 38 p, Mackenzie Delta Research Project Paper 4.

Makale, Holloway & Associates, (1968), **Planning Report: Village of Inuvik,** Edmonton, Makale, Holloway & Associates.

Makale, Holloway & Associates, (1973), **Capital Budgeting Program for Inuvik from 1973 to 1981,** Edmonton, Makale, Holloway & Associates, 42 p. Study prepared with Associated Engineering Services Ltd of Edmonton.

Makale, Holloway and Assoc, (1972), **General Plan, Town of Inuvik,** Edmonton, Makale, Holloway and Associates.

Makale, Holloway & Associates Ltd, (1970), **Improvement and Development Plan, Central Business District, Inuvik, NWT,** Edmonton, Makale, Holloway and Associates Ltd., 19 p.

Malcolm, Andrew H., (1980), **In Brief, Pallid Summer of the Arctic Circle a New Canadian Town Fails to Take Root,** New York, New York Times 9 September 1980.

Manning, Sally, (2006), **Guts and Glory: The Arctic Skiers Who Challenged the World,** Yellowknife, Outcrop, 144 p., ISBN 0919315348.

Massey, Vincent, (1956), **Visit of the Rt Hon Vincent Massey, Governor General, to the Canadian Arctic, March 20 to April 5, 1956,** Ottawa, Canada, Dept Northern Affairs and National Resources, 94 p.

McCourt, Edward, (1969), **Yukon and Northwest Territories,** New York, St Martin's Press, 236 p, Pages 205 to 211 on Inuvik.

McDermit, Margo, (1983), **Origins Of Inuvik,** Inuvik, CBC Radio 25 May 1983. Interview with Gordon Robertson and Eric Nielsen on the founding of Inuvik on the occasion of Inuvik's 25th Anniversary.

McNeil (ed), Tony, (1986), **CFS Inuvik Commemerative Year Book 1961-1986,** Ottawa. Available on internet. Published on closure of the station. Assisted by Kel McGreavy, Mike Hauka and Larry Lambourne.

Mead, Robert Douglas, (1976), **Ultimate North: Canoeing Mackenzie's Great River,** Garden City, Double Day, 312 p. Chapter on Inuvik p 228-237.

Meidler, S.S., (1962), **Seismic Activity in the Canadian Arctic 1899-1955,** Ottawa, Dominion Observatory, Dept Mines & Technical Surveys.

Merrill, C.L., (1955), **Physiography of the Mackenzie Delta Region and its relation to relocation of Aklavik, NWT,** Geological Society of America, Bulletin Dec 1955, 2 p.

Merrill, C.L., (1956), **Notes on Aklavik Relocation Project, 1954,** Canadian Geographer, 1956, No 7, 1 p. From April to August 1954 a team of five engineers and three specialists in geology and geography investigated possible sites for a new Aklavik on the Mackenzie Delta. A location 33 air miles east of the present town was selected. Early start of the survey permitted examination of each site during the winter, break-up and summer conditions. Aerial reconnaissance was made by helicopter; ground survey was done by tractor, dog team, and boat. Various tests made on the sites are noted. AB 46721.

Merrill, C.L., (1985), **Merrill Fond,** Yellowknife, Northern Heritage Museum. Mainly photos.

Merrill, C.L., J.A. Pihlainen and R.F. Legget, (1956), **The New Aklavik – Search For The Site,** Ottawa, National Research Council, Division of Building Research, 6 p, NRC Paper 5573. DBR Technical Paper No 89, reprinted from The Engineering Journal, January 1960, p 52-57.

Mitchell, D.C., (2003), **Sold American: The Story of the Alaska Natives and Their Land 1867-1959,** Fairbanks, University of Alaska Press.

Morrison, David, (1997), **Inuvialuit of the Western Arctic,** Ottawa, Archaeological Survey of Canada, Internet site www.civilization.ca.

Mowat, Farley, (1952), **People of the Deer,** Boston, Little, Brown and Company. With drawings by Samuel Bryant. HB.

Mowat, Farley, (1967), **Canada North,** Boston, Little, Brown and Company, 128 p. With B&W and colour photographs.

Murphy (ed), Helen, (1970), **Man In The North Conference on Community Development,** Montreal, Arctic Institute of North America, Proceedings of a conference held in Inuvik on 18-21 November 1970 co-sponsored by the Mackenzie Institute and the AINA.

National Energy Board, (1977), **Reasons for Decisions on Northern Pipelines,** Ottawa, National Energy Board, Vol 1, 2 &3. Inuvik hearing 20-22 Sept 1976.

Nelson et al, Walter H., (1959), **Report of the Commission Appointed to Investigate the Unfulfilled Provisions of Treaties 8 and 11 as they Apply to the Indians of the Mackenzie District,** Ottawa, Government of Canada. The report was reprinted by the Indian-Eskimo Association of Canada in 1970.

Newman, Peter, (1963), **Renegade In Power: The Diefenbaker Years,** Toronto, McClelland & Stewart.

Nicholls, Graburn, (1964), **Permafrost preservation value proved by Inuvik, NWT experience,** Ottawa, Public Works In Canada, v 12, no 3, Sept 1964, 2 p. The construction experience at Inuvik has shown that piles driven through the active top layer of soil into permanently frozen ground successfully resist uplifting and settling of structures built on permafrost.

Nielsen, Frederik, (1963), **Impressions from a Journey to Northern Canada 1963,** Ottawa, Northern Affairs & National Resources, 5 p. Copy in the Northern Affairs library. Nielsen was a Danish visitor with Greenland connections.

Nolan, Stephanie, (2000), **Letter From Inuvik,** Toronto, Globe and Mail. Articles published on 20 & 21 March 2000.

North Magazine, (1962), **Mackenzie Delta Logging Project,** Ottawa, North, Jan-Feb 1962, 1 p. Describes the Department of Northern Affairs project initiated in 1960 as a work-relief measure which developed into a lumbering operation with industrial potential. Log delivery, milling and lumber yardage are carried on by local Indians and Eskimos.

North Pacific Planning Project, (1948), **Canada's New Northwest: A study of the present and future development of the Mackenzie District of the Northwest Territories, Yukon Territory and northern parts of Alberta and British Columbia, 1947,** Ottawa, King's Printer, 155 p. Narrative summary of work by the project, initiated in the US and Canada in 1943 to explore economic possibilties, development of natural resources, welfare of native peoples and defence of the region.

North, Sandra, (1962), **Story of Inuvik,** Inuvik, Sir Alexander Mackenzie School, 6 p. Student report on the development of Inuvik.

Northern Affairs & National Resources, (1956), **Gov Gen Vincent Massey visit to East Three,** Ottawa, Northern Affairs and National Resources, 2 p. Visit through the Canadian North, March 20 to April 5, 1956. Report of travels.

Novacorp Engineering Services Ltd, (1984), **Feasibility of Greenhousing In Inuvik,** Calgary, Novacorp Engineering Services Ltd., Submitted to Beaufort Food Services Ltd.

Nowasad, F.S., (1958), **Agricultural Research in Sub-Arctic and Arctic Canada,** Ottawa, Canadian Geographical Journal, Sept 1958, 3 p. Discusses agricultural possibilities on the basis of findings of the Dept of Agriculture's experimental sub-stations. The Fort Simpson sub-station is supervising the landscape and garden work at the new town of Inuvik. AB53671.

Nowasad, F.S., (1959), **Farming in the Sub-Arctic,** Agricultural Institure Review, Jan-Feb 1959, 5 p. Considers the acreage and potential of the Mackenzie River Valley, in particular, Fort Simpson, Aklavik and Inuvik.

Nowasad, Frank S., (1970), **Handbook for Northern Gardeners,** Ottawa, Canada Agriculture, 26 p. First printed in 1960.

Nowasad, F.S. and A. Leahey, (1960), **Soils of the Arctic and Sub-Arctic Regions of Canada,** Agriculture Institute Review, Mar-Apr 1960, 4 p. Prospects for agricultural development in the Mackenzie River valley are evaluated and the results of research at the field experiment station at Inuvik are summarized.

Nowosad, F.S., (1958), **Agricultural Research in Sub-Arctic and Arctic Canada,** Canadian Geographical Journal, Sept 1958, 4 p. Discusses agricultural possibilities on basis of research at the new town of Inuvik.

Nowosad, F.S., (1963), **Growing Vegetables on Permafrost,** Ottawa, North, 4 p. Success of growing garden crops on permafrost in Aklavik and Inuvik.

Nuligak (Bob Cockney), (1966), **I, Nuligak,** Toronto, Peter Martin Associates, 208 p. An autobiography of Nuligak (Bob Cockney b.1895, d.1966). Translated from the Eskimo by Maurice Metayer. Illustrations by Ekootak. Nuligak was a member of the Kitigariukmeut tribe.

NWT Council, (1958), **Name for Aklavik East Three,** Ottawa, Northern Affairs and National Resources, 15h Session, 14-18 July 1958, Ottawa.

NWT Council, (1963), **25th Session, Inuvik, NWT, 8 July 1963,** Ottawa, Northern Affairs and National Resources.

O'Bonsawin, Christine, (2002), **Olympian Firth Sisters,** 6th International Symposium for Olympic Research 2002.

O'Reilly, Kevin, (1987), **NWT Postal Cancellations,** Yellowknife.

Oilweek, (1977), **Northern Canadian Mythology Claimed to be Overdone,** Calgary, Oilweek Magazine 1 August 1977, Report of Business Opportunities Board members Dick Hill, Grant Hinchey and Len Cardinal to Certified General Accounts, Calgary Chapter.

Page, Robert, (1986), **Northern Development, The Canadian Dilemma,** Toronto, McClelland & Stewart, 361 p.

Pan American Petroleum Corp, (1969), **Mackenzie River Operation,** Houston, Pan American Petroleum Corp, 7 p, vertical. AMOCO Canada sets up a rig at Inuvik in August 1969. In HORIZONS company magazine.

Pantenburg, Vitalis, (1957), **A Town Is Relocated: Aklavik, Canada's First Modern Town In The Arctic,** Kosmos, December 1957, 6 p. In German. Outlines development of the Aklavik settlement around an HBC trading post. Ground conditions restricted construction and lack of year-round aircraft landing facilities in postwar years, made impossible any development of Aklavik into an administrative and communications centre for northwest Canada. Another site, on more stable ground, was found for this town of 700 inhabitants, on the east bank of an eastern arm of the Mackenzie Delta, 56.5 km from the old location. On the new site, named Inuvik, the buildings are erected on 6-9 m piles, frozen 5-8 m into the ground. Water supply and electric power lines are laid in a utilidor, a well-insulated main on piles well above the ground. The installations are kept frost-free by a hot-water pipe in the same main. Work at the new location started in 1955. The new town is planned for 2500-3000 inhabitants, is to be completed by 1961. AB53858.

Parker, John, (1996), **Arctic Power: The Path To Responsible Government In Canada's North,** Peterborough, Cider Press, 85 p. The book consists of four lectures given at Trent University in 1992, while Parker occupied the Chair of Northern Studies. The first two lectures offer a demographic, geographic, and historical perspective, which is essential for an understanding of the contemporary scene. The last two cover the period of "transformation," the building of a province-like government in the Northwest Territories.

Parsons, G.F., (1970), **Arctic Suburb: A Look at the North's Newcomers,** Ottawa, Northern Science Research Group, IA&ND, 94 p, Mackenzie Delta Research Project No 8.

Patty, Stanton H., (1970), **New Town Illustrates Potential of Canadian Arctic,** Seattle, The Seattle Times, 9Aug70.

Pedersen, Georgi Lind, (1979), **Journey To The Northwest Territories,** Copenhagen, Greenland Technical Organization.

Pennington, Janet, (1994), **Curtis L. Merrill Inventory September 1994,** Yellowknife, NWT Archives, NWT Government.

Peterson, Norma, (1976), **Report on Land Use Problems and Restoration Techniques in the Inuvik District, July 28-August 8, 1976,** Yellowknife, DINA Land Use Section.

Petrone, Penny, (1988), **Northern Voices: Inuit Writing In English,** Toronto, University of Toronto Press. Includes Victor Allen, Nellie Cournoyea and Abe Okpik.

Pettersen, Bjorger, V., (1971), **TEST Program Progress Report 1970-71,** Inuvik, TEST Program, 28 p.

Pettersen, Bjorger V., (1969), **Story of the TEST Program,** Inuvik, TEST Program, 84 p.

Pettersen, Bjorger V., (1969), **TEST Program Progress Report 1968-69,** Inuvik, TEST Program, 28 p.

Pettersen, . Bjorger V., (1970), **TEST Progress Report 1969-70,** Inuvik, TEST Program, 28 p.

Phillips, A., (1957), **Checkered career of an arctic priest,** MacLean's Magazine, 1957, 5 p. Describes the activities of Father Bernard Brown, based at Aklavik and Inuvik.

Pihlainen, J.A., (1951), **Building Foundations In Permafrost, Mackenzie Valley, NWT,** Ottawa, National Research Council, Division of Building Research, 48 p, NRC 5902, Tech Report 8.

Pihlainen, J.A., (1959), **Pile Construction in Permafrost,** American Society of Civil Engineers, Soil Mechanics and Foundations Division, Journal, Dec 1959, 6 p. Discusses design considerations for pile foundations with data on costs at Aklavik and Inuvik.

Pihlainen, J.A., (1962), **Inuvik, NWT Engineering Site Information,** Ottawa, National Research Council, Division of Building Research, 36 p, NRC 6557, DRB Tech Paper 135, August 1962.

Pihlainen, J.A., R.J.E. Brown and G.H Johnson, (1956), **Soils In Some Areas of the Mackenzie Delta Region,** Ottawa, National Research Council, Division of Building Research, Aklavik Relocation Project, NRC 4096, DBR Tech paper 43.

Pihlainen, J.A., R.J. E. Brown and R.F. Legget, (1956), **Pingo In The Mackenzie Delta, NWT,** Ottawa, National Research Council, Division of Building Research, 4 p, NRC 4009, Research Paper No 27, Bulletin of the Geological Society of America, August 1966, p 111-1122.

Pihlainen, J.A. and G.H. Johnston, (1953), **Permafrost At Aklavik,** Ottawa, National Rsearch Council, Division of Building Research.

Pilon, Jean-Luc, (1993), **Inuvik,** Ottawa, Canadian Museum of Civilization, 2 p. Part of Retracing a 1992 Archaeological Expedition on the Canadian Museum of Civilization internet site.

Plummer, Harry Chapin, (1954), **Aklavik Airfield,** Toronto, Canadian Aviation, 2 p. Discusses plan for construction of an airfield when a townsite for relocation of Aklavik in the Mackenzie District is decided upon; also factors involved in the relocation program generally. The airfield will enable flight from Yellowknife, 1200 miles to the southeast, of heavy passenger and cargo transports of Canadian Pacific, and others, into the new townsite. AB41895.

Polar Record, (1956), **Reasons For Transfer of Aklavik,** Cambridge, Scott Polar Institute, Reasons for transfer of Aklavik, Mackenzie District, from West to East Channel of Mackenzie River, and factors by which suitability of potential sites was judged during relocation survey (Polar Record, News Notes,1956, p 178-79, AB E47384).

Porsild, A.E., (1943), **Birds of the Mackenzie Delta,** Ottawa, Canadian Field Naturalist, 6 p. Feb-Mar 1943, v 57, p 19-35.

Pritchard, Gordon B., (1962), **Inuvik – Canada's New Arctic Town,** Ottawa, Canadian Geographic Journal, June 1962, p 201-210.

Pritchard, Gordon B., (1964), **New Town in the Far North,** London, Geographical Magazine, Sept 1964, 15 p.

Pritchard, Gordon R., (1962), **Inuvik, Canada's New Arctic Town,** Cambridge, Polar Record, Jan 1962, p 145-155.

Public Works, Canada, (1961), **Inuvik: Place of Man,** Ottawa, Dept Public Works, Brochure for official dedication on July 21, 1961.

RCMP Quarterly, (1954), **Moving – One Arctic Town!,** Ottawa, RCMP, 3 p, RCMP Quarterly, April 1954. From Editorial and Information Division, Dept of Resources and Development.

Reguly, Robert, (1964a), **Inuvik: It's Canada's grand monument to segregation,** Toronto, Toronto Star, 23 Sep 63.

Reguly, Robert, (1964b), **Even School Split Down Middle In Our Segregated Arctic,** Toronto, Toronto Star, 25 September 1963.

Reguly, Robert, (1964c), **Our 'Welfare State' Arctic Has Only A Dim Hope For The Future,** Toronto, Toronto Star, 27 September 1963.

Rensaa, E.M., (1959), **Building at Inuvik: The school and hostel project,** Ottawa, Indian and Northern Affairs, Northern Affairs Bulletin, Nov-Dec 1959, 5 p. Reprinted from Canadian Consulting Engineer. Describes the construction of three wooden buildings, the largest at Inuvik, each divided into three sections by fire-resistant cross walls and equipped with sprinkler systems. They have sloping roofs (18°) covered with aluminum inter-locking shingles, stop fences along the eves to prevent snow sliding. The interior sheetings are mostly fir and poplar plywood; the exterior wall-finishing consists of color-stained cedar shingles. The buildings rest on piles, steam-jetted into the (permanently frozen) ground and have approx. 2.5 ft. free air space below the lowest floor. The ground floors are about 7.5 ft. above the ground and a 4.5 ft "crawl" space is provided under the main ground floor to house ducts, piping, etc. Pipes for water and sewage are laid in utilidors together with hot-water pipes from the community's central heating plant. (Rensaa, E.M., Canadian Consulting Engineer, 1959, AB61164).

Richardson, Boyce, (1965), **The Indian In the Northwest Territories,** Montreal, Montreal Star, 30 p, Inuvik section p 25-29.

Richardson, Boyce, (1969), **Does Inuvik Exemplify Civil Service Planning – or Lack of It?,** Montreal, Montreal Star, 4 p, article published April 16, 1969.

Richardson, Sir John, (1851), **Arctic Searching Expedition,** London.

Ridge, Frank Gerald, (1953), **General Principles for the Planning of Sub-arctic Settlements,** Montreal, Dept Geography, McGill Univiersity, 569 p, PhD Thesis. Contains a study of the most important settlements of the Yukon Territory and Mackenzie District to show present conditions and development, and to indicate scope and direction of planned future development. In three parts, of which the first deals with the regional environment affecting settlement in the western sub-arctic, part 2 consists of nine intensive settlement studies based on three month's field work including Aklavik, part 3 presents fundamental considerations, administrative organization, and general principles for planning based on problems encountered in the nine settlements.

Ritchie, J.C., (1976), **Campbell Dolomite Upland Near Inuvik, NWT: A Unique Scientific Resource,** Saskatoon, University of Saskatchewan, Muskox 1976.

Roberts, L., (1949), **Mackenzie,** New York, Rinehart Roberts, 276 p. Sketch of geography, history and native peoples of the Mackenzie Basin, discovery of the river, exploratory expeditions, etc.

Robertson, Chris, (1998), **To The Top Of Canada,** Oakville, 202 p, ISBN 096849506.

Robertson, Gordon, (1955), **Aklavik, A Problem and Its Solution,** Ottawa, Canadian Geographical Journal, June 1955, 9 p. Discusses the present town site and problems of transport, building, water supply and sewage disposal resulting from mud during the break-up to freeze-up period. The search for, and choice of, the new site are discussed. AB42105.

Robertson, Gordon, (1956), **Moving An Arctic Town – The Problems of Aklavik,** Ottawa, Northern Affairs and National Resources, 14 p. Presentation to The Royal Canadian Institute, Convocation Hall, Toronto, March 10, 1956.

Robertson, Gordon, (2000), **Memoirs of a Very Civil Servant: Mackenzie King to Pierre Trudeau,** Toronto, University of Toronto Press.

Rowley, G.W., (1957), **Settlement and Transportation in the Canadian North,** Montreal, Arctic Institute of North America, 7 p, ISBN Vert file, Arctic, 1957, p 336-342. Rowley writes on the problems of Aklavik and the need for a new townsite. He was secretary of the Advisory Committee on Northern Development.

Rowley, G.W., (1959), **Aklavik-Inuvik Relocation,** Ottawa, Indian Affairs and Northern Development, c44 p, outsize. Single copy located in the DINA Library 711.414.

Rowley, G.W., (1972), **Canadian Eskimo Today,** Cambridge, Scott Polar Institute, 5 p, Polar Record 16, 1972.

Roy, Geoffrey, (2000), **North Canada,** Bucks, Bradt Publications, 276 p.

Sainville, Count Eduard de, (1898), **Journey To The Mouth of the Mackenzie River 1889-1894,** Paris, Société de Geographie, Bulletin, 1898, 16 p. deSainville was a French explorer who spent 1889-1894 in the Mackenzie Delta area. An article in Science, 19Apr1889 referred to deSainville as an English explorer.

Savoie (ed), Donat, (1970), **Tchiglit Eskimos: Amerindians of the Canadian Northwest in the 19th Century, as seen by Emile Petitot: Vol I,** Ottawa, Northern Science Research Group, 228 p, Mackenzie Delta Research Project No 9.

Savoie (ed), Donat, (1971), **Loucheux Indians: Amerindians of the Canadian Northwest in the 19th Century as seen by Emile Petitot: Vol II,** Ottawa, Northern Science Research Group, 228 p. Proceded by general observations on the Dene-dindjie Indians. Mackenzie Delta Research Project Publication 10.

Schwartz, Herbert, (1970), **Elik and other stories of the Mackenzie Eskimos,** Toronto, McClelland and Stewart, 79 p.

Scotter, G.W., (1968), **Study of the Range Resources and Management of the Canadian Reindeer Operation,** Edmonton, Canadian Wildlife Service, 65 p.

Scotter, G.W., (1969), **Reindeer Husbandry as a Land Use in Northern Canada,** International Union for the Conservation of Nature and Natural Resources, 10 p. Proceedings of the Conference on Productivity and Conservation in Northern Lands, IUCN publication N.S. 16, p 159-169.

Scotter, G.W., (1972), **Chemical Composition of Forage Plants from the Reindeer Reserve,** Arctic 25, p 21-27.

Scotter, G.W., (1972), **Reindeer Ranching In Canada,** Journal of Range Management, p 167-174.

Scotter, G.W. and J.E. Miltimore, (1973), **Mineral Content of Forage Plants from the Reindeer Preserve, NWT, Canada,** Canadian Journal of Plant Science 53, p 263-268.

Sen, Amartya, (1999), **Development As Freedom,** New York, Knopf, 304 p, ISBN 0375406190.

Sexton, J.K., P. Hail and D.F. Murphy, (1960), **Pile Construction In Permafrost,** American Society of Civil Engineers, Soil Mechanics and Foundation Division, Journal, June 1960, 3 p. Few cases of pile movement have been observed one year after construction at Inuvik. The piles were steamed in and frozen into the permafrost to a depth twice that of the active layer.

Smith, Derek G., (1967), **Mackenzie Delta – domestic economy of the native peoples, a preliminary study,** Ottawa, Indian Affairs and Northern Development, Northern Coordination and Research Centre, 59 p, Mackenzie Delta Research Project, No 3.

Smith, Derek G., (1975), **Natives and Outsiders: Pluralism in the Mackenzie River Delta, Northwest Territories,** Ottawa, Mackenzie Delta Research Project, 173 p.

Smith, Michael, (1976), **Permafrost in the Mackenzie Delta, NWT,** Ottawa, Geological Survey of Canada, 54 p, GSC Paper 75-28.

Spence, I., (1961), **Human Adaptation in the Mackenzie Delta: A study in facilitating and adjustment of the northern Indian and Eskimo to rapid social change,** Montreal, McGill University, 262 p, MA Thesis. Cultural adjustment problems of the Indians and Eskimos in Aklavik and Inuvik including an experimental project designed to test community development procedures as a means of solving these problems.

Spirling (director), Gordon, (1961), **Building In The North, NFB Film,** Ottawa, National Film Board, 25 minutes. This film is about the construction of Inuvik and shows the techniques of building-site selection in the north, and outlines the important measures that must be taken to build successfully.

Stabler, J.C. and M.R. Olfert, (1980), **Gaslight Follies: The Political Economy of the Western Arctic,** Toronto, Canadian Public Policy, Spring 1980, p 374-388. The oil discoveries at Prudhoe Bay on Alaska's Arctic coast in 1968 intensified interest in the oil and gas potential of the Canadian Arctic and led to consideration of a means of transporting northern oil and gas to southern markets. Following the energy crisis of the early 1970s, industry and the Canadian federal government began to plan a transportation corridor along the Mackenzie River Valley. Opposition soon developed. Native residents pressed for the settlement of land claims as a minimum prerequisite to further development of the petroleum and gas industry in the north. Environmentalists feared that speedy development would occur at the expense of adequate environmental protection. This paper reviews the bases for the conflicting concerns and analyzes and evaluates the process chosen by government to reach a decision concerning a northern gas pipeline.

Stanley, D.R., (1958), **Modern Communities in the North,** Western Miner and Oil Review, Dec 1958, 3 p.

Stewart, D., (1965), **Summer Fun for Inuvik,** North, 1965, v 12, No 1, 4 p. Formation and program of the Inuvik Summer Recreation Program for children 6 to 12. Teenagers provided the leadership and supervision for the two-week program.

Stewart, P., (1972), **Beware Of Southern Bias,** Edmonton, Edmonton Journal 19 December 1972. Criticism of wild statements by David Hamilton in the CBC documentary film "Mackenzie Road".

Stinson, Cathy, (2000), **King Of The Castle,** Toronto, Second Story Press, 63 p. Dedicated to Elijah Allen, SAMS head caretaker.

Stoneman-McNichol, Jane, (1983), **On Blue Ice: The Inuvik Adventure,** Yellowknife, Outcrop, 80 p. The history of Inuvik. SB. With photographs.

Struzik, Ed, (2001), **Greening of Inuvik,** Edmonton, Edmonton Journal, 20 Aug 2001. Part of a series "Down the Mackenzie".

Sullivan, Michael, (1960), **Down North: The Story of Inuvik,** Ottawa, Habitat, 4 p. Reprinted in North, 1960, v 7, nos 4-5. Describes Inuvik on the east channel of the Mackenzie Delta, built to replace Aklavik on the west channel.

Sutherland s.g.m., Agnes, (1995), **Bishop Who Cared.**

Swaney, Deanna, (1999), **The Arctic Tour Guide,** Melbourne, Lonely Planet, 456 p, ISBN 0864426658.

Szabo, Chris, Vicky Paraschak and Gary Cauerte, (2001), **TEST Symposium Report, Inuvik, March 21-23, 2001,** Yellowknife, GNWT Municipal & Community Affair, 70 p.

Appendix I: References & Bibliography

Taylor, Don, (1965), **Special Report on the Yukon and NWT,** Winnipeg, Trade and Commerce Magazine.

Taylor, Phyllis M., (1960), **Dog Team and School Desk,** London, H. Jenkins, 160 p. Description of Aklavik in the 1950s. Includes many community leaders involved in the creation of Inuvik. Mentions a story by Tommy Gordon when he was 10 years old.

Taylor, Wilf, (1989), **Beating About The Bush: A Life In The Northern Forest,** Madeira Park, Harbour. With Alan Fry.

Tener, John S., (1984), **Beaufort Sea Hydrocarbon Production and Transportation,** Ottawa, Federal Environmental Assessment Review Office, 146 p, ISBN 066253123X, Final Report of the Assessment Panel, July 1984.

Terpening, Rex, (2003), **Bent Props and Blow Pots: A Pioneer Remembers Northern Bush Flying,** Vancouver, Harbour, 338 p, ISBN 1550172875.

Thorstansson (ed), (1964), **Education North of 60,** Toronto, Ryerson Press, A report prepared by members of the Canadian Association of School Superintendents and Inspectors in the Department of Northern Affairs and National Resources.

Thrasher, Anthony Apakark, (1976), **Thrasher: Skid Row Eskimo,** Toronto, Griffin House, 164 p. Autobiography.

Time Magazine, (1956), **The North ... The Rites of Spring,** 23 April 1956. Move of Aklavik.

Time Magazine, (1969), **In The Great Tomorrow Country, Tomorrow is Now,** Time Magazine 2 May 1969.

Tower, Courtney, (1970), **What's Happened to our Northern Dream?,** Toronto, Maclean's Magazine, May 70.

Turnbull, Andy, (1999), **By Truck To The North,** Toronto, Annick Press, 88 p. ISBN 1550375504, With Debora Pearson.

Tyndale, George, (1970), **Frozen Northland – Land of Golden Opportunity,** Manchester, Manchester Guardian. But there is resentment among the indigenous people of the transient whites – "bloody whites" is the label given them by Nellie Cournoyea, the beautiful, blue-eyed blonde Eskimo manager of the local radio station. She is particularly resentful that migrants are buying up property that will escalate in value as Inuvik develops – as it must – in the first arctic city. And she is apprehensive that when the new generation of indigenous people materializes they will find themselves second-class citizens in economic terms.

UMA Engineering Ltd, (1985), **Town of Inuvik Expansion Plan,** Edmonton, UMA Engineering Ltd., A NOGAP report.

University of Calgary, (1997), **Rule Wynn and Rule Architectural Drawings,** Calgary, University of Calgary Press, 321 p, ISBN 1895176816. An inventory of the collecttion at the Canadian Architectural Archives, University of Cakgary Library, Linda M. Fraser, compiler, Kathy E.Zimon, editor.

University of Canada North, (1971), **Concepts Conference, University of Canada North, Inuvik, NWT November 19-22, 1971,** Inuvik, University of Canada North, 16 p. Edited by John M. Hallward.

Usher, Peter J., (1971), **Fur Trade Posts of the Northwest Territories 1870-1970,** Ottawa, Indian Affairs and Northern Development, 180 p. Northern Science Research Group 71-4.

Usher, Peter J., (1973), **Committee for Original Peoples Entitlement,** Inuvik, Committee for Original Peoples Entitlement.

Van Ginkel Associates, (1975), **Communities of the Mackenzie: Effects of the Hydrocarbon Industry,** Montreal, Van Ginkel Associates, 131 p. Sponsored by Canadian Arctic Gas Study Ltd., Gulf Oil Canada, Imperial Oil and Shell Canada.

Van Ginkel Associates, (1976), **Building In The North: Experience and Projects,** Montreal, Van Ginkel Associates.

Vaughan, Richard, (1994), **Arctic: A History,** New York, Alan Sutton. Comment on Inuvik p 276.

Wade, P.J., (2006), **Convention Centres As Ambassadors: Inuvik & The Petroleum Show,** New York, Realty Times, September 19, 2006.

Waterman, Jonathan, (2001), **Arctic Crossing: A Journey Through the Northwest Passage and Inuit Culture,** Toronto, Random House, ISBN 0679310908.

Webster, Rev. J.H., (1987), **Arctic Adventure,** Ridgetown, Dominion Press Ltd., 132 p. An Anglican minister's experiences, Mackenzie Delta, Coppermine, Coronation Gulf area 1927-1940. In collaboration with Edna H. Craven. "Due to the ever-increasing amount of air traffic there was a need for airports. In 1952 plans to construct an airport near Aklavik were made. A large bulldozer was brought in by boat to level the land before gravel would make a landing strip. The bulldozer removed all the tundra and within a few days the area was a quagmire."

Wein, Ross W., (2002), **Forest Fires and Northern Communities: Lessons from the 1968 Inuvik Fire,** Inuvik, Aurora Research Institute, 20 p, Scientific Report No. 8, June 2002.

Wein, R.W and L.C. Bliss, (1973), **Experimental Crude Oil Spills on Arctic Plant Communities,** Journal of Applied Ecology, 1973, p 671-682, 9 p. The objectives of this study were to determine the initial and long term effects of crude oil on the survival and re-invasion of Low Arctic plant species. The research was conducted at Inuvik, Tuktoyaktuk and Tununuk.

Western Arctic Handbook Committee, (2002), **Natural History of the Western Arctic,** Inuvik, Western Arctic Handbook Committee, 98 p, ISBN 0968791018, Edited by Scott Black and Alan Fehr.

Wilkins, J.E., (1964), **Planning Investigation for Inuvik, NWT,** Ottawa, Dept Public Works, Northern Construction Group, 13 p, ISBN Vert File.

Williams, G.P., (1967), **Ice Dusting experiments to increase the rate of melting ice,** Ottawa, National Research Council, Division of Building Research, Tech Paper No 239, 21 p. Value of ice dusting to speed melting of ice base on experiments conducted at Inuvik in 1964 and 1965.

Williams, Penny, (1991), **Talented Women of Inuvik,** Yellowknife, Above & Beyond, 3 p. Featuring Cynthia Hill, Cece McCauley and Mo Grant.

Wolforth, John, (1965), **Mackenzie Delta, Its Economic Base and Development, A Preliminary Study,** Ottawa, Northern Coordination and Research Centre, Indian Affairs and Northern Development, 85 p, Mackenzie Delta Research Project 1. This study was undertaken to provide background data and analysis necessary for a general understanding of the economic realities of life in the Mackenzie Delta..

Wolforth, John, (1971), **Evolution and Economy of the Delta Community,** Ottawa, Northern Science Research Group, Indian Affairs and Northern Development, 163 p, Mackenzie Delta Research Project 11. Historical analysis shows that agents of change – the trading companies and mission churches – focussed the activities of native Eskimo and Indian peoples in the

Mackenzie Delta. In 1950, the trapping camps were evenly distributed throughout the Delta. After the building of the new planned settlement of Inuvik, the numbers of trapping camps diminished. For the mid-sixties a grouping procedure used to dichotomize serious and part-time trappers, shows that a large proportion of the latter maintained trapping camps. Analysis of the employment in Inuvik also shows a divided commitment to land and town. High income and high status jobs were occupied predominantly by white transient workers since they required skills and levels of educational achievement possessed by few native people, though native people of Metis origin showed some success in more menial jobs. A comparison of employment in government and non-government sectors indicates that native involvement in the latter was growing, many people in both sectors shifted jobs frequently, or between jobs and land-based activities. The town economy, like the land economy, showed signs of adaption to the dual allegience felt by native people to the land and town.

Wolforth, John R., (1964), **New Towns of the Frontier – A Case Study from Inuvik,** Vancouver, University of British Columbia, 2 p.

Wonders, William C., (1960), **Postwar Settlement Trends in the Mackenzie Valley Area,** Geografiska Annaler, No. 4, 1960, ISBN Vert File.

Wright, S. Walter, (1967), **Settlement Planning Based on Functional Analysis,** Waterloo, University of Waterloo, Masters thesis, 254 p. The settlement of Inuvik was chosen to demonstrate the author's proposed planning method based on the systems approach to problem solving.

Wyatt, Colin, (1958), **North of Sixty,** London, Hodder & Stoughton, 223 p. "A picture of the happy, lovable people in Canada's Far North and of the way they are being affected by its sudden development." With photographs.

Yip, Mike, (1971), **Inuvik,** Inuvik, Mike Yip, c50 p, A photo essay of Inuvik. HB. With lots of B&W photographs.

Zaslow, Morris, (1984), **Northwest Territories 1905-1980,** Ottawa, Canadian Historical Association, 25 p, Canadian Historical Association No 38.

Zaslow, Morris, (1988), **Northward Expansion of Canada, 1914-1967,** Toronto, McClelland and Stewart, 421 p. A history of northern Canada from 1914 to 1967. The Canadian Centenary Series: 17. With photographs.

Zellen, Barry Scott, (2008), **Breaking the Ice: From Land Claims to Tribal Sovereignty in the Arctic,** Lanham, Maryland, Lexington Books, 420 p, ISBN 9780739114919. Forewords by Dick Hill and Eddie Kolausok.

Printed in the United States
By Bookmasters